Heartsick

Heartsick

THREE STORIES

ABOUT LOVE, PAIN, AND

WHAT HAPPENS IN BETWEEN

Jessie Stephens

Ⓗ

HENRY HOLT AND COMPANY

NEW YORK

Henry Holt and Company
Publishers since 1866
120 Broadway
New York, NY 10271
www.henryholt.com

Henry Holt ® and ⓗ ® are registered trademarks of Macmillan Publishing
Group, LLC.

Distributed in Canada by Raincoast Book Distribution Limited

First published 2021 in Macmillan by Pan Macmillan Australia Pty Ltd

Library of Congress Cataloging-in-Publication Data

Names: Stephens, Jessie, author.
Title: Heartsick : three stories about love, pain, and what happens in
  between / Jessie Stephens.
Description: First U.S. edition. | New York : Henry Holt and Company,
  2022.
Identifiers: LCCN 2021060764 (print) | LCCN 2021060765 (ebook) |
  ISBN 9781250838360 (hardcover) | ISBN 9781250838353 (ebook)
Subjects: LCSH: Man-woman relationships. | Couples. | Interpersonal
  relations. | Separation (Psychology) | Love.
Classification: LCC HQ801 .S8145 2022 (print) | LCC HQ801
  (ebook) | DDC 306.7—dc23/eng/20220127
LC record available at https://lccn.loc.gov/2021060764
LC ebook record available at https://lccn.loc.gov/2021060765

Our books may be purchased in bulk for promotional, educational,
or business use. Please contact your local bookseller or the Macmillan
Corporate and Premium Sales Department at (800) 221-7945, extension
5442, or by e-mail at MacmillanSpecialMarkets@macmillan.com.

First U.S. Edition 2022

Designed by Meryl Sussman Levavi

Printed in the United States of America

1   3   5   7   9   10   8   6   4   2

To my twin sister, Clare. The love of my life.

Preface

I'M IN AN AIRPORT BOOKSHOP.

A shop assistant asks if I need a hand with anything and I shake my head, knowing that if I speak my voice will crack—and when the tears come they tend not to stop.

I'm looking for a book I'm fairly certain doesn't exist. I want something that will put into words how I'm feeling right now—a sensation I have no vocabulary for.

You see, I'm not meant to be in this bookshop alone, waiting for my sister and a friend to finish up at some jewelry shop next door. This isn't what this moment is supposed to look like. I'm still attached to another set of moments, ones I'd played out in my head until they'd become fact. I'm being tortured by a parallel existence: one in which my boyfriend hasn't broken up with me and we're on the trip we planned, taking turns sleeping on each other's shoulder in our cramped economy seats.

I want a book that puts words around how I'm feeling and doesn't try to make me feel something different. That provides no instructions. That reminds me that this experience—and the unholy blend of grief and self-loathing that accompanies it—is as old as humans are. Some of the first stories humans ever told were about this feeling. So why am I, a twenty-first-century woman, eight days after being dumped on an otherwise unexceptional Tuesday, certain I'm the only person ever to have felt like this?

I get on that plane—without a book—and experience a holiday devoid of color and taste. I look for his face in the lantern-filled markets of Hội An and in the crowded museums of Ho Chi Minh City. I'm suffocating inside Sylvia Plath's bell jar, clamped shut over me no matter where I go. I know there's a vibrant new world on the other side of the glass, but I'm unable to touch it. I'm obsessed with my phone. I check and post and check again and beg it to ring and look to see if he's reacted to my photo. My life has become an empty performance for the one person who isn't watching.

For a while, I thought that was where the idea for this book began. But an idea doesn't arrive once. It haunts you, finding its way into your past and future, tapping you on the shoulder until you do something with it.

So this book probably started well before that.

I'M INTERVIEWING A man for my master's thesis. He's sixty-five, tall, has a hint of a Scottish accent, and has been married to the same woman for more than half his life. I ask him about his first relationship. He says he was fourteen. I see his eyes go glassy. He coughs. Tries to compose himself. But his eyes just get wetter and the tip of his nose turns pink.

He tells me her name was Patricia and she broke up with him suddenly, and that he then had to ride the bus with her every day for the rest of the year.

"Now that I think about it, I was terribly heartbroken," he says, shocked by his proximity to his own pain from more than fifty years ago. The feeling is still right there, living in his chest. It's not because he doesn't love the woman he married. He says, "She's been the most wonderful thing for me. Everything I hoped for. She's smart, she's loving, she's just a wonderful companion for me. And it's just been . . . it's been one of the real treasures of my life."

But inside him, there is space for both. Love for the woman he married and sorrow for the girl who left him.

There are three things I learn from that man, tall and broad, wearing a well-fitted tan coat.

The first is that heartbreak doesn't belong to women.

The second is that heartbreak doesn't belong to the young.

And the third is that heartbreak might never really leave you. Even if you fall in love again. Even if the years wear on and you forget the color of their eyes or what you talked about. Even if it was never right and your life went in the direction it needed to. Even then, the part that was broken by someone else when you were fourteen never quite heals.

But then, this book probably started before that.

I'm nineteen. the hot water is turning cold as I am curled in the fetal position in the shower, unable to grasp how much this hurts. I've been broken up with by a boyfriend I thought I'd marry. He's told me he doesn't love me anymore, and I think there's probably someone else. I'll later learn there is. I can't eat and I barely sleep, sure that this event has confirmed something I already know about myself: I'm fundamentally unlovable. An empty sack of flesh, uninteresting and vacuous, playing the part of a girlfriend but never quite being enough. I feel embarrassed about what he knows about me. Ashamed. Stupid that I let someone get close enough to see all the ugly parts.

But then, this book probably started before that.

I'm fifteen. the study is dark because the curtains are drawn and my friends and I are checking MSN Messenger. I have a boyfriend at the time. I've noticed that people look at me differently when I tell them that. His name is Jordan and I like how he smells. I remember considering my face from every angle the first time we met, how it would look if he was sitting to my right or to my left, how my nose bulges at the end from straight on. Boys had called me ugly before— boys who saw my pictures over MSN Messenger and who'd then been horrified when I'd shown up in real life. But Jordan was the first boy to tell me I was beautiful. And for a few months, I let myself believe him.

But on this Sunday afternoon in our dark study, I notice that Jordan has changed his name on MSN. It once had a love heart and my name following his. It still has the love heart. But now it's followed by a different name. The name of a friend I'd introduced him to the day before. I think I might be dreaming and that this is a nightmare I'll wake up from. It isn't.

But then, this book probably started before that.

I'M SEVEN AND I know I like boys. I notice that there's a certain kind of girl they like—and that girl isn't me. It's a slow heartbreak, I suppose, watching the boy I think is funny and handsome watch someone else. At a Friday night disco, the boys line up to dance with the prettiest girl in the class. They do not line up to dance with me. One day, I give the boy I like a packet of chips from my lunch box and he pays me a fair bit of attention for the rest of the afternoon. But once Mum stops putting chips in my lunch box, the sandy-haired boy in my year loses interest in hanging out. It takes me a while, but eventually I figure he might have been using me for the chips.

THIS BOOK WAS born in the hours I've waited for men to message me back and who never did. In the years full of almost-relationships, where I thought *I cannot handle another rejection* and then found myself turned down by someone I wasn't even sure I liked. This book was forged over hundreds of conversations with people who cried and yelled and laughed as they watched their lives be upended by a breakup.

They taught me that heartbreak has nothing to do with who you are. What you have or don't have, whether you could have or should have been better. Katy Perry's been dumped and serial killers serving life sentences have been known to have three girlfriends. Love doesn't make any sense. And having experienced romantic rejection doesn't say anything about the quality of a person. Relationships are not some test we fail or pass. They have a little to do with luck. A lot to do with timing. There are few things we control less than how someone else feels about us. And, just as love's magic can appear from nowhere and cast a spell on two unsuspecting people, so too can it disappear for no reason at all. So I wrote the book I wanted to find in that airport bookshop.

A book that didn't explain away heartbreak, forcing it into the past tense even though it was still present.

I wrote a book about scars. The ones that never quite heal. That we walk around with until the day we die. Somehow, that's less sad than it sounds. Everyone we love, particularly those we love so much we design our lives around them, lives inside us. And when they leave us, we can't just force them out.

I wrote this book for the person who doesn't want to be told that this too shall pass. Not yet. Who wants to sit in it. Sit with it. And see it for what it is. Who wants to know they're not alone. That their pain is at once unique and universal. Belonging to them and everyone.

I wrote this book to say: you don't need to look very far—heartbreak lives in all of us. Deeper in some than in others. It doesn't mean we don't love now. It just means we've loved before. And that comes with us wherever we go.

I wrote this book for people who know that a self-help book won't fix it. No book will. And for the people who know there's no such thing as distraction, because there's someone living behind your eyes and they shape everything you see.

I wrote this book because I know what it is to feel fundamentally unlovable. Like there's something wrong with you.

It is their story—Claire's and Ana's and Patrick's . But it is also my story and our story.

I hope within it you find echoes of yourself.

Introduction

❧

THERE ARE A FEW THINGS YOU SHOULD KNOW BEFORE YOU
meet Claire, Ana, and Patrick.

The first is that they are real people, although I have not used
their real names. All names used are pseudonyms. And while this
book is predominantly nonfiction, parts have been fictionalized to
varying degrees. Human memory is not chronological, nor does it
provide perfect dialogue or neat scenes. In the pages that follow, I
have turned people's lives into stories, and at times that has required
artistic license. I do not invent plot and I have done my best not to

invent feelings. Where memory has left gaps, I've filled the story with color that seems to fit. I've sculpted these narratives out of the clay that was handed to me.

The journalist Peter FitzSimons once said to me that whenever he reads fiction, he finds himself distracted by a voice in the back of his head that whispers, "This didn't happen." When I considered the subject of heartbreak, I knew I didn't have to make this story up. If I'd tried to make something up, it wouldn't have been anywhere near as interesting as the stories that were playing out in people's real lives all around me. The plot didn't have to be manufactured. It was buried inside most people I knew.

The stories had to be true, because within them would be nuances I'd never noticed before and realities I couldn't have invented. I didn't want to be limited by what I, as a thirty-year-old, happened to know about love and loss. I wanted to learn from people as I wrote, injecting wisdoms from different places and genders and ages into the pages of this book.

Long-form nonfiction storytelling, in my experience, elicits compassion and empathy most powerfully. There are few activities as intimate as reading a book, the words invisible to everyone around you. The characters and story lines might be dancing on a page, but they're dancing to a song playing in your head. In the solitariness that reading a book demands, one is forced to reflect on one's own life. After all, every time we explore others, we're mostly just exploring ourselves.

Claire, Ana, and Patrick have all read the book and have consented to their stories being shared. I interviewed them—for the most part—while the world was locked down in the midst of a global pandemic, which made the logistics harder than they would have been otherwise. During this process, I was struck by the generosity of each of them and their willingness to answer questions I had no right to ask, to share with me parts of themselves that were vulnerable, and to open up about experiences that were painful.

They gave me one of the most precious and personal things any person can offer another, which is their time. We spoke on the phone and on video chat, we emailed and messaged, and when it was possible, we met face-to-face. They sent me diary entries and text exchanges and emails they'd kept. They shared photographs and videos. They invited me into their worlds—each expressing surprise that someone would find the details of their love lives interesting.

All three, at one time or another, thanked me. Our conversations were cathartic. Maybe even healing. There comes a time after suffering when our friends stop listening. Our family grows impatient. I tried to play the part of a living journal—listening without judgment. My very presence, I hope, told them that their stories and how they interpreted them mattered.

The poet and novelist Ben Okri said, "The face of storytelling hints at a fundamental human unease, hints at human imperfection. Where there is perfection there is no story to tell."

And is there anything more imperfect than the decay of a romantic relationship? So, this is heartbreak, three ways. I wanted to tell these stories to put forward a new theory about heartbreak and the lasting effect it has on a person. It is only through sharing our vulnerabilities and the most tormented parts of ourselves that we're able to discover how much we have in common. How alike we all are.

Claire is in her twenties and has moved to London to start over. She meets Maggie and they strike up a close relationship. One night in Claire's apartment, everything between them changes and she finds herself caught up in a current she can't free herself from.

Ana is in her early forties and is married to a man she's been with for twenty-five years and with whom she has three children. She loves him, she thinks. She just sometimes wonders whether she actually likes him. She loves another man, and he's been there all along.

Patrick is in his early twenties and has never had a girlfriend before. He meets Caitlin during a university group assignment and the thought of her creeps into his sleep and contours his conversations. Before long, every thought takes the shape of her face. He hasn't considered that she might have a boyfriend.

Heartsick

Claire

THE ROOM SMELLS LIKE DUST AND SOUR SWEAT. SHE STANDS up straight and rolls her shoulders back. Click. Doesn't sound good. Maryanne, her mum, keeps telling her to stand up straight or she'll end up like that hunched old lady with the blue eye shadow they sometimes see on Ruthven Street. She spits back that she's an adult and can stand however she likes. Then she remembers she's thirty and living at home in Toowoomba and having an argument with her mum about her posture, and swallows down the lump in her throat that says, *You're embarrassing, Claire. Your life is embarrassing.*

The head of the vacuum cleaner hits the metal legs of the chair and she resists the urge to ram it into the stupid chair again and again and again until it falls over. The vacuum itself sits between her shoulder blades and the black straps holding it to her body are tangy with the body odor of whoever wore it last. By the time she leaves tonight, the smell will have stuck to her cheap black cotton T-shirt. The kind of smell that doesn't really go away, even after you wash it.

She pulls her phone out of her pocket, checks the time, then stuffs it back in and keeps vacuuming. Forty-eight minutes until she can go home. Her shifts are only three hours but they feel longer than the minimum eight-hour days she used to work in an office. She blinks her eyes hard, trying not to think about those days. Trying not to think about how much a life can change in two years. Past Claire, who lived in a North London flat with a job as a sales manager in a glass skyscraper, would pity future Claire. She owed her an apology for messing it all up.

Back then, life had a rhythm that she felt nostalgic for even as she was living it. Monday to Friday was all soy cappuccinos and overflowing sandwiches from the bakery down the road and meetings where she felt useful and brainstorming sessions that went well into the evening though it seemed no time had passed. It's funny how memories can trick us. They reflect back moments of our lives, but without the discomfort or anxiety, the sweat or cold hands. Memories are like well-framed photographs, where all the mess is just out of focus.

A buzz inside her pocket. She retrieves it without breathing—a habit she still can't break. Her stomach sinks. It's just Charlie, who wants to know how she's doing and when she's coming back to London like she promised. They were meant to do that Portugal trip. And Joel's thirtieth is next month. She always said she'd be back for that.

Claire ignores the message, annoyed Charlie would even ask, would pretend like nothing at all had changed. As she runs the vacuum along the dark gray carpet, Claire fantasizes about writing back: "Leave me alone. I'm obviously never coming back to London."

Her thoughts race loudly through her head. When she'd first started this job a few weeks back, she'd thought she might listen to music and be transported someplace else while she wiped down glass doors and mopped the scuffed dance floor. Maybe it wouldn't be so bad. But within minutes of having her earphones in, she'd begun hyperventilating, sure she was going to pass out before she made it to the bathroom. Her vision had tunneled and her mouth had turned to cotton. Her heart was thumping faster. Faster. Faster. Harder. She had breathed through it, trying to hurry the process along, repeating "Get it together" to herself. Telling the boss that she hadn't quite got around to cleaning the bar because she'd had a panic attack wasn't an option. It had been her first day of work in nine months. Glenda, a friend of her mum's, had offered her some hours cleaning the clubhouse at Toowoomba Bowls Club a few nights a week, and as quickly as she had said no, her mother had exclaimed "Yes," and now here she was. Completely on her own, except for a checklist of tasks to complete, unable to listen to music lest it make her feel anything.

As she pulls the vacuum cleaner off her back and balances it on the edge of a table, her phone vibrates again. This time it's an email. Her body registers who the sender is before her brain does. The way the letters of the name curl sends an electric shock from her fingertips all the way down to her toes. Her thumb hovers over the notification. Eight-fifty on a Thursday night. Why now? What could she want? She looks around at the empty clubhouse, the mopped wooden dance floor and the L-shaped bar swarming with fruit flies even though she's just sprayed all the metal surfaces. *Imagine if she knew this is what my life looks like*, she thinks, before quickly realizing that she probably does.

The phone is bright, her name clear. Maggie Stuart. No subject line. She clicks on the email and immediately wishes she hadn't.

Ana

❦

On matching wicker deck chairs, angled in such a way as to encourage conversation between the two people occupying them, sit Ana and, beside her, the wrong man. *If I told him*, she wonders, *would it ruin my life?*

She opens her mouth and closes it again. Picks up the glass of Riesling to her right and takes a sip. This moment is almost perfect. The southern New South Wales sky is fairy-floss pink and a warm breeze tickles her hairline. It's starting to smell like summer—citronella and faraway traces of backburning. The kids—Rachael, seventeen, and the twins, eleven—are at their grandparents' until seven. Billy, the dog, is curled up beside her, waiting for dinnertime. She lives in the house with the swimming pool and the French doors and the deck looking out onto dense bushland, just like she'd always wanted. The deck he'd built with his calloused hands. She looks down at the dark timber panels. Him. The foundation upon which her whole life has been built. He'd tell her that if you muck around with the foundations of anything, the structure will collapse. And you'll have to start again. "Not very efficient," he'd mumble, before climbing into his truck to tear down a perfectly beautiful cottage to make way for a lifeless monstrosity.

She hears him breathe a forced sigh from the chair beside her and fury rises in her chest. For a moment she thinks she might hate him, and then remembers, slowly, that she doesn't.

If you asked Ana what her first memory was, she'd answer as if she'd been thinking about it. She's in her baba's backyard and there's a hole in the fence and she can see a spider. It's growing. Getting bigger and bigger. But the memory isn't really about the spider. It's about the people behind her. Her baba and deda. The way Baba always shook her head when Deda made her laugh. How she sat with her knitting needles and yarn, lost in her fingers, while he sat across from her, reading another book about World War II. And how one of them would look up, every so often, and smile at the other. As if to say: *Even after sixty years, I miss you when you're someplace else.* That's what love is to Ana.

Her parents were the same. And Ana, for most of her marriage, had been the same. Until it all went wrong.

Tonight, as tended to happen, the tone of the sky changes, a reminder that some things don't stay good for long. Twilight falls and darkness envelops the bushland laid out before them. With her elbow propped up on the dusty armrest, her head resting heavily on her hand, she notices things she hasn't before.

The breeze has begun to bite, its coolness snatching the color and warmth from her legs. The ice cubes in her Riesling have melted faster than she'd drunk—the remaining two mouthfuls will taste more like water than wine now. The glass itself is chipped, which she ordinarily wouldn't notice, but the light has turned ugly and suddenly everything looks much worse.

In half an hour, the kids will be home and then she'll serve dinner and yell at them to help her wash up while already doing it all herself. She'll tell Rachael to have a shower and Rachael will lie and say she had one this morning and then she'll say "No you didn't" and Rachael will ask whether she is calling her a liar.

And then the kids will go to bed, closely followed by Paul, who has the sleeping patterns of a ninety-year-old man, and she will sit on the couch and half watch some late-night American show full of jokes she doesn't understand.

And then she will turn it off, climb into the left side of a bed that never feels big enough, and think to herself, *I married the wrong man*.

And as she drifts into sleep, she'll be given the space she's desired all day to think about the one thing she isn't really allowed to.

The right one.

Patrick

⚘

*I*F THIS WERE A MOVIE, HE WOULD NOTICE HER HAZEL EYES first. How they look like the big bang—brown matter spilling into a green galaxy. The beginning and the end of the earth. But this is not a movie. And they are not the first thing he notices.

The first thing he notices is that the person walking through the door is a girl. A black bag hangs over her right shoulder and rests just above the curve of her hip. Long hair falls over her narrow shoulders. He doesn't want you to imagine her in slow motion, because she's not. Time doesn't stand still. No one trips over or runs their fingers through their hair. One person simply walks into a room and another person notices. All his eyes deliver to his brain, as though he is a caveman incapable of higher-order thinking, is: *Girl.*

In Patrick's defense, he's never seen one in the lab before. He's not being sexist, that's just a fact. It would be like seeing a polar bear wandering along St Georges Terrace. Nothing against the polar bear—he'd be welcome to stay, of course—but you'd be lying if you said you didn't notice it.

He's not proud of what his mind does next, but it's probably best he be honest. He screens her from the ground up, like one of those full-body scanner machines at the airport. Narrow feet sit inside white trainers. Legs hugged by tight denim jeans. A loose red-and-white-striped shirt. Long, brown hair, almost to her elbows. He can't tell you much more than that. Certainly not the color of her eyes. Just that there is a girl unpacking her things inside the software engineering lab and he would like to keep looking at her. It is enough for him to think, *Hmm, that's an unusual occurrence*, and file it neatly away in his memory.

A few days later, he finds himself sitting opposite the girl in the library, his mind registering slightly more than *Girl* this time. Her bracelets, which look like pieces of ragged string you find tied around a leg of ham, circle her slender wrists. There are a dozen of them. All different colors, standing out against the bright white of the desk.

"Where's Thomas?" Girl asks, checking the time on her phone.

"I'll text him now," the other girl says.

Yes. By this stage, there are two girls—and they've found themselves in the same group for this interface design assignment. Two years he's been studying software engineering and he has never worked with a female on a group project. Now he has two.

He's learned that Girl One—the one with the bracelets—is

named Caitlin. Her cheeks are flushed from the heat outside and she keeps lifting her hair up, waving cool air toward the back of her neck. Every time he instructs his eyes to look elsewhere, they find her again, searching for he doesn't know what.

Girl Two sits beside him and looks like the kind of person who went to a private school—modestly dressed in expensive-looking clothes, shiny hair finely streaked with a blend of blond and gold. Her skin is clear and fair, her big, toothy smile likely corrected by years of dental work. Patrick can't tell you what it is exactly, but there's something fundamentally different about these two women. One is Caitlin and the other—her name might be Emma or Emily, he forgot immediately after she said it—is not.

After she sends the text, Emma—he's decided her name is Emma—begins to tell a story about her weekend. He's always admired that about women. Their ability to pluck a story out of absolutely nowhere and decide that now would be a good time to tell it. He'd never been much good at small talk. When he tunes in again, she's recounting how someone got so blind drunk they knocked their two front teeth out on the edge of a gutter. Her voice echoes through the library, all tapping keys and humming printers, and he wonders how she could be so unaware of how loudly she's speaking. He glances at the students around him. One is highlighting a textbook, shifting in his seat. Another has taken out one earphone and is glaring at them.

Caitlin nods politely without asking any follow-up questions. She fiddles with her bracelets, avoiding eye contact as much as possible.

He is struck by a desire to know her. To ask her all the questions Emma is answering unprompted. Was she at a house party last weekend too? Where was she before this moment? Where will she be afterward? Who is she outside of these walls?

She begins muttering under her breath and he realizes she's reading out the project outline. He leans back in his chair. Smirks. She sees it.

"Sorry, just trying to work out what we're actually meant to do here." She rubs her forehead. "I reckon we just split it up rather than all trying to meet . . ."

"That's the point of a group assignment, though," Emma snaps, looking at him for reassurance.

To be entirely honest, he's never understood the point of group assignments, but he doubts it's for four people to sit in front of the same computer screen and debate every step of designing an interface. He's done enough of these to know that they'll meet a few times a week for a month. Emma will tell her stories. Thomas won't turn up. He doesn't know about Caitlin. But one person—probably he—will actually do the assignment but will put all four names on it anyway. Thomas might pat him on the back as they leave class, utter a quick "Thanks, mate."

"Yeah, I'm with you." He tilts his head toward Caitlin. "I've got a lot on this week . . ." He trails off. Doesn't know why he said that. He does not have a lot on this week.

Caitlin looks at him and nods. He realizes he likes it when he has her attention. It makes him feel like he exists.

It's decided that he and Caitlin will design the web formats. The other tasks are divided between Emma and Thomas—even though, at this stage, Thomas might very well be dead.

"We'll need to meet at the labs sometime this week to work out what needs to be done and then we can divide it up. Thursday works for me. I'm sure I saw you in there the other day, actually," Caitlin says, he realizes after a beat, to him.

The top of his ears feel hot. "Did you?" he asks. Another lie.

Emma and her shiny hair have somewhere else to be, so she packs up her things and says that she'll see them later. He watches her walk through the glass sliding doors into the warm, still afternoon.

"You off too?" he asks Caitlin, both of them still looking at their laptop screens.

"Yeah." Her fingers play with her bottom lip. "I feel so rude . . . I'm checking that email to see what her name is."

He laughs. Tells her he's been trying to work it out too, but he's fairly certain it's Emma. Then she laughs. It's not. It's Alice. He makes her show him the email to prove it. He pulls a face. Guilty.

"And what's my name then?" she asks. A test.

"Caitlin," he says. Her eyes are hazel. Like the big bang. "You're Caitlin."

Claire

It's a saturday evening and the last dregs of sunlight are making their way into the foyer of the Empire Theatre. To everyone but Claire, there's an energy in the air. Women with chunky necklaces sip their prosecco and complain about the day's unbearable heat. A handful of people buy overpriced programs, people who are most likely related to someone on the pages inside. The chatter and clinks and music make her feel like she's suffocating and, for a moment, she considers hiding in a toilet cubicle, but then she sees the line of women snaking around the corner.

Maryanne is lining up at the bar. Claire thinks she's probably looking around, wishing anyone else here were her daughter. Someone who gets out of bed before noon. Who works full-time as a nurse or a teacher or for the local paper. She'd never say it. But imagine the disappointment of having your thirty-year-old daughter move back in with you, unable even to walk to the shops to get a loaf of bread. Sick. But not the kind of sick other people understand. The kind of sick that sounds made-up. That most people think could be cured with a stern talking-to and some perspective. "Oh yes," Maryanne must say to her friends, "my daughter has moved back in with us because she's lazy and sad."

And now her mother has to walk back from the bar, bypassing laughter and stories that make a tableful of people lean in, only to stand in the dark orbit of her daughter. Not even Claire wants to be in Claire's presence. Other people are like bright, flickering candles and she is a draft of cold air, blowing them out if they come too close.

They're seeing a play called *The Wrong Side*. "I think it'll be great," Maryanne had said as she applied her lipstick in the hallway mirror. "You'll love it," she'd added, rubbing the sides of Claire's arms and leading her out the door.

In London, Claire had spent most of her Friday and Saturday nights at the theater. The London Palladium, the London Coliseum, the Royal Festival Hall, Hammersmith Apollo, and countless tiny underground playhouses she can't remember the names of. She'd look forward to it all week—a group of them would turn up early for a few drinks and a catch-up. Everything had been so easy then. She hadn't had to pretend to be interested and words would fall out of her mouth without her second-guessing them. Afterward, she'd walk back out onto the cold, dark street and feel like she'd just woken from a trance. She can't let herself go like that anymore, carefree and in the moment. When you're wearing a crown of thorns firmly nestled into the top of your head, hot blood trickling down your forehead and into your eyes, it becomes impossible to think of anything else.

By the time her mum has finally made it to the front of the bar queue, Claire's given up trying not to think about the email. She hasn't replied yet. Doesn't have the words. Why would Maggie even send her an email? It's so formal. Cold. A place reserved for business inquiries and spam. They'd never emailed. It had always been texts and calls. She's been trying to draft a response in the notes section of her phone for three days but nothing she writes makes sense. All she can see, clear and with perfect punctuation, is Maggie's final line: "I've moved on, Claire. And it's about time you did too."

That's why when she looks toward a crowded table to her right and sees the back of Maggie's head, she thinks she must be imagining things. She already knows she's crazy but seeing people who aren't there is alarming even for her. But there's that sway she does with her hips. Brown hair to her shoulders, longer than she'd ever seen it. It looks as if she's lost weight. And she recognizes that white T-shirt, baggier than it once was. She'd bought it for her when they'd first arrived in Toowoomba.

She needs to get away.

She puts her head down and weaves through groups of people, saying nothing as she pushes past. She can't breathe. Heads are turning, sensing a change of energy in the room, and she just hopes one of them isn't Maggie's. It's like two hands have clamped around her throat. Her feet are unsteady and she has to count the steps as she races down them, the glass doors finally in sight.

Once she's out on the street, she buckles over, hands on thighs, sure she's about to vomit on the footpath. She's panting and can feel her chest and neck turning red, every breath harder to find than the last. She's sure she's about to die. She will pass out and hit her head. Or have a heart attack. There's a knife twisting its way through her chest and there's no way a heart is meant to beat this fast. Isn't every heart only given a certain number of beats? Her body is using them all up. Faster. Thumping in her ears. She's about to spontaneously combust all over Neil Street but at least then this will be over. Let this be over. Black dots obscure her vision and it's like two curtains from her peripheral vision are closing in on her.

"Claire?" It's Maryanne. Her mum knows why she's out here. But there's a tone of exasperation anyway.

"I know, darling. I know. Deep breaths." Maryanne rubs her back, just like she used to when Claire was sick as a child. Circular motions. Gentle.

"I'm . . . I'm sorry, Mum," Claire says, her voice cracking. "I'm sorry. I can't do this."

"I didn't think she'd be here."

"I did," Claire whispers. She's focused on Maryanne's glossy pink sandals, her pink painted toenails, wedged into the shoe a little too tightly. "Can we get Dad to pick me up? I need to go home. I need to be at home."

Maryanne tries to talk Claire into returning inside. "Everyone is about to be seated," she says, "and there are hundreds of people. You won't see her again."

But fifteen minutes later, Claire is in the passenger seat of her dad's Ford Fiesta. Her pupils are dilated, her eyes barely blinking. She looks like she's just seen a ghost.

Ana

❦

TWO YEARS EARLIER

ANA IS WEARING A NAVY SILK DRESS THAT COMES HALF-way down her shins and has a scooped neck that displays more cleavage than she's comfortable with. It's the first time in a long time that she has bought a dress instead of just borrowing one from a friend who has recently been to a wedding.

"Does this look all right?"

"Better than all right," he says, kissing her on the cheek. He doesn't look at her, eyes instead on his phone screen.

"Sorry, that's Rob. Jenny can't come tonight. She's got a cold or something."

"That's annoying. You pay per head, don't you?" She fastens the delicate buckle on the strap around her ankle.

Paul nods. Shrugs. Gives her a look that says they're both thinking the same thing. They'd known that Jenny would find some excuse not to come to the Durnham Rugby Ball at the last minute. She hates this stuff. And Ana knows it well, mostly because of how many times Jenny has told her.

Still, Jenny and Rob are only in town for a month. For the ball. But mostly for Rob to see his parents, who fade away a little more every time he visits. They're here a few times a year maybe, when Rob can get the time off work in Sri Lanka. And every time they arrive Jenny consults her book of excuses—jet lag, colds caught on flights, a meal that didn't agree with her—and cancels a plan that's been in their diaries for months.

But if she's honest with herself, Ana is relieved Jenny won't be there. Jenny's been married to Rob for years now. Seven maybe. Or eight. But, still, it never feels right when she's there. They'll talk about something that happened twenty years ago and halfway through Jenny will wander off to the bathroom. Or Rob will turn to her, filling her in on a detail of the story—like how during their trip to the United States, Ana had meant to book a youth hostel on Fourth Street in Manhattan, but accidentally booked Fourth Street in St. Petersburg, Florida—and Jenny will nod vacantly, as if she's been listening all along.

"How long do you reckon since we saw Robbie?" Paul asks once they're in a taxi, pulling his seat belt on.

It must've been six months, Ana realizes. But it didn't feel that long. When you've known someone for twenty-five years, your memories become all mixed up and something that happened a decade ago can feel like it was just last week. She feels a pang of guilt—she should make more of an effort to keep in touch. Rob's her closest friend, the kind who tells you that you look like shit when you do, in fact, look like shit.

When they arrive at Hyatt House—a glorified function center that does the odd wedding but mostly school formals—Ana watches as women enter with their husbands, almost always trailing a step or two behind. One woman stops at the entrance and mouths something to a middle-aged man while throwing her arms up in frustration. She looks at the ground and shakes her head and he puts his hands in his pockets, like a schoolboy standing in front of the principal.

Ana and Paul don't treat each other like that. He still rests his hand on her thigh at the dinner table and kisses her on the cheek when he comes home from work. They say each other's name without contempt and whenever Ana meets someone she doesn't like, Paul asks her what she thought of that Maureen they met tonight, and they both inevitably agree.

As they walk toward the front terrace, she sees Rob standing on his own. He's playing with the cuffs on his shirt and when he looks up, his smile takes up the majority of his face.

"Mate, how've you been?" Paul puts his arms around him, gives him a firm pat on the back.

"Can't complain," Rob says, pulling in Ana. "Haven't seen you in too long."

The room is a sea of white, the silk chair coverings a shade slightly different from the thick table linen. There's already a smattering of glasses on the tabletops, well-dressed women already having poured themselves just a mouthful of wine—a splash that will be topped up a dozen, maybe more, times throughout the night.

"It's a shame Jenny's not here," Ana says convincingly while they wait in line at the bar, the men gesturing at the tap marked Stella Artois.

"You know what she's like." Rob makes a face, his tone suggesting there's more to the story. He asks after the kids, one by one.

"They've been asking when they're going to see Uncle Rob next," she says. "Careful or they'll forget you."

Once they sit down, Paul comes and goes, eating when a course arrives, and leaning toward them. There are other couples seated at their table of eight, but the women are huddled together talking about the kids' school, and the men have gone off to smoke on the terrace. Mostly, it's just Ana and Rob, remembering halfway through sentences all the things they've forgotten to tell each other since they last spoke. Unlike most men she knows, Rob actually listens to her. Sometimes he pauses after she speaks, looks over her shoulder, and says, "Hadn't thought about it that way," even though she's sure he's thought about it in every way possible. He's just being kind.

When Rob leads her out the glass terrace doors after the dessert neither of them really touched, a cold gust of air slaps her awake. Light floods out from the function room, illuminating the skeletons of a few leafless branches. Everything else is inky black and silent. They settle at a small outdoor table with their generously filled glasses of red wine. There's an energy in the air. The kind that compels them to say things out loud they ordinarily wouldn't.

"She cheated on me last year," Rob says after a while. He sniffs.

Jenny had had an affair with a man she worked with. Rob had been getting ready for bed when he'd heard the notification sound on her laptop, pinging over and over again. He'd typed in the password, only meaning to turn the sound off, and a conversation had flashed up—words that didn't belong jumping out at him. Jenny was downstairs messaging Kevin about all the things she wanted to do to him, unaware that her phone was synced up to her computer. Words and phrases emerged that she'd never used with Rob. She wanted to slide his cock into her mouth and then sit on top of it, feeling him deep inside her.

He'd thought he might be sick, his body splitting from the inside. A sob had come from somewhere, the sound one might make if they were punched hard in the stomach. Kevin had sat inside their home with his wife and children. Eaten with the cutlery Rob's parents had bought them as a wedding gift.

Jenny's face had fallen, white and childlike, her lips in a thin straight line, as Rob had stormed down the stairs, yelling "What the fuck?" over and over. She'd walked out, but it hadn't lasted long. They'd both known it wouldn't. The apology came a few days later, with a commitment to not only end things with Kevin but to also resign from her job. There had been excuses made about a desire for attention that he hadn't been meeting. Rob worked too much. He didn't put his arm around her like he once had. And so they'd gone to therapy and the therapist had said, "There's good stuff here."

Ana doesn't know what to say. She shakes her head. "And is there good stuff?"

"Yeah. Sort of. I don't know. We don't argue much. But I think that might be because we don't really talk." He smiles ruefully.

"Paul and I don't really talk either," Ana says, joining Rob in looking out into the blackness. "Like, *really* talk. You know what he's like, though. He's never really been a talker."

"He's crazy about you, though, you know that. He'd never fuck someone else."

"No, I know. But maybe we've run out. We've just run out of things to say to each other . . ." She doesn't know why she's saying any of this. She'd never even really thought it until now.

She feels a tightness in her throat when she thinks of how Paul slid a takeaway coffee across the bench for her this morning. How he'd spilled a few drops of his own down his white T-shirt, the one he'd owned for fifteen years.

At some point, she gets up to go to the bathroom and feels like she's on one of those theme-park rides that spins too quickly and suddenly you're stuck to the walls. When she clumsily lands on the toilet seat, feet pointed inward, she has a stern word with herself. *You seriously need to go home.*

But when she returns to the terrace, spotting Paul sitting with half a dozen guys by the fireplace on her way through, Rob has already poured them another drink. Oh well.

After a large gulp—her sips do seem to be getting much bigger, her mouth numb—she says, "All right then. So tell me. How are you really? Not your business. Not even your marriage. How are you?" She's not sure what compelled her to ask that question. Maybe the look on his face. Who did she think she was? Dr. Phil?

"Bleurgh," he says, shaking his head. "It's been a shitty year."

He uses the word "depression," which shocks her. There was a night in January, he tells her, looking into his wineglass, when he'd wanted to end it all. But then he'd thought of his mother and what it would do to her.

"I was too much of a coward. But that night, I honestly couldn't imagine having to wake up all over again."

She asks how he feels now and if he's been seeing anyone, getting help. He has. Once or twice. But the therapist wanted to talk about his relationship with his parents and his family history and kept telling him how long this process was going to take and he didn't see how any of it was going to help him feel better tomorrow. Instead, he tells her, he just went through the motions. Got back into exercise. He's going to the gym every day and sleeping more.

"I am feeling better," he assures her, playing with the edge of his cardboard coaster. "Sorry, I don't know why I told you any of that."

Paul's footsteps are loud and clumsy, his grin lopsided. The bar's closed, he announces, and he's ready to call a taxi. He plants a wet kiss on Ana's head and asks how long they've been sitting out here. It's bloody freezing. But neither of them can feel it.

As she rests her head against the squeaky leather of the backseat on the way home, Ana thinks about Rob. *What would I have done if something had happened to him? Did I say enough?* There's something else that's troubling her, though. She tells herself she'll call him tomorrow. Make sure everything is all right. But, deep down, perhaps she already knows that everything is not all right. Her life, neatly stitched over twenty-five years, is coming undone. And once one thread is unpicked, the rest tends to tear apart, with even the smallest tug.

Patrick

᪥

THE LECTURE HALL IS HUMID AND DIM FOR TWO IN THE afternoon. While students shuffle in, the lecturer flicks through his notes, wet patches growing under his arms.

He sees her on the far left-hand side, settled between two empty seats. Her hair is up today, a messy ponytail hanging down her back. He catches her eye just as he looks down at his feet and decides to give her a moment to choose to ignore him if she'd like. They'd only met in the library the other day—she might not remember his face. But when he looks up again, he sees her arm waving, gesturing for him to join her.

He slides in next to her and moves his feet the wrong way when she tries to tuck her bag under the seat.

"I feel so sorry for him," she says, staring at the lecturer dabbing himself on the forehead, then down the sides of his face, with a handkerchief. The Perth sun is beating down on the black ceramic-tiled roof and he looks like an ice cream that's been abandoned on the footpath, melting beneath it.

Patrick laughs, feeling the dampness of his own body, holding his arms in close to his sides. As he tries to ask what time they should meet at the labs tomorrow, the lecturer begins to hush the room and he doesn't get to finish his sentence.

Sitting beside her, he can't get his breathing right. He's too aware of it now. *Just breathe in. And then out. Like that. But don't think about it. Why are you out of breath? Why are everyone else's lungs doing it unconsciously? Focus. On the chair in front. Shit. Forgot to breathe.* He feels watched, as though her eyes are needles ready to pierce through his skin. His legs shift and his arms cross and then rest in his lap. He needs a pen. Something to hold. He rustles through his backpack and finds one, along with a notebook. For a few minutes, he writes—focusing himself. Performing studious Patrick to a person who probably isn't taking any notice.

"You don't have to take notes," she whispers, her words hot against his ear. "All the slides are online." He knows that, of course. Everyone knows that. But taking notes puts ideas in his own words, which helps him remember things.

"Really? Awesome," he mouths back, closing his notebook.

He can't tell you what the lecture is about. The words skim his ears, but his mind fails to catch them. He does learn that Caitlin bites her nails. And that her nail polish is chipped pink. And that's more than he could've hoped to get out of a lecture on a Wednesday afternoon.

When the lecture finishes, she asks if he wants to grab a coffee before their next class at four. He says yes even though he doesn't drink coffee—he actually hates how the bitterness clings to your tongue. But he orders a latte because she does. They sit by the window right beside an air-conditioning vent working so hard it's leaking droplets of water into a bucket beneath it. It's the first relief he's had from the heat all day and the beads of sweat under his arms begin to dry out. Once their coffees arrive, he brings up the assignment in an attempt to avoid any silence. The other component he'd only discovered last night is a presentation with all four of them.

He gulps. "Yeah, presenting in front of people probably isn't my strong point."

"Does it make you nervous?"

"I hate it. And I'm just not good at finding the right words." He pops off the lid of his takeaway coffee and then puts it back on again.

Coding he can do. Concepts he can understand. But he often feels like words are butterflies, flying away whenever he gets too close to the right one. His brother is the same. So is his dad. They get the same tortured expression whenever they find themselves the center of attention, a question directed their way. His mum isn't much better. Neither of his parents are native English speakers. It's always as though they're thinking in one language and trying to translate it into another, tormented that the word they want doesn't exist. He didn't realize until high school that a silent dinner table wasn't normal, when he started staying at friends' places. He was so envious of how they spoke, their ideas so urgent you could see the food they'd just put into their mouths. They'd argue and tease, carrying jokes from one dinnertime to the next. And then he'd go back to his house, his mother speaking in Mandarin, before sitting down to watch some soap opera set in a world she'd left.

But Caitlin asks him questions he's never considered before. Like "What makes you nervous about it?" and "Don't you think most people in the room are only half listening anyway?" and "What's the worst that can happen?" And when he answers, she leans in, asking him to clarify when she doesn't quite understand what he means. He notices a scar just under her right eyebrow and wonders if he likes it because he likes her or if it really is as beautiful as it seems to him.

She asks if he'd like to send her through what he's written so far. She says she'll help him. She did a writing course last semester and likes putting together presentations.

"I'm going to need a hand with the web formats, though . . . so we'll be even," she says matter-of-factly.

They swap numbers. He takes his last gulp of coffee, no longer noticing that it tastes like an ashtray. Over the next few days, he will examine everything that happened in that café. How her hand held his phone, tapping in her number; how she'd laughed when he impersonated the overheating lecturer whose mouth had become audibly dry. He will wince at how he'd knocked over his water bottle and it had nearly taken the coffee cup with it, and how it had made him feel clumsy and self-conscious. But mostly he will think about how in her eyes he saw parts of himself, which felt like nothing short of a miracle.

THE LAB IS empty except for them. It smells like his cologne, the traces of which are still foreign to him.

"You smell nice today."

"Do I?" he asks, as though it were by accident.

They've been there all afternoon, finishing off the web formats. There are no windows, the crooked clock on the wall the only hint that any time has passed. Fluorescent downlights are fitted to the ceiling, casting a hospital yellow across the room. His eyes sting. It's getting late and they should probably go home, but he doesn't want to. They've met more often than they needed to in the last three weeks. She must know that too. They're meant to be getting this assignment done but mostly they talk, their laptop screens fading to an idle black. These moments—working beside her in the lab or seeing her in lectures—have become the scaffold upon which his life is now built. They are the points that determine the shape of his week. Wednesday is Caitlin. Thursday is No Caitlin. And it is only on this day—a Caitlin Wednesday—that he learns she has a boyfriend.

She glances up at the black hands on the clock. "I better run." There's a pause. A breath. A glance. Maybe there's not. Maybe he's imagining it. "I told my boyfriend I'd cook tonight and I've got to grab a bunch of stuff from the shop."

The admission of a partner in the middle of a conversation never quite fits. No matter how naturally it rolls off the tongue, it always sounds like a confession. Like it requires an answer.

"Oh, cool. Special occasion?" He raises his eyebrows and looks up at her. Sounds too interested.

"No." She piles her exercise book and laptop into a large canvas bag covered in colorful stitched diamonds. He likes it. Much more than those shiny leather handbags other girls carry. The kind with brand names emblazoned on them in gold.

Before Caitlin, he wouldn't have noticed. But now everything he sees, from the way she messily bundles her thick hair into a ponytail to how her bottom teeth are slightly crooked, makes him think: *This is what I've always wanted.* A girl who throws her head back when she laughs. Who can rub her eyes when she's concentrating because there's nothing black applied to them. Who uses words like "facetious" without stopping for a moment to scan for it.

Everything he discovers about her is a new thing he wants. He never really understood the word "infatuation" until last week, when he watched *The Beach* with his housemates, some Leonardo DiCaprio movie everyone except him had seen half a dozen times. At one point, the main character says that when you become infatuated with someone, you'll find a reason to believe that they're exactly the person for you. You'll convince yourself that everything they do—the way they take photographs, the way their voice sounds when they're tired, how their socks sit beneath the bone in their ankle—is just what you've always been searching for. Yes. He understands infatuation now. How it creeps into your sleep and contours your conversations. It makes you sick. Tired. Derails the rest of your life. Every thought takes the shape of their face.

He hadn't known what it meant to want something before now. Really want something.

He's watched friends barely able to follow a conversation, checking their phone again and again to see if the girl they're seeing has texted back. Watching from the outside, he couldn't stand it. But now he understands that they couldn't give a shit about him. For them, the vibration against their thigh was from the axis upon which the earth was spinning. Anything else could wait.

Caitlin tells him that Nick—a name that helps him form a picture of a guy who is tall, broad, and plays rugby but has a bad shoulder that's always held him back—can't cook. *Interesting*, he thinks. They live together. He can't work out whether her voice carries resentment or affection. Maybe a little bit of both. What would he know?

He walks to the station with his head low, the wind picking up as the sun disappears behind clouds. He's riddled with a sense of vicarious embarrassment for himself. Of course she's in a relationship. Having coffee with a girl doesn't mean she likes you. He should have learned all this by now.

A knot tightening in his chest, he wonders what she's doing. He sees her hanging up her canvas tote on a hat stand, and then reasons that people his age don't have hat stands. She probably hangs it over a chair. He sees her letting out a deep exhale, kicking off her shoes. Nick jumps up from somewhere, kissing her and making a fuss, holding her tight around her narrow waist. She pushes him off playfully before pulling out a saucepan, filling it with hot water. But it's her and she's magnetic, so Nick follows her and wraps his arms around her, kissing her on the side of her neck. They say things like "I love you" and "I missed you." He says he's not hungry yet. She rolls her eyes. He pulls up the dress she was wearing today, purple, with a tie around the middle. They have sex right there in the kitchen, knowing each other's bodies better than they know their own. Her skin, the color of sparkling sand, is dripping with sweat.

The train is mostly empty. His head rests on the cool window, the oil from his forehead leaving a round mark. A jolt of anxiety lands in his stomach. He'll be the last one home, meaning the kitchen will be chaos. His housemate Tai will have cooked chicken and vegetables and left evidence of every step on the bench. Joey hardly leaves the house, so he'll be settled in front of the TV, legs spread, Xbox controller in his clammy hands, pots and plates stacked up in the sink. Their house on Marlborough Avenue has never felt like home. When he'd moved in almost two years ago, he'd imagined they'd have parties, faceless people spilling out into their tiny courtyard. But that had never happened. Not least because he didn't actually know enough people to fill a party. And he'd be horrified for anyone to see the state of their living room, stale chips and dark hairs buried between the worn couch cushions.

What would Caitlin think of their place? Tai sometimes calls it a "bachelor pad," which is mortifying because a bachelor pad conjures up a mahogany coffee table, black leather couches, and a shelf boasting a bottle of Macallan whisky. A bachelor pad is also meant to have women in it occasionally. As far as he knows, there has never been a woman in their Marlborough Avenue town house.

In fact, in his twenty-one years, Patrick has never had a woman—besides his own mother—step foot inside his bedroom. This certainly isn't by choice. He'd fantasized about bringing someone home and how they'd creep up the sunken stairs, shushing each other. He assumed this would be the period of his life when he finally found someone who was his. A companion to sit with him in the corner at his weird family Christmas. And watch *Air Crash Investigation* with him on a Saturday night so it didn't feel so sad.

When he arrives home, he sees the state of it through her eyes. The kitchen looks exactly how he'd predicted it would. It's dark and the air is stale. The smell of grease and animal fat and of Joey, who is still wearing the shirt he sleeps in, makes him decide he's no longer hungry. As he lies in bed that night, he is visited by the thought that he won't be able to sleep. Once it arrives, it refuses to leave. It haunts him until it becomes true. He rolls to his right and thinks about Caitlin, hearing the thump of his heart in his ears. Then he rolls to the left and wonders what her family is like and whether she has a pet dog and whether she can dance. He wants to know her as well as he knows himself. Nick must know everything about her. What she looks like when she sleeps. How she curls up when she's sick. Fears you only share with someone when it's so dark you feel like you're floating.

His imagination dances with his sleep and he sees flashes of them, like out-of-focus photographs coming to life. They're lying under the stars in a sleeping bag, her head in the crook of his neck. A park. A flash of her teeth. They're in bed and it's too hot and their bodies are moving so fast, like the friction of sticks on the brink of creating fire. There's a fireplace and a rug and he feels at home.

Just past three o'clock, he decides that this person is driving him mad.

When he wakes up four hours later, eyes barely open, he grabs his phone from beside his bed. There's one message. The name in blue. It's her.

Ana

❧

Multigrain bread is dropped into the toaster and orange juice is poured for nine-year-olds who can do it themselves.

According to their school reports, Oliver and Louis are "capable" but "distracted," more often than not by each other. Rachael, unlike her brothers, is focused and considered but entirely devoid of any self-esteem, like just about all fifteen-year-old girls. Sometimes she spends an entire Saturday experimenting with makeup in her bedroom, taking photos to post somewhere Ana doesn't like to think about too much. She could read it as creative. An attempt at self-expression. But she knows Rachael better than that. Her daughter hates her face so much that she wants a new one. The makeup isn't about highlighting the features she loves but erasing the ones she hates. Which is all of them.

If you asked Ana on this particular Saturday morning—as the sun floods in through the back doors onto a family of five eating toast at a cluttered timber table, a washing basket sitting on one side—if she is happy, she would say yes. Without hesitation. And she would mean it. This is better than any life she could have imagined. The kind of life where you don't have time to stop and ask yourself if you're truly happy because you're too attached to living it.

She sings along to an awful song she loves on the radio as she drives Rachael to netball and stands dutifully on the sideline in a jacket that isn't warm enough. When they arrive home a few hours later, with a loaf of bread and a roast chicken, she still feels distracted. Not quite herself. Paul's playing a round of golf with some mates from the club, making the most of Rob being in town. She wonders what they're talking about.

She spends the day wiping down benches with too much Ajax and washing school uniforms and walking the dog and paying phone bills that have blown out and inquiring about a maths tutor for Rachael. By the time she looks at the clock again, it's time to pick the boys up from Hayden's down the road, and she's back in her Toyota Kluger, with the same song playing on the radio again.

She sees an accident on the way. A car has collided with a motorbike on Orwell Road. Shards of steel and aluminum have traveled hundreds of meters, and now there are little cones placed alongside each one. Although she can't see blood, she can tell that whoever was on the motorcycle is no longer in one piece. Police are standing next to a dented Audi, and passersby walk more slowly than usual, craning their necks to see something they don't want to.

"Thank God Paul doesn't ride a motorbike," she mutters under her breath to an empty car, racking her brain to work out if anyone she knows does. They don't, which confirms something she has secretly always known.

Bad things—complicated things—don't happen to her. She can never say that out loud, of course. But she dares herself to think it. But now that she's forty, this is beginning to make her more anxious than relieved. Surely it is only a matter of time until the universe realizes it has forgotten her in its dishing out of tragedy. Close friends have buried their parents or found themselves diagnosed with aggressive cancers or been cheated on by a husband who'd found someone else twice as attractive and half their age. Last year, Nathaniel in the twins' year had died of leukemia. Another girl in their year had lost her father to brain cancer. The worst thing that has ever happened to Ana is losing her grandparents, which seemed to happen at the precise moment she was ready for it.

She watches the grim faces of three police officers, one taking down notes. She breathes a sigh of relief. She drives past this sadness and leaves it on the corner of Orwell Road. And for another day, bad things don't happen to Ana O'Donnelly.

By seven, they have eaten spaghetti Bolognese and the kids have dropped plates into the sink when they should have gone straight into the dishwasher. As she rinses, then stacks them, her phone vibrates on the bench. It's Paul. Could she pick him up from the club? They'd stayed and had a few beers after golf. She suspects Rob is still there too. She's been meaning to text him today but didn't quite know what to say.

After calling out to Rachael that she's ducking out, she lifts the keys off their hook and takes the fifteen-minute drive into town. When she walks into the club, in black tights, thongs, no bra, and a Bonds jumper with remnants of her dinner (or is it someone else's?) on it, she suddenly feels self-conscious. She probably should've changed, or at least pulled a bra on, she thinks. As she jingles her keys and scans the room, she spots Paul and Rob in the far corner.

Paul is sitting back, arms crossed over his chest—a pose men adopt only after their forty-fifth birthday. She imagines how horrified he'd be if she snapped a photograph, his stomach bulging against a snug red polo shirt.

And then there is Rob, leaning in, telling Paul a story she desperately wishes she could overhear. Although speckles of gray now creep up the sides of his hair, his profile has barely changed in twenty-five years. His nose is the first thing you notice—so distinctive he has no choice but to joke about it. She has always thought it was oddly attractive, in a masculine way. Had a woman been born with a feature of that size in the middle of her face, she'd have cried "deviated septum" and had it hacked at until it was petite and upturned. But Rob's face would not make sense without it.

Rob notices her before Paul does. He waves at her, his smile so pronounced that creases from the corners of his eyes reach the corners of his mouth. And that's when she feels it. But how to put it into words. A bird trapped in a too-small cage, its wings thrashing the metal bars, fast and certain and unrelenting. Then there's a drop. The feeling of drifting off to sleep and you're falling but you don't know quite where and what will happen if you hit the bottom.

Has he always looked like that? His hair has grown longer—is that it? His neck looks narrower, his Adam's apple bulging from its base, giving way to a wide chest she thinks she might like to touch with her fingertips.

But it isn't how he looks. It is the way he stands up. The way his arms move and the way his spine rolls and his chin lifts as she walks toward him. She can't tell where she feels it. In her stomach, maybe. In her lips, curling upward. Behind her eyes, whispering thoughts that feel like a different language but which she understands anyway. The translation, though imperfect, is something like the word "possibility."

All she knows is that this is a feeling she thought belonged in adolescence. But now it is back, and energy and life emanate from this six-foot-two man in front of her whom she's known since she was eighteen. It feels dangerous and it steals her breath for a moment. She hates it but also wants to feel just like this every day until she dies.

His eyes stare into her as he says, "Hello again!" and bends down to embrace her in a hug and plant a warm kiss on her left cheek. She feels his hard chest on hers, curses herself for the second time that night for not slipping on a bra on her way out. Paul doesn't get up but pats the bench next to him, indicating for her to sit down.

She slides in next to Paul, who cheerily kisses her cheek, and Rob sits back down opposite them. They only speak for about ten minutes. Rob asks about Rachael's netball but it feels like they're not talking about netball at all. He laughs at her in a way no one else does, and when he speaks, he looks only at her. As though Paul isn't sitting just to her left.

But it's getting late and Paul has to be up early for Sunday morning soccer, so they walk together to the car park and say goodbye. Rob wraps his arms around her, his cologne—woody and expensive smelling, maybe Armani—sets on her spaghetti-stained cotton jumper.

She knows she won't see him for a long while. He lives more than eight thousand kilometers away.

Driving home, she barely says a word to Paul. She is with someone else in her head. And when she walks back through the door, she tosses the keys on the kitchen bench and decides not to shower or change into her pajamas. Instead, she crawls into bed wearing her dirty over-sized jumper that smells like something new and old and far and close. She is still when Paul climbs in beside her.

She lies there all night, unable to get comfortable, until the sun begins to creep under the curtains and lively birds start to whistle, as though trying to trick her into believing that today will be no different from the one before it. But somewhere between two and three in the morning, she'd realized that things could never be the same again. It is like one of those optical illusions, where all of a sudden you can only see the faces and not the vase and, no matter how hard you try, you can't switch back. You're stuck looking through the world with different eyes at an image that no longer makes sense.

Claire

‌❧

SIX YEARS EARLIER

CLAIRE IS SITTING ON THE TUBE. SHE'S WEARING A COAT she bought from Miss Selfridge last week because, even though it's spring, it gets so cold when the sun goes down that she can't feel her hands. Staring at the woman standing in front of her wearing a short floral dress and Dr. Martens, she wonders if any of this will ever feel normal. Her. In London. British accents and double-decker buses and police who look like they're straight off the set of *The Bill*,

Buckingham Palace in the distance. She feels like she's in a movie and this is all an elaborate set bustling with actors. Everything is interesting. Buying tampons from Boots. Topping up her Oyster card. The streets smell different here. Clean. Crisper.

She still thinks about Vanessa, which she hoped would stop when she landed in another country, half a world away from her. Not because she wants her back. More just out of habit. In quiet moments, she considers sending her a message, just so she might have an opportunity to tell her how she's never been happier and London is the best decision she ever made. She knows whatever reply she receives from Vanessa will be unsatisfying. Every time they speak, Vanessa seems further from the person Claire had known. Like a mirage that disappears the closer you get. Vanessa would probably ask if she left because of her, and she'd reply and say, "No, not everything is about you." Even though she did leave because of her. Because Toowoomba is too small a place, especially when you both work in theater and are—as they always used to say—the only gays in the village.

The train pulls up at Camden Town tube station and she wishes they hadn't arranged to meet in the middle of the day. She's more relaxed at night. As she stands on the escalator, she chews on her thumbnail. Why does this feel like a date? It's not a date. Her friend Yazmin just knew she was alone in London and suggested she meet up with a friend of hers called Maggie. Yazmin would normally be here but she's currently gallivanting around Europe, and so here she is, about to meet a stranger in Camden who would probably rather be doing just about anything else. *This is what you have to do*, Claire coaches herself silently. *Meet new people. That's the whole point.* She buries her hands deep into her coat pockets, picks at the stitching.

As soon as she reaches the street, she sees her. Standing outside the HSBC like she'd said she would be. Claire recognizes her from Facebook, but she looks smaller in real life. More awkward.

"Hey, Maggie," Claire says when she reaches her, offering a stiff wave.

"Oh, hey! You recognized me." Maggie smiles but her eyes don't move.

"So, are you from here?"

"Here as in . . . England?" asks Maggie. "Or, like, London?"

"Both. I guess. Did you grow up in London?"

"Does it sound like I grew up in London?"

Claire is trying to read her. She thinks the correct answer is no.

"I grew up in Birkenhead, in the Wirral," Maggie says, as though that should mean something to Claire. Her voice has a different melody from that of other people she's met in London. Rougher. An upward inflection at the end of every sentence, as though she's always asking a question.

"It's sorta northwest, just outside of Liverpool. Daniel Craig— like, James Bond—grew up there."

"That's cool," she says.

"No, it's not."

They stand in silence for a few seconds until Claire asks how Maggie knows Yazmin, even though she already knows the answer. They talk about the last time they spoke to Yazmin. How she's funny. How she has a new girlfriend. When is she coming back from Spain? Oh, not sure, think she's going to Italy first. It becomes clear that this is all they have. Claire has a sudden urge to climb back down the escalator she's just come up, get back on the train, and go back to the hostel.

"So, what ya wanna do? Are you hungry?"

Claire can't think of anything worse than sitting across from a stranger in a restaurant and trying to fill silences until their plates are cleared. "Would it be weird to go to the pub?" she says. "I feel like I need a drink."

Maggie studies her, then nods. "Yeah, right then, let's do it. I know a cheap place down on the next corner."

It's a Saturday and the sun is peeking out from between two heavy gray clouds. Swarms of people are charging down the street, so much so that Claire keeps sidestepping into rather than around them. They start conversations—"So, whereabouts do you live?"— but then get separated, before they rejoin and ask a new question— "Have you got a job yet?"—without answering any of them.

The pub has a look and atmosphere that Australian pubs try but fail to create. Stone floors and arch windows and a dark oak bar that smells like history. The glass cathedral ceiling reveals a sea of whites and grays. Looking up at the miserable sky makes it feel warmer inside. Cozier.

They find a table with a pair of red leather stools by a window and Claire offers to buy first drinks. She orders them both vodka and lemonades because she doesn't know what else you're meant to drink at lunchtime on a Saturday. Maggie raises her eyebrows and Claire doesn't know how to interpret it.

Maggie tells her she's a personal trainer. Claire tries to think of a question to ask. She's not particularly into exercise. She's always thought of gyms as sterile and depressing. Who wants to run on the spot, legs pounding on a moving piece of rubber, while looking out onto a main road banked up with peak-hour traffic?

She tells Maggie that she worked in theater back home. Maggie doesn't like theater. She doesn't say so explicitly but she just nods and changes the subject, so Claire can tell. A few minutes later she asks, "Is Yazmin into that theater stuff?" and Claire fumbles her way through an answer before excusing herself to go to the bathroom.

One more drink, she tells herself, *and then you can leave*. Have a shower. Watch *Breaking Bad* on your laptop in bed. But when she sits back down, Maggie asks, "Should we get somethin' to eat?"

"*Should we get somethin' to eat?*" Claire repeats, imitating her accent. She's surprised even as she says it. Surprised because she's fairly certain it's rude to impersonate an accent and she's never had a compulsion to do so before—and surprised at how much it really did sound like Maggie.

Maggie looks back at her. Blinks. And then starts to laugh. Her face softens and for the first time Claire notices the dimples that frame the edges of her mouth, her eyes coming alive in a way they weren't before.

Things change after that.

They sit on their high stools for hours, talking about everything and nothing. Yazmin doesn't come up again. Maggie tries to say "You reckon?" in Claire's accent, but they both gasp at how terrible it is and she promises not to do it again.

The sounds of dusk are emerging as they walk back toward Camden station. This is why she came to London. To meet people who know nothing about her. She can start over. She can be Claire-at-Twenty-Four, rather than always having to be the Claire of the year before, and of the year before that, glued to every little thing she's ever done. She's not Vanessa's ex. Or Maryanne and Greg's only child. She's just Claire. And that can mean whatever she'd like it to.

Patrick

⳾

*T*HE NIGHT BEGAN TERRIBLY.

The tail end of summer has quickly turned into an unusually cool autumn, and a bitter breeze clips at his cheeks and hands in a way that doesn't often happen in Perth. He bounces on the balls of his feet and wishes he'd worn something warmer. He pulls at the cuffs of his thin black cotton hoodie, the only thing between him and the night air.

He is standing outside the Brass Monkey Hotel, his lower back resting on a dark cyan baluster. Taxis and buses speed past, the city loud with life. He watches a group of women, probably his age, twenty or twenty-one, stumble toward him in heels that make their entire bodies lean forward. One rolls her ankle and he flinches, but then hears a chorus of squealing. Someone caught her. Another pulls a water bottle out of her bag and takes a swig. Her eyes squeeze shut and she screws up her face, rubbing her lips with the back of her hand. As they clomp past, laughing and clutching at each other's arms, they don't so much as glance at him. He is invisible. Like another post holding up the building behind him.

As they pass by the entrance, they begin to whisper. Two guys, older than him but not by much, sit on a stone step a little farther up the street—one is wearing a leather jacket, the other is in denim. One by one like falling dominos, the women turn their attention to the pair. There's more laughter. And then a "Hey," followed by giggling and playful nudges. The men laugh back. And the women keep stumbling on, probably to a club that will let them in even though they shouldn't.

"Patrick!" he hears, and when he turns around, it's her.

For a moment, he feels embarrassed. The last time he saw her face was late last night, lit up on his laptop, while he stalked her boyfriend on Facebook. He tried to gauge who Nick was, what kind of relationship they had, by flicking through a handful of photos. One was from a few years back. It must have been someone's Year Twelve formal. Nick's arm was draped around Caitlin's right shoulder, her right hand clutching his, a white corsage hanging from her wrist. It looked ragged. Like he'd tucked it away in his pocket and nearly forgot about it until she asked. A few of the leaves were bent the wrong way and the tips of the petals were already turning brown. She was smiling, the muscles in her neck clenching. Tight ringlets fell past her shoulders, her skin tinged an artificial orange. Nick looked even younger than she did, his chin soft and round but jutting out like he was looking for a fight. Nick's black eyes peered into him, as if he could see the pillow propping up Patrick's head late at night. Someone had written beneath the picture, "You two look HOT," and Nick had replied, "Yeah, she scrubs up all right." The words might have been exchanged two years ago, but Patrick decided he hated him.

Tonight, her skin looks golden and warm against an off-white jumper, and the tip of her nose is pink.

He doesn't know why but he opens his arms and says "Caitlin" too loudly, and they share an awkward, stiff hug, her face brushing his face.

"Where are the others?"

"Not sure, I only just got here," he says. He didn't. He'd gotten here half an hour ago and had walked up and down the street a few times before pacing the aisles of the supermarket on the corner, pretending to look at different brands of pasta.

They're going to Lucio's, a local pizza place Alice has been raving about. On Monday, their results for the interface design project had come through. A high distinction. So they'd decided to go out to dinner and maybe a bar on Barrack Street. He has a feeling Caitlin gets a lot of high distinctions. When she'd helped him with his part of the presentation, he'd seen how she wrote and how easily words spun from the cogs in her brain out onto the page. She'd replaced connecting words with full stops and had made sentences that'd felt clunky and confused sound fluid. When he'd stood in front of the tutorial, two dozen or so twentysomethings half-asleep at their desks, he'd glanced over at her standing in the corner. There was something about the way she looked at him. A nod. A curl of the lips. He'd felt just as nervous as always. But she was calm, sure that everything would be okay. He could see her silhouette in his peripheral vision as he spoke and noticed that his shaking hands had stilled and his shoulders dropped as he did. He'd let himself think for a moment that maybe he could do anything if she were right there beside him.

He asks what she got up to today. Studying, she says. And she went to a café on her own in an effort to get away from Nick. She never says anything nice about him, really. He refuses to learn how to drive. He sleeps in late on weekends. He doesn't get along with her family and her mum tells her she's outgrown him. She'd wanted to hike the Bibbulmun Track in Kalamunda last weekend, but when their alarm had gone off, Nick had refused to get out of bed. When Alice had asked her why she didn't just go by herself, she'd shrugged. She was probably sick of doing things on her own, he'd thought. She'd met Nick when she was in Year Ten, and when she'd decided to move to Perth for university, he'd come too. Now they lived in a run-down apartment in East Perth where the cracked paint on her bedroom walls made her feel like she was being buried alive, every day a new brick being laid across her chest, making it almost impossible to move.

He knows all of this because she has told him. Mostly through text messages late at night when neither of them can sleep. It began at 3:00 a.m. with her asking if he'd started the essay for their Internet of Things subject, another class they were in together. He'd replied in the morning with a "No" before asking why she had been up so late. She'd said she had trouble sleeping. A lot on her mind.

Where is everyone? he is thinking, just as she says, "Wait, was it seven we were meant to meet?"

It's nearly seven thirty.

He checks his phone. Two messages. His stomach drops. One from Thomas. Sick. Another from Alice. Assignment due on Monday. Hasn't started. She's out.

"Anything?"

"Looks like they've both bailed," he says, raising his eyebrows. He can feel redness spreading to his cheeks and the more he wishes it away, the worse it gets. As much as he has wanted time alone with Caitlin, he suddenly has a desire to run away. Having other people around when he is with her makes him feel safe, less exposed. But now he feels like raw flesh, pink and damp, and she can see the way his stomach churns and what he ate for breakfast. It's just them and, despite how many times he's rehearsed conversations with her— questions he wants to ask, stories he wants to tell—he has nothing at all to say. He's overwhelmed by the responsibility to say something interesting. To be fully himself but not really because that could never be enough.

"Well, aren't we popular." She smiles, her teeth big and bright. "Is it bad that I'm sort of relieved?"

When they arrive at Lucio's, he realizes this is the first time he's been to dinner with a girl one-on-one and wonders whether the other diners assume they're dating. They must look mismatched. She walks unselfconsciously, like it has never occurred to her not to, her head high, emphasizing her long, thin neck. He trails behind her, not sure where to put his hands, like a man who's just discovered he has them. One finds his pocket. The other pushes his glasses higher on the bridge of his nose. Then that hand finds a pocket too. The other hand comes out, touches his stomach. Then scratches his cheek, even though it isn't itchy and he feels like a firework that's been lit from both ends. He lets himself imagine for a moment who he could be if this person beside him were his girlfriend—what life might be possible.

When he sits, a menu to occupy him and later a glass of water, he relaxes. He remembers parts of the script he'd rehearsed. They start to chat and he learns that she grew up in Brisbane and always knew that she wanted to do something in software. "Everywhere you look, there's a problem waiting to be solved," she says. They talk about their parents. How computer systems are a language they were never taught to speak. Nick comes up. He's always there, sitting at the table with them, a ghost they can sense but can't see. She sips her Diet Coke and says, as though she's commenting on the crust of her pizza, that she knows she needs to end it.

"You'd be so surprised if you met him," she says. "We don't have anything in common."

She and Patrick do, though. They both like to run. Both own bikes they wish they used more. Then there's music. The Wombats. Arctic Monkeys. Rüfüs Du Sol. And movies. And how they both like to go to bed early, even though they struggle to sleep, and wake up before their alarm. They both sometimes get that thing where your mind wakes up before your body and you're paralyzed. It's almost like you're suffocating and you're sure something really bad is about to happen and there's nothing you can do to stop it. Caitlin says she's never met someone before who understands that feeling. Neither has Patrick.

As much as they convince themselves these similarities matter—common interests that would make them seem compatible on a dating app—they know they don't. They simply fill the space. Give them something to talk about. Their likeness will play into the myth they spin about how their story started. "We liked the same music," they'll say. But by this point, they're both already hypnotized. They don't know it yet, but they're open to all suggestions. It isn't the coincidences that build the trance, but the trance that builds the coincidences, finding parallels in places they wouldn't ordinarily look. They imprint destiny on each other, a kind of teleology, the early work of merging two stories into one.

As they leave the restaurant, she walks closer to him than before. He can smell her clothes, like clean, warm laundry. When they pass Russell Square on their way back to the station, she asks if he would like to sit. She's not ready to go home yet. The bandstand in the center of the park is lit up from the inside. Soft yellows illuminate the open-air platform, the concrete stairs left with its shadows. He sits on a step, second from the top, and she shuffles over beside him. Darkness cloaks them. They can hear the thumps of a beat from a nearby bar, just enough to make out the song. "Dreams" by Fleetwood Mac. He knows this song will always make him think of her. He doesn't say anything and the silence is comfortable. A relief.

She rests her head on his upper arm, her hair so close he doesn't have to strain to smell it. He's never smelled anything so good. Like coconut and honey. He tries to steady his breathing. Work out what to do next. He considers resting his head on top of her head but thinks it would probably be uncomfortable. He wants to do whatever it takes for her to stay there, like that, and never move. Attached to his arm like this forever.

If he's honest, Nick doesn't cross his mind. Nick who won't even get out of bed to go hiking. Who didn't give her a birthday present last year because he had to wait to get paid, and then it was "on its way" and then it never came. Who makes her leave early whenever they go to one of her friends' houses, because suddenly he's just stopped speaking and has picked up his phone and is scrolling through Facebook.

His heart is beating so fast that Patrick thinks she can probably hear it pounding against his skinny ribs. *Badum. Badum. Badum.* There's a sense he's dreaming even though he knows he isn't. Part of him feels like he knew this would happen. Sitting on this concrete step, the smell of her mixed with dewy grass. This had to happen—

like life set him on a certain path where this was the inevitable end point. It makes everything that's come before worth it. His mind keeps leaving his body, watching from above, as though to check and confirm that this moment really belongs to him.

Not much is said. The angle of his shoulder starts to hurt, but he doesn't say anything. She's the one who eventually says it's time to go. They walk to the station together, a looseness to their bodies that didn't exist a few hours ago. *How interesting*, he thinks. That you can go years without anything much changing at all, monotony as far as the eye can see, and then in a matter of hours your life becomes unrecognizable.

He asks what she's doing tomorrow. She says nothing planned. He says for him neither. She asks if he wants to do something. He says yes and knows he won't be able to sleep. The person beside him is the gatekeeper to paradise—a place that feels so close and yet entirely out of reach.

Ana

The plane smells like a hospital and the feet of someone who couldn't wait until takeoff to remove their shabby Nike runners.

Stuck in seat 52B (she didn't even know planes went back that far), she can see the feet in question. They belong to a man positioned in the same row, but in seat E. Right in the center. The smell couldn't offend more nostrils if it tried.

She thinks she might like to complain. Catch the attention of one of the Qantas flight attendants—they'd understand—and just suggest that they kindly ask the man to put his shoes back on. They are going to be stuck in this aluminum box for almost twelve hours and she, along with no doubt a dozen or so others, is beginning to feel nauseous. Not only will they be inhaling this stench while they eat and sleep and read and watch, but by the time they get off the plane, the scent will probably have made its way into the fibers of all their clothing. Their hair. Their breath. And they will all arrive in Sri Lanka smelling like another man's foot.

But she doesn't want to be *that* woman. Planes are full of forty-something women beginning sentences with "Excuse me" and "Sorry, I just," and she has vowed that she will never become one of them. So she huffs and asks Paul, probably not quietly enough, "Can you smell that?"

He looks up from his book and says, "What?" and then, "No." Of course he can't.

It is not two minutes later that Rachael turns and self-consciously whispers to her from the row in front, nose scrunched up, "Mum, can you smell that?" and she has never loved anybody so much in her entire life.

The flight map blinks in front of her. Eleven hours and fifteen minutes. Five and a bit movies and they'll be there.

She has thought about Rob every day for almost seven months. He has gone from sitting in the background of her life, popping up when he posts some blurry photo of a golf course on Instagram, to the foreground, occupying the place of a problem that demands solving.

Her phone suddenly vibrates in her back pocket and she knows who it is before she even looks at it. "Can't wait to see you all. We'll have dinner waiting. Hope the flight isn't too torturous x."

Hiding her phone in the gap between her and Paul, she types out "Hungry already" but then deletes it because it sounds weird and uncomfortably sexual, before settling on "See you soon x."

As she feels the wheels turn beneath her, she finally switches her phone to airplane mode and lets her body relax. She closes her eyes and leans her head back into the seat, deepening her breathing, noticing the way her stomach dances and her chest thumps and something crawls low inside her pelvis, a part of her body she almost forgot she had.

She thinks about the last time she saw him—that final night at the club—the smell of his embrace that had lingered on her skin and the text he sent her a few days later. He missed her, he'd written. He wanted her and the family to come and visit him in Sri Lanka. He'd "cover the cost," was how he'd put it. Anyone else might have been insulted, but she knew he had more money than he knew what to do with. She'd often heard him ask what the point of earning money was if you didn't spend it on the ones you love.

And so they spoke hypothetically for weeks, until late one night Rob had said he had the flights up on his screen, ready to book. Whether they agreed or not, he'd written, there would be five tickets for them to Sri Lanka in April. So she'd taken a gulp of her Riesling, looked at the ceiling for a moment, and then typed back with two tense thumbs, "We'll be there."

Something had shifted in the way they spoke to each other. There were more *x*'s and *was just thinking about you*s—and there was more complaining about their partners. They had begun Face-Timing, and increasingly she found herself fixing her hair and then putting on a little bit of lipstick, dabbing some on her cheeks, and should she put mascara on? No. That would be too obvious.

She'd send him photos of mundane, everyday things, like the kids swimming in the pool. But she would rearrange her legs a few times until they looked thinner and more toned in the foreground of the shot. Every time something happened in her life—if she watched a TV show she couldn't stop thinking about or had a confrontation with a teacher or had a funny conversation with one of the kids—she'd rush to tell Rob, who made her feel like everything mattered a little more. Her life suddenly felt interesting, like a movie that Rob was watching, and she got to decide which scenes were cut and which ones were drawn out. For the first time in twenty years, her life had an audience. It was no longer just her trying to find joy in the mundanity. It all meant something to someone else.

And Rob—this person whom she'd known forever yet never really known. Pockets of his life were a mystery to her and she enjoyed nothing more than to imagine what he was doing at any given time. She liked thinking about him at work, wearing a Hugo Boss suit, surrounded by women who wanted him. It was the things he did alone that most intrigued her. Exercising and driving and sitting in his enormous office, overflowing with natural light and smelling of freshly vacuumed carpet. What was he thinking about? Who was he when no one else was around?

As she feels the plane dancing on waves of wind, she lets herself imagine Rob's hands on her body, firm and warm and intentional. She knows—as we so often do, if we allow ourselves to be truly honest—exactly what is going to happen next. A voice with no sound tells us. We just mostly choose to ignore it.

When they land in Sri Lanka, she knows it is the start of something. And she also knows there is always only one way it can ever end.

ROB STANDS, THE fingertips of both hands on the glass dining table, as though he is about to announce a corporate restructure. "All right, it's our last night together," he says seriously. "And we all need more to drink."

There's a murmur of approval around the table.

"Are you red?" he asks Paul, pointing at him firmly. Paul nods yes and holds up his empty glass, the remnants of his last drink gravelly in the bottom. "White or red?" he asks Jenny, turning to her slightly groggily.

"Hmmm, no, I think I'm done," she decides, taking far too long for Rob's liking to make her decision.

"How about me?" Ana laughs as he jogs to the kitchen. It is getting late—the kids collapsed into their beds hours ago—but Ana isn't tired at all.

"You're white," he shouts back. "You're always white."

She smiles and looks down at her sandy-brown legs. It's rare in life that you know how much you're enjoying something at the precise moment you're enjoying it. Happiness is something more often felt in retrospect—a sensation you later ascribe to memories. But she knows, at this moment, that this trip has been one of the best of her life.

She'd slept deeply on sheets she didn't have to wash. She'd climbed out of bed when she felt like it, usually met by Rob in the kitchen, who'd demand she sit while he made her a cappuccino better than anything you'd get in a café. They'd been on safari and seen elephants and cheetahs and leopards and water buffalo, and hours had passed where she'd thought about nothing else but what was directly in front of her.

The kids had had a ball. Paul too. They'd never done anything like it. Rob had sat with the boys in the jeep, explaining how to tell a male deer from a female one or spotting toque macaque monkeys hidden in trees. One early morning, as the white sun pierced through the blue of dawn and they were still rubbing sleep from their eyes, he'd told them that Sri Lanka was the land of serendipity.

Sri Lanka was once named Serendip, he'd explained, his sunglasses nestled on top of his tousled, overgrown hair. He went on to say that it was based on a Persian fairy tale called *The Three Princes of Serendip*, in which the princes were always finding things—incredible things—they hadn't been looking for. He'd paused and slowly rubbed the side of his face, covered in days-old stubble.

"And that's what serendipity means," Rob had said to Ana and the three kids, as he'd seemed to realize that Paul was no longer listening. "Finding exactly what you want. By accident."

Over the last two weeks, Ana's body had found a new awareness of Rob. She felt that even if her eyes were closed, she'd know exactly where he was, how many steps away from her he stood, and whether or not he was watching her. If she was next to him, her body would react, as naturally as sweat pools on your lower back on a hot day. Most of the time, she'd feign distraction and find a reason why she needed to be elsewhere. To twirl Rachael's ponytail, perhaps, or stand behind one of her boys, her arms hanging across their chest, her chin resting on a reluctant head. Rob's presence felt like the sun. You wanted to lie in it and feel it gently caress your skin, but after a few minutes it became too much. It stung and it suffocated and its intensity was unbearable.

When he'd touched the tops of her arms one night as he'd circled the table to get to his seat at a restaurant, she'd frozen. For hours afterward, his hands had felt imprinted on her, like his gentle brush had actually been a slap, leaving a red raw mark.

Rob returns from the kitchen with a fresh bottle of white and looks at Ana expectantly. She is reaching for the empty glass to her left when Jenny says, "No, this is yours," and laughs, sliding the glass to Ana's right toward her. "I can tell, see?" she adds, lifting the glass to the light. "I don't touch the glass. Only the stem," she explains, as though she's being helpful. The second glass, now in front of Ana, is covered in fingerprints, wearing the greasiness of dinner.

Ana offers a forced laugh, which comes from her throat and not her chest, and says, "That'd be me!" while Rob reaches for his own, lifts it above his head, and says, "It'd be me too," laughing.

"Whoops, me too," Paul adds, looking at the glass in front of him, and then Jenny tells a dull story about her grandmother and etiquette and being reprimanded as a child for adding salt to her meal without first having a mouthful.

And so they sit and drink and reminisce about old nights at the Durnham Hotel, where Rob always used to drink too many bourbon and Cokes and make out with someone he'd just met on the worn couch in the corner with suspect stains all over it.

"I used to think you were creepy," Ana says, sitting back in her seat as if it were a question.

"Oh," Rob replies, straight-faced. "That's because I absolutely was."

Jenny and Paul laugh as if they understand, but they don't. They don't know that before Ana and Paul even met, Rob used to stare at her from across the room, looking away only when she caught him. They don't know what Rob said to her the first time she showed him her engagement ring. There was a part of themselves that they'd only ever shared with each other.

Later, as Rob rinses dishes at the kitchen sink, the sleeves of his shirt rolled up, Jenny yawns at the table and says she's tired. It's past her bedtime. As Paul indulges her, asking what time she has to be up in the morning, Ana thinks that if she didn't know Jenny, she'd probably find her quite beautiful.

Blond blow-dried hair frames a thin face and her eyes are an arresting green. Her skin is bronze but sunspots stain her cheekbones and forehead, betraying her age. She doesn't look forty, though, probably because she's had fantastic Botox inserted into her forehead and around the sides of her mouth. Rob had told Ana that.

But she has a mean smile. And her voice is high-pitched. Grating. Even though she is Australian, she has begun to adopt the accents of the British friends they've made in Sri Lanka. Ana finds it mortifying.

"Yeah, I'm off to bed too," Paul announces, letting out an exaggerated exhale as he stands up, taking his wineglass inside with him. Rob protests. Doesn't he want one more? But Paul laughs that he can barely keep his eyes open and wanders to the guest room shouting "Night" after him.

"The last ones standing," Rob says as he pours Ana an absurdly generous glass of wine, then tops his up before putting the bottle back down.

They talk about the day they first met. Well, properly met. Ana can't remember what day of the week it would have been, but she knows it must have been summer. It had been hot and dry, the train platform offering no relief.

When the young man with light brown coarse hair, dusty skin, and a nose that appeared to have been broken a few times had looked up at her as she'd approached the bench he was sitting on at Durnham station, she'd recognized him immediately. *He looks different in daylight*, she'd thought.

Self-consciousness curved the top of his spine, his elbows resting on his knees, his fingers interlaced and hanging between them. The business shirt he wore, which was at least two sizes too big, made him look younger. He'd tucked it furiously into belted pants that looked like they'd been purchased by his mother. His eyes— blue-gray, maybe—were less intense than when she'd caught them a few times in the past.

As she'd gotten closer, Ana had become painfully aware of her ill-fitting black pencil skirt that sat too high and made her waist look thicker than it actually was. She'd bought it, along with the pink blouse she had on, from a secondhand shop she was embarrassed to have ever visited. But when a temp role had opened up in a leafy corner of Sydney's Central Business District in Wynyard, she'd leapt at the opportunity. She'd imagined meticulously organized filing cabinets and expensive stationery used to mark documents in manila folders. She'd wear a high bun, she fantasized, fastened with bobby pins and hair spray, and she'd routinely apply bright lipstick and flit around in high heels like Fiona's older sister, Wendy, did.

Often when she'd been at her best friend Fiona's house, Wendy would arrive home, usually after they'd all eaten dinner, with a veneer of dewiness glazing her forehead and cheeks—not enough to be unsightly, but enough to indicate that she'd done something meaningful that day. Ana had thought there were few things more attractive than a woman like Wendy, with her eyeliner slightly smudged under each eye and her bun now loose, who lived with that kind of purpose.

And so the day after she'd sat her final Year Twelve exam, Ana had sprawled every newspaper she could find across the laminate dining table and told her mother she had two criteria. The first was that she had a desk and the second was that it was a desk inside an office in the city. She'd applied for more than two dozen positions in a week. Eventually, after months of hovering around the phone every time it rang, Sweeneys, an advertising agency, called to say they had some temporary work available if she could start next Monday. Office attire, they specified.

It turned out Ana hadn't actually been able to afford the silk blouses and fitted trousers she'd imagined, so she'd had to settle for clothes she resented, living in constant fear of being spotted by someone she actually knew. And here she was.

"Hi," Ana said, feeling an awkward jolt of visibility as he looked at her.

Shuffling over to make space on the warm blue bench, Rob grinned and said, "Well, fancy seeing you here."

His breath smelled like toothpaste as he told her about the job he hated, forcing him to get up four hours before he was ready to, five too many days a week. She teased him that mornings must be hard when you didn't go to bed until dawn on the weekend.

"I admit it," he'd said, laughing. "I've probably been going a bit hard lately. Mum's convinced a full-time job will be the thing that makes me grow up." He pulled a face. Unlikely.

At nine minutes to eight, their train had groaned to a halt at the platform. It was six minutes late, though neither of them had cared. Without bothering to check whether there were any vacant seats up- or downstairs, Rob had made his way into the vestibule and grabbed on to a pole casually as the train pulled away.

"Did I see you at the pub with Paul the other week?" he'd asked, roughing up the front of his floppy thick hair with his free hand.

"Yeah, we're there all the time," she'd responded, her gaze reflected in the glass as suburbs flashed by. They'd been dating since late last year.

With her head resting on the inside of her left arm, her hand clutching the railing overhead, Ana had told him a story about how the previous weekend, Paul had woken up in the middle of the night and demanded she "brush her teeth because Monkey will freeze them if you don't drink the chicken." He'd been sleep-talking—Monkey was the family dog. She'd known she was babbling a little, but it was a pretty funny story.

Rob had thought that Ana laughed about Paul in a way that had showed that she loved him—at least that's what he told her years later. How it had made him realize that Ana and Paul's relationship was different from the one he had with Melissa, the girl he'd been dating back then—it was a real relationship, not a superficial one like his was. *Imagine thinking that's adorable*, Rob said he'd been thinking, not without envy.

"How about you?" Ana had asked. "Paul mentioned a while back you were seeing Melissa?"

Rob hadn't answered straightaway, which had made Ana wonder whether Paul had told her something he hadn't been meant to. The footy boys—the Dingos, as they called themselves—had always abided by unwritten rules she didn't understand, nor really care about much. Anyway, she'd been sure that she'd seen Rob out with Melissa, dancing to some TLC song as the lights were being turned on. She'd thought it was quite sweet.

Eventually, he'd answered. "Not really," he'd said. "Haven't seen her for a while . . . Been busy with work and footy . . ." Rob trailed off, scratching his ear on the inside of his arm.

Ana later learned that what Rob had meant was that it would never have been cute if Melissa had woken him in the middle of the night with nonsensical sleep-talk. It would have been irritating. He would've sighed and rolled over, wishing she hadn't stayed the night and anticipating the hour she would finally sneak out.

The train had come to a halt, stopping at one of the several suburban stations between Durnham and Wynyard, and Ana had lurched clumsily forward, falling into Rob's chest before quickly recovering her balance. More people had climbed on board, pushing the two into a tighter pocket of the carriage. She could feel a droplet of sweat trickling down her armpit, the air in the carriage now steamy and thick.

Ana reached up again and wrapped a hand around the railing

above her, swaying slightly again as the train started to move again. But not once did she suggest they look downstairs or upstairs to see if there might be somewhere to sit.

And here they were, twenty-five years later, after children and marriages, funerals and overseas holidays, the same two people. Ana looking at Rob with endless curiosity, and Rob looking at her like she might be the most remarkable thing he's ever seen.

Claire

~

THE NEXT FEW MONTHS GO BY IN A HAZE. CLAIRE'S IN IRE-land for St. Patrick's Day, and Berlin the day after. She stands in front of the *Mona Lisa*, smaller than she'd imagined, and inside the Colosseum, bigger than she'd dreamed. She thinks about theater and how she'd like to write—and less about Vanessa. By the time she gets back to London, the name is no longer attached to a feeling.

But London doesn't care about any of that. It welcomes her back with rain that never stops, with wind that knots her hair and a list of things to do. She's staying at a hostel and needs to find a place to rent. And a job. Her days are spent trying to win a game where the odds are stacked against her. Yazmin has returned from Europe and they sit behind her computer screen, applying for whatever jobs are available. But her phone doesn't ring. The nights are long, loneliness creeping in once the sun goes down. Letting go of Vanessa had been freeing at first, but now it just makes her feel empty.

When she thinks about love or sex, it no longer takes on a certain shape or smell. It's just blank. A thing she is unable to imagine. She doesn't ever remember feeling like that. Even in primary school, there would have been a boy she'd tricked herself into believing she wanted. Claire had always seen herself and her life as gray and monotonous— she knew that she borrowed color from other people, that she clung to it a little too tightly. She had loved Vanessa a lot more than she'd loved herself. And so had Vanessa. The majority of their relationship had felt like a waiting game—Claire waiting for Vanessa to grow tired of her. She had. Then the next day, Vanessa would change her mind and so it went on until Claire had moved so far away that she couldn't say yes when Vanessa asked to come over at midnight.

When Maggie first asked if Claire wanted to come and train with her at the gym, she politely said no. They had lunch one day. And went to the movies another. But eventually, Maggie asked again, and Claire knew she couldn't pretend she had anything else on. That was the problem with being unemployed and in a city without many friends or family. You couldn't lie and say you had other plans.

She'd warned Maggie that she hadn't done any serious exercise since school, and even then, she mostly pretended she had period pain or forgot her sports uniform so she could get out of it. She hated how it felt. To not be able to catch your breath. The way your heartbeat throbbed in your head and your ankles ached. Maggie had promised she'd go easy on her but smiled as she said it.

And that's why Claire finds herself at Genesis North End Road on a day that is bright and edging toward warm. Almost.

The gym is mostly empty because it's just before lunchtime on a Thursday. "I Gotta Feeling" by the Black Eyed Peas is playing on the television and if she hears this song one more time, she'll scream. It smells like rubber and salt and she can see Maggie standing in the far corner with another trainer, studying a clipboard. They're wearing the same red cotton shirt and black sports shorts. It's the first time Claire has ever seen her bare legs. They're lean and strong, her skin honey-colored. She turns to face the mirrored wall to her right and hopes it will deliver her something she wants to see. It doesn't. Her black cotton leggings look worn and stretched and she's not wearing the right bra under her oversized white T-shirt. She makes the woman in the mirror promise never to wear white again. All it does is make her D cup look like an F.

Maggie turns around and waves. "I'm excited," she says, smiling and bouncing over and rubbing her hands together.

She throws her arms around Claire, who says tonelessly, "I hope you know what you're dealing with."

Watching Maggie is mesmerizing. She makes everything look easy. Her back straight. Feet shoulder-width apart. Eyes looking straight ahead. Thinking about a dozen things at once. Claire fantasizes about what it might feel like to occupy a body like that, with muscles in the right places and arms and legs that do what they're supposed to. Imagine respecting your body and not resenting it. Wearing it like something you earned, rather than lugging it around because you have no other choice.

At first, Claire feels strong. She remembers that she's competitive. She pushes herself far beyond what she probably should. But then Maggie says they've only got ten minutes left, and her legs go numb.

When she stands up, black spots obscure her vision. She tries to blink them away. Takes a sip of water. Pleads for the head spins to pass. But the dots are getting bigger and bigger and gulps of air aren't making it to her lungs.

Maggie's voice—"Hey, you okay?"—sounds far away and every part of her is trying to resist this from happening. Not here. Maggie gestures for her to lie down just in time and everything goes dark and silent. She's floating. She sees people and things that don't make sense and she's back in her bed in Toowoomba and her mother is there and then she hears a voice she doesn't recognize.

"You're okay." A hand rests on her clammy forehead.

Her eyes open slowly and a few seconds later, she can hear the music again. Louder and louder. Where is she? And why is it daytime? Fluorescent lights glare at her from the ceiling and a dumbbell rack appears in her peripheral vision. Maggie is cross-legged beside her.

Claire covers her face with her hands. "I'm so sorry. I'm a fainter. It's just a bit stuffy in here . . . I probably needed some fresh air."

"You went completely gray for a moment there. Probably pushed you a little hard. Here, sit up. Have some water."

Maggie doesn't fuss or panic. She strokes her hair. Tells her about the time she fainted on a crowded bus passing by Oxford Circus and hit her head hard on the pole she'd been grasping on to. "Nice try, though," she adds. "This better not mean you won't come back."

"I'm clearly allergic to exercise. How much clearer can I be!" Claire says, gesturing to her body, still flat against the mat.

"Let's do a bit of shavasana just to round out the session." Maggie lies down beside her, directing her to breathe in and breathe out.

As Claire closes her eyes, trying to erase the memory of what's just happened, she has the impulse to reach over and hold Maggie's hand. To say thank you for being kind.

"Okay, corpse." Maggie swings up to her feet and claps her hands. "You hungry?"

They walk to Pret a Manger and sit by the window. People passing by wear shorts and T-shirts, searching for a park to sunbake in. Claire is quieter than usual. She pretends she's still feeling light-headed, but she's not.

"You been to Candy Bar yet?" Maggie asks, with a mouthful of baguette. Claire's heard of Candy Bar, a lesbian bar in Soho. The kind of place that doesn't exist in Toowoomba.

"Not yet. I want to though." Yazmin had said she'd take her when she got back. There were a bunch of bars along that strip, Soho's gay drag.

"We should. You free this weekend? I'll message Yazmin."

They finish their lunch and Maggie goes back to work. Claire spends the rest of the afternoon in her bunk bed at the hostel, scrolling through jobs she isn't qualified for and places she can't afford. When she goes to the bathroom the next morning, she groans at the pain in her hamstrings. Maggie's words from yesterday echo in her head. As her legs had trembled, she'd said: "You'll think of me tomorrow when you sit down on the loo."

Patrick

⁂

It's just past two in the morning when the pull of his bladder wakes him up. He waits to see if he can ignore it, flipping over his pillow and rearranging his legs. It doesn't work. He climbs out of bed, barely opening his eyes, hoping to preserve whatever sleep is left in them.

When he falls back into bed, the darkness of the room is interrupted by a gleam of light. His phone, facing up on the carpet, thumps silently, the name Caitlin bright on his screen.

She's never called him this late before. They've spoken a few times on the phone since that night in Russell Square, but a phone call without a text first is unusual.

"Hello?" His voice is husky and dry.

She sniffles through the line and her voice is unsteady, trembling as she clears her throat. "I broke up with Nick." He can sense her throwing her head back, shaking it side to side in an effort to compose herself. She pauses. Apologizes for calling. Just needed to speak to someone who didn't know Nick.

His stomach sinks, abandoning the hope that there was another reason he was the first person she'd called. She says he didn't see it coming and she doesn't know how that could be.

"It's awful to know you're the reason someone else is in so much pain. It hurt for me too. But it hurt a long time ago. He's only just catching up."

He asks where she is.

"I'm just in my car." She half laughs. "No, it's okay. I'm just going to sleep here tonight and then sort out what to do next in the morning."

"What?" he asks. "You can't sleep in your car. That's ridiculous. It's too cold—"

"It's not that bad," she interrupts.

"Caitlin, you're not sleeping in your car. Drive to mine. I'm around the corner. You can sleep on the couch. Actually, you take my bed and I'll sleep on the couch . . ."

"No—that's not why I called," she says.

"I know, but seriously. I'm wide awake. I'm already moving my stuff downstairs, so my bed is free."

She asks if he's sure and then apologizes again. But within fifteen minutes, she's on his doorstep in a gray hoodie, tracksuit pants, and Ugg boots. They hug awkwardly and her head rests on his chest—he doesn't know what to do when people cry. It makes him uncomfortable. Like he should be looking somewhere else.

They sit on either end of the couch. She hugs her knees, takes sips of the hot chocolate he's made for her. They're in a cocoon, sharing the same blanket, the whole world still and silent except for them. He tells her he can't imagine how she feels. He's never been in love. Never had a girlfriend.

"What? Seriously?"

"Yeah. Maybe I kissed a girl in Year Seven or something but nothing since then."

She asks why that is. Whether it was a choice. Or if he's just never met anyone he likes enough.

"I've never really thought about it. I probably don't really know how to talk to girls. It's just me and my brother, and my parents aren't particularly . . . talkative. Or emotional. Maybe I'm just not what girls are looking for. I don't know."

"I don't think that's true," she says. "And, anyway, being in a bad relationship is way, way worse than not being in one at all."

For her, she tells him, the relationship she's left was dark and small, dead plants rotting in the corner, the hands of a familiar stranger clawing at her at night. She knew this world so well that when she was there, it was like she was nowhere—suspended in time, nothing good happening but nothing particularly bad either. The quiet was slowly killing her, the walls moving an inch inward every day, and the voice in her head that had once whispered had begun to yell, *Get out*. More frequently. Louder. Until the voice didn't sound like it belonged to her anymore. It was a command from someone else. She knew she didn't have a choice. There were no questions anymore. Just *run*. She begged it to be quiet. It would have been much easier if this place could be home, and she could learn to love the other person within it all over again. But moment by moment, she felt everything they had slipping away, water between her fingers, unable to be scooped back up. That was its own grief, the loss of something you gave away, perfect to the eyes but not to the heart.

When her eyelids start to blink more slowly, the whites of her eyes turning pink, he shows her upstairs. It's now the early hours of Saturday morning. He tells her to sleep for as long as she wants, and he'll see her when she wakes up. When he closes the door, he resists the urge to walk straight back in.

SHE STAYS THE following night. And the one after that. That first night, once all the lights were off, he lay on the couch, listening to the hum of the fridge. With his legs bent at an awkward angle, he watched the stairs. Maybe if he wished hard enough, her right foot would appear, squeaking the stair beneath it.

It's the third night and she's leaving in the morning. She's going back home to Brisbane for a few days to stay with her mum. Her hair is wet from the shower, her skin pink and bright. Joey is downstairs playing a game that's too loud, and they're both propped up on pillows in his bed. He spent most of the day downloading *Silver Linings Playbook* and now his laptop, the screen cracked at the right-hand corner, is positioned between them. She snuggles down under the covers and his hands are white and cold like glass, his fingers stiff on the keyboard.

"It's freezing," she says. "Get in under the blanket."

He does and stops himself from saying how much he's missed his white cotton sheets.

The movie begins but he can't focus. His mind is in so many different places, the screen not one of them. He is thinking about her legs, a few centimeters from his. About the way her body is facing his, her wrist holding up her head. About the dark brown freckles scattered along her forearm that look like stars in the galaxy, dots that you could connect to make shapes, like a face or a Christmas tree. About her breath, sweet and hot. About how her body is shuffling to get comfortable, her hips landing closer, the hem of her pajama pants tickling his ankle. He dares himself to look over at her. To see what expression is written on her face.

When he does, he sees that her eyes are already on him. Then her face comes closer and her lips are soft and warm. He tries to use his tongue at first, but she doesn't so he just mirrors her. Lips on lips. Her mouth is small. Did he kiss her or did she kiss him? He doesn't know. The thoughts are running so fast he can't catch them. They are just words now. Breath. Wet. Warm. Eyes. Hand on hand.

She pulls away and wipes her bottom lip with her thumb. He fills his lungs back up. Dizzy.

"Is this too soon?" he asks.

She shakes her head no.

Hands clutch his face and he dives in again, lost underwater in a current that makes it impossible to see. His mind speaks as though it exists separate from his body—stunned that it is his own hand touching her, fingers tracing along her bare back. She kisses his neck, all the way down to his collarbone, and he wants to touch all of her at once.

Is this actually going to happen?

She knows he's never had sex. They had talked about it the other night. He'd said he didn't know why—he's been interested in girls as long as anyone else. Since he was in primary school. But he'd always sat back and waited for the moment to present itself. Then it never did.

Everything is on fast-forward and the voice in his head can't keep up. There are flashes. Tops come off. Pants come off. Nothing is said. Just lips and moans and writhing bodies, her hips rising to meet his hand. He doesn't know if he's doing any of this right. He listens to when she makes sounds and when she falls silent, when her body moves quickly and when it becomes still. She's the one who says to get a condom, and once he does his body can't stand it.

"I can't believe this is happening," he says into her hair, sprawled across his pillow.

He falls onto her, panting into her shoulder. Limbs like lead, the bitter air drying the sweat from his back.

They stay in his bed together that night. Burrowing under his arm, she asks him to tell her a story. He tells her one about stealing a Kinder Surprise from a shop when he was a kid and his mother found out and yelled and he hadn't thought about that memory in years. With her, he's more himself than when he's by himself. She reaches into him and finds things he didn't even know were there.

He doesn't sleep much, his mind half-awake all night, conscious there's a warm body beside him. At one point, his thoughts float away, taking him to the edge of a precipice, white water foaming around rocks coated in moss. The wind hisses past him, smashing waves against the cliff face. *Jump*, his mind whispers, an urge building. He hesitates. It's too high. But the choice is being made by someone else. A voice he doesn't recognize. *You'll jump*, it says. Beneath him is life, ferocious and savage. One day he might regret jumping. But it will be too late. Nothing will ever return him to that spot peering down, dry and unscathed.

No matter how much he wishes things had turned out differently.

Ana

⸙

ANA STARES AT THE BACK OF THE BATHROOM DOOR AND listens to the silence of a house where almost everyone is asleep. The air conditioner murmurs and she imagines Rob shifting on the couch as he waits for her. She knows Paul isn't going to have so much as flinched since he fell into bed two hours ago. He'll be fast asleep, his snoring rattling the bedhead, the smell of red wine seeping from every pore of his damp skin.

Her eyes are heavy but her mind is buzzing, desperate to sit up all night talking to the person who makes her feel like the world is a little bigger. As she washes her hands, she notices the darkness of mascara smudged under each eye. She wipes them gently outward, struck by the blotchiness of her nose and cheeks, warmed by too many glasses of white wine. *I really should go to bed*, she thinks. They've got to be up in six hours and the kids still aren't fully packed. She feels an odd twinge of nostalgia for a moment that hasn't quite passed and realizes that it's not for a place but for a person.

Walking back out into the living room, she thinks for a moment that Rob might have gone to bed, the back of his head no longer visible from behind the white leather sofa. But as she approaches, she sees him slumped low, grinning up at her, his eyes barely open. As he shifts forward, the fabric squeaks beneath him, his forearm stuck to the surface. He reaches a hand toward her and next thing she knows she's kneeling in front of him, laughing in order to break the silence hanging in the air. He's looking her in the eye, as if to tell her something, and slowly he props up his elbow and rests his head on it, in line with hers. She doesn't know who leans in first but suddenly his lips are on her lips and his hand is gently touching the back of her head and she feels like she can't breathe. Her heart is beating so fast she swears she can hear it and why does this feel like it is the right thing when it is objectively the wrong thing?

He pulls away for a moment and slowly opens his eyes, staring as though he can see something in her she can't. When he kisses her again, she can taste wine but also something new. His tongue is cool and fresh and everything about him is gentle yet assured, like he is leading her in a dance he knows every step to. When he touches her lightly on the wrist, she can feel his pulse through every fingertip—transmitted from him to her. She lets herself surrender to how much she wants this, but it's the discovery of how much he wants this that shoots desire down into her stomach so deep that it stings. He touches her like she is a sublime creature, not the woman she just saw staring back at her in the bathroom mirror. This woman, the one he is kissing, doesn't have silvery stretch marks or a purple C-section scar or a paunchy stomach that folds beneath her clothing. Instead, she is flawless. And she can see herself through his eyes, just for a moment.

Then, there's the flick of a doorknob. A shuffle. The slow and broad steps of Paul walking toward the back of the house, a sound you recognize instantly after living with someone for more than half your life. Rob is lying on the couch and Ana is still kneeling in front of him. Their eyes widen at each other but by the time Paul pokes his head out and says, "An?" she is half sitting, half standing, while Rob sits uncomfortably behind her.

"I was just coming to bed," she says, certain that Paul knows. He must know.

"Good night," Rob mumbles, his voice thick and caught in his throat.

And so she puts the glasses in the dishwasher, while Paul fills up a glass of water and mutters something about how late it is. She detours to the bathroom and sits down on the toilet again, head in her hands, desperate to go. But she can't. Her body is tied up in knots and now not even her bladder knows what to do anymore. *What the fuck was that?* she mouths to herself, suddenly completely sober. And she sits there a little longer, prolonging a moment she doesn't know what to do with. From nowhere, her mind delivers a picture of Paul's sister, Kelly. They'd gone out for Thai just before this trip. They'd laughed so hard Ana had gotten the hiccups, with Kelly frantically googling how to make them stop. She'd thought on the way home that there were few people whose company she enjoyed more. How lucky she was. *What would she think of me?* she finds herself asking. She'd be disgusted. She'd say to people, "Have you heard what she did?" and she wouldn't be angry so much as disappointed in someone she'd thought of as family. Ana feels repulsed to be inside her own skin, crawling with the fingertips of a man who is not her husband.

But she composes herself, brushes her teeth, and then climbs into bed with the man she'll love until the day he dies.

Claire

There's eight of them sitting on cushions on Yazmin's living room floor, drinking Smirnoff Double Blacks, while Bridge sits at the windowsill smoking a cigarette, the direction of the wind blowing it right back into the cramped flat.

"My roommates are going to kill you if this place smells like smoke," Yazmin says, pouring chips into a bowl.

"It won't," Bridge whines, flicking her cigarette onto the street below.

Maggie decides to tell them about what happened at the gym,

but Claire clambers over her, the palm of her hand trying to cover her mouth.

"I was just really good . . . is what . . . Maggie is trying to tell you," she says, wrestling Maggie to the ground.

"You . . ." Maggie starts tickling her, playing with the sides of her stomach. "Literally. Died. You died in the gym." The room erupts in laughter and Charlie, sitting cross-legged across from them, demands Claire get off Maggie so she can give them more details. Already, Claire likes these people. They're a group of girls she's always watched enviously at restaurants but never really been a part of. It feels as good as it looks from the outside.

When Claire sits back up and looks at them, she notices Yazmin's face is the only one that's still.

Just after ten, they leave for Soho, the cold air nipping at Claire's bare legs. Maggie makes a comment about what she's wearing. Something like, "Look at you with heels on." A whistle. Raised eyebrows. She bumps her with the side of her hip.

Up ahead, Claire notices Yazmin whispering to Bridge, gesturing back toward them. When Claire had tried to ask her a question as they were walking out the door, Yazmin had avoided her eyes, as though worried if she met them, she'd say something she would regret. She wonders what's up with her and replays the night so far in her head, trying to pinpoint a moment where she might've inadvertently said something to upset her.

Once they get to Candy's, Yazmin takes her by the arm and they line up to order drinks. "I need to talk to you," she says, her eyes dark and accusing.

Claire just looks back at her blankly.

"Maggie. What's going on with Maggie?" Yazmin presses.

"What? Nothing's going on. We've just hung out a few times.

Other than you, she's literally the only person I know in London . . ." She feels defensive. Patronized. Next to her, a woman picking up a couple of shot glasses is elbowed from behind and Claire feels a dribble of liquid on her shin.

"Just be careful. Seriously."

"Be careful about Maggie? Why? You're the one who introduced us."

The bartender asks what they want. Yazmin orders. Claire looks down at her hands, picks at her nails. She gets that guilty feeling like she's done something wrong, but she still isn't sure what.

As they turn around and head back to the table, Yazmin cranes her neck and whispers in her ear, "She's got a lot of problems. You don't want to get caught up in that."

"Okay, well, we *all* have problems," Claire snaps back. "What do you mean by problems, anyway?" She tries to sound less curious than she is.

Yazmin stops and turns to her, balancing three drinks in her hands. "Not that long ago, she had a drug problem. She's just getting over it now. She had a bit of a fucked-up upbringing, I think, and I've seen her lose her shit. She's fine at arm's length but you don't want to get too close."

"Yeah." Claire's voice is steady. "I know all that, actually. We've talked about it. And I've got my own stuff too."

Yazmin looks away and Claire feels bad. She knows Yazmin is wary because she's seen Claire in relationships before.

"I know what you're saying, Yazmin. And nothing is going on. We're just friends. But thank you for looking out for me."

They sit down at a pink booth and suddenly there are eight overflowing blue shots, one being pushed toward her. It burns the back of her throat. She drinks and talks to Yazmin about how she can't find a job but this week landed on a place. She moves in two weeks from today. More shots come followed by vodka sunrises, one of which Claire spills on the booth table. Charlie tries to lick it up and they all laugh.

Around her are a sea of women. Femme. Butch. Young. Not so young. "I Gotta Feeling" comes on and her eyes catch Maggie's from across the table. *This fucking song*. Someone yells that they're getting up to dance and Yazmin grabs her by the hand. The dance floor is crowded and the speakers are so loud she can feel the music in her chest. She tries to move like everybody else but the voice in her head is loud and mean. *What was that? Just do what that person is doing. Try to make it look like you're not trying so hard*. Maybe she needs more to drink.

She looks around and sees Maggie—in a world of her own, unaware that anyone is watching her. Her shirt is baggy and her forehead is slick with sweat. Her mouth is slightly open and she runs a hand through her short hair, pushing it back off her face. The song changes to "Party in the U.S.A." by Miley Cyrus and while she dances with Yazmin, she can feel Maggie's eyes on her, the whites of her eyes visible in a sea of black. She likes it. Her mind stops taunting her and her limbs start doing things without her having to tell them to.

The next thing she knows she's across from Maggie. Their hands touch. They move closer. Their faces are only centimeters away from each other. She can smell her perfume. It's spicy. Almost masculine. She isn't sure what will happen if she looks up at Maggie, so she focuses on her feet. And then over Maggie's shoulder. She hopes Yazmin is in the bathroom.

They spend the rest of the night dancing and waiting at the bar. She's sure Maggie is going to kiss her, but she doesn't. She just half smiles every time they make eye contact.

That's what she thinks about when she is back on her stiff hostel mattress a few hours later, unable to sleep, music still pounding in her ears. She imagines what it might feel like to have Maggie touch her. To have her tongue trace its way down her body. She floats into a sleep and dreams that Maggie is under the blanket, between her legs, bringing her to orgasm.

ON MONDAY NIGHTS, they watch *Glee*.

Maggie comes over to Claire's after work, picking up Thai on the way. They eat out of containers on her cream corduroy sofa, silent until the ad break comes on. There's one commercial that comes on every time. It's for butter. Or cheese. They're not sure exactly. But there's a cow running across a beach in slow motion and a woman with long hair sitting on a rock. The song "Can't Fight This Feeling" comes on partway through, and Claire has perfected the timing. The cow. The woman. Claire belting out "Can't Fight This Feeling" with a mouthful of pad thai and Maggie laughing, even though she does it every Monday night.

After they're finished eating, they curl up on the sofa and watch the rest of the episode. Usually Claire lies on Maggie's lap, and Maggie runs her fingers through her hair. Afterward, they talk about the episode. Distractedly watch whatever's on next. And then Maggie goes home.

Yazmin doesn't know, but really there's nothing to know. They just spend time together. Claire thinks about Monday nights all week long and tidies up for them on Sunday afternoons. She vacuums the floors and rearranges the cushions on the couch. She waters her fiddle-leaf fig and does a basket of washing. Clean clothes are folded into her set of white Ikea drawers and she tries to get rid of the mold that lives in her shower. She lights a scented candle but blows it out before Maggie arrives because she doesn't want to seem like she is putting in too much effort. Maggie is what she thinks about when her mind drifts, filling her with warmth and possibility.

On this particular Monday night, Maggie seems distracted. They talk about work. Claire has just started a customer service role, which is basically fielding complaints for a restaurant. Maggie theorizes that Brits love to moan so much they've had to dedicate an entire job to it. She's not wrong. Claire doesn't mind it, though. It doesn't pay too badly and it's the first time she's ever worked in a city.

When they are sitting next to each other on the couch, Claire can barely concentrate. She's aware of the outline of Maggie's face in her peripheral vision. The way her jaw tenses when she chews. Her presence is so much bigger than her body, Claire thinks, a field of energy surrounding her limbs, felt by anyone who gets close. It pulls you and pushes you at the same time. Claire's stomach is fluttering, wings of hundreds of butterflies flapping against the insides of her gut, desperate to get out.

Eventually they finish their food, dumping the mostly empty containers on the side table. Claire rolls into Maggie's lap, lightly touching her denim jeans, the only thing between her fingertips and Maggie's bare skin. She tries to focus on the episode. It's all about Santana, a closeted lesbian, who wants to be prom queen so that her best friend will fall in love with her. A bunch of them sing "Born This Way" and she sings along, doing the dance moves badly with her arms. Maggie tries to grab her wrists to stop her but she keeps going, purposely obscuring her view of the TV. Ad break.

"When did you know you were a lesbian?" Maggie asks her.

"I don't know," she says, thinking aloud. "As a kid, I always liked boys who looked a little bit like girls. And then as I grew up, I felt attracted to women who looked like men. It's weird."

"Have you had sex with men before?"

"Yeah, I have. I think I'm just not that into penis, though?" She screws up her face. "I came out to my mum just before I moved here. And she didn't say much. Just 'Don't tell your father.' So I still haven't."

"Why do you think she said that?" Maggie pushes the hair off Claire's face.

"I reckon she thinks this is all just a phase and that I'll grow out of it. And I'm like, 'Mum, I don't know how to tell you this, but I don't ever want to see a dick again in my life.' The funny thing is, I reckon Dad wouldn't even care." She pauses. "When did you know?"

"I knew before I started school, I s'pose. I always dressed like this." She looks down at her loose-fitting jeans and gray shirt, which is hanging low on one shoulder, revealing the strap of a sports bra. "Mum was cool. Like, when I told her as a teenager, she just looked at me funny as if to say, *Yeah . . . and the sky is blue*. Dad was awful about it, though. I don't think he bargained on a gay daughter. He was in the air force so wasn't really around much, but when he was, he'd make fun of how I dressed. Say no boy would look at me if I didn't put any effort in." She leans her head back and stares up at the ceiling.

"School was the worst, though. I was the first openly gay kid at St. John's College and I got so much shit for it. None of the girls would even sit with me because they were all so paranoid I'd make a move. Like, they weren't even hot?" She smiles.

Claire begins to ask a question but Maggie interrupts. "Shut up, it's back on."

They turn back to *Glee*. Claire imagines Maggie, an awkward teenager, eating lunch on her own, cross-legged on cold bitumen. It makes her feel sick. She has a compulsion to be as close to her as she can. Grip on to the thigh she's resting her head on. They're both quiet.

Then the stupid cheese ad comes on. The cow. Running in slow motion on the beach. And the song. Claire counts herself in and belts out the chorus, hitting the notes perfectly like she knew she would. She closes her eyes and ad-libs lyrics about the cow being in love with the woman on the rock, and he's escaped from his paddock to kiss her with his dribbly mouth, and she can hear Maggie wheezing with laughter as she keeps going.

When the song reaches its final line, she holds the last note as long as she can. She looks up at Maggie, whose eyes are shining and cheeks are flushed. And then her face turns serious. Claire is still smiling when Maggie leans down and kisses her, soft lips that taste like Thai food.

Maggie pulls away and watches her for a moment.

Claire sits up and then climbs on top of Maggie, straddling her legs either side of Maggie's waist, and kisses her again, letting herself dive in to how good it feels. Her body can't stand how much she wants this, her hands exploring all the parts of Maggie she's suddenly allowed to touch.

They talk between kisses. Confessions. Spilling out of them. Involuntary. The tingling feeling in Claire's stomach rises. She wants all of her. Now. She pulls Maggie's shirt off and then tugs off her sports bra, kissing Maggie's bare chest, playing with her nipples. Wanting to bite them but holding back. Her breath shakes and she can smell her saliva on Maggie's skin.

Maggie rolls Claire off her, positions her to sit.

"When is your roommate home?" she asks, kneeling in front of her.

"She's not . . . not tonight. She's away."

Maggie pulls off Claire's red harem pants, which she'd bought in Paris last month and has hardly taken off since. She kisses up the inside of Claire's thigh, teasing her. Claire can't sit still. She just wants to be touched. For Maggie to feel how wet she is. How much she wants this. Finally, Maggie peels off Claire's underwear and Claire can't help but groan as she does, opening her legs wider. It feels like Maggie is everywhere. The rhythm makes her whole body shake and before Maggie's lips climb any further, she pulls at Maggie, wanting to unbutton her jeans.

"I can't . . . my period just started today."

"I don't care," Claire says. "Seriously, I don't care."

Maggie shakes her head, her eyes smiling. And then she disappears again and Claire doesn't protest. She's someplace else. Floating. She opens her eyes to remind herself what's happening. And who it's happening with. She closes them again. Her hips move on their own. She's not thinking anymore. Colors. Bright colors. Everything tenses. Then release.

They curl up on the sofa for hours afterward, swimming in the soft light from the lamp beside them. Whispering even though no one else is home. They talk about the things you're not meant to. The last people they slept with. Claire tells Maggie what it feels like to have sex with a man. How it's more aggressive. Sometimes it hurts. Sex with a woman never hurts. They talk about when they knew this would happen. Not when they met. Maggie wasn't Claire's type. They go over, moment by moment, how awkward that day in Camden had been.

"What is Yazmin going to think?" Maggie asks.

"Who cares what Yazmin thinks? And why would it bother her? She loves you." Claire tries to sound convincing.

"I don't think . . ." She trails off. Claire gets the sense that Maggie knows more about how Yazmin feels than she's letting on. She changes the subject.

Their voices grow husky, and it's after midnight when Maggie closes the front door behind her, leaving Claire alone in the dark hallway.

Patrick

⁒

NINE MONTHS LATER

THERE ARE A LOT OF THINGS PATRICK IS SURPRISED TO learn about love.

He didn't expect it to be the broken parts of someone you find yourself falling for. The parts they feel self-conscious about. The parts they hate. How her hair dries curly after the beach and how she gets the hiccups every time she drinks. How her eyes disappear in photos and how she always overcooks pasta, making it taste rubbery. How she watches hours of reality TV where women screech at each other and how she always gets a pimple in the same place, right between her eyebrows.

He loves her in a new way the first time she tells him about her dad and how one night he threw a pile of plates stacked up in the sink hard against the white kitchen tiles. The details of her relationship with him begin to leak into their conversations. Walking home from the pub on a Friday night after drinks with her friends, she tells him how her dad used to pick fights with her mum's friends, calling them names and shouting down the phone at them when they called at dinnertime. During a movie where a man comes home drunk and pushes his wife to the floor, she asked if they could turn it off. He nodded and they went to sleep wrapped around each other, limbs tied together like a knot. When they play that stupid game where they force each other to say what they love most about the other, she says: "I love you because you are gentle. My dad was never gentle."

Her dad used to smash windows and punch holes through plaster walls. Neighbors would knock on the door, arms folded on the other side of a screen door, saying they'd heard shouting and was everything okay. Caitlin had heard it too. Words she didn't know the meaning of yet. When they fought, she'd tiptoe to her brother's room and he would turn the television up as loud as it would go and they'd sit beside each other without saying anything. Once, her dad caught her creeping to Isaac's room. Called her a rat. Said to get back to her room and that if she didn't, he'd belt her until she was black and blue. She knew he was telling the truth.

Patrick doesn't always know how to respond when she tells him these kinds of things and sometimes he feels like it's a test he's failing. Every day, he learns there is more to this person and, honestly, he doesn't know what to do with it all. There are times when she pauses, maybe waiting for him to ask a question, but it feels like he always asks the wrong one. Sometimes when she finishes a story, he hasn't prepared a response. So he changes the subject. Or kisses her on the top of the head.

It's just after Christmas when they leave for their first holiday, just the two of them. They fly to Brisbane and then get a smaller plane to Hervey Bay before taking the ferry across to Fraser Island, off the southern coast of Queensland. It's where Caitlin spent some of her summer holidays as a kid, camping with family friends, bathing in Lake McKenzie. He's never been. Never even heard of it.

When they arrive, they hire a four-wheel drive, the only car that won't get bogged in the sand.

"You know, we're the world's largest sand island," the woman handing over the keys tells them, her top lip wrinkled from the sun, "and we've got the cleanest lakes you'll see in your life."

They pile their gear into the car, backpacks filled with sleeping bags and instant noodles and a tent. She drives while he sits in the passenger seat, barely able to keep his eyes open. For a few moments he falls into a light sleep, clutching at a dream he never quite touches. When he opens his eyes, he forgets where he is for a moment and then sees the water's edge to his left and the grassy sand dunes to his right. He looks over to her and she smiles at him, one hand out the car window, feeling the breeze. The sand running alongside them looks singed by the sun, white specks floating above it, almost like fog. He can taste the salt. The shoreline pulls in and out, flat until the horizon, sparkling like roughly cut diamonds.

Once they arrive at the campsite, the air is starting to cool and clouds are rolling in overhead. She's the one who knows how to pitch the tent, placing pegs in all four corners, and sliding foldout poles into exactly the right places. He just does what he's told. Within fifteen minutes, their tent is standing.

"Welcome to our front veranda," Caitlin says, gesturing to the small enclave at the front where she's put their backpacks. They unpack and set down their sleeping bags and lie side by side, staring up at the inside of their perfectly erected dark green tent. They hear the distant chatter of another conversation, maybe half a dozen men, opening beers and playing Bob Marley on a set of tinny speakers. He thinks there is no one he would rather be here with.

Every Christmas and every New Year's Eve and all the other days that you're meant to spend with the people you love, he's always felt an overwhelming sense of failure. He's not doing it right. He's not spending it in the right place or drinking the right beer or having the right conversation. But here, with her, he realizes there's nothing for him outside of this tent. There is no better life going unlived.

That night, they have sex in the tent, Caitlin holding her hand over his mouth, giggling that they have to be quiet. Afterward, they unzip the front mesh door and lie on their bellies, feeling the breeze on their sweaty bodies. The campsite has fallen silent by the time they try to sleep and the silence turns up the volume on his thoughts. This is how life is meant to be. Full. Overflowing. Technicolor. There's a feeling in his stomach. Anticipation. Everything is exciting. Tomorrow is exciting and so is next year and the one after that. Life has a pulse it's never had before. There's too much potential for his mind to fully capture.

They wake early and swim in Lake McKenzie. The water's edge is aqua green, before a darker drop-off, the temperature cooler the deeper you go. They sit on the sand, leaning into each other, as they listen to the calls of the blue-faced honeyeaters, signaling for the entire island to come alive.

The next three days are a delicious cycle of morning dips and afternoon naps. Of accelerating in their four-wheel drive along Seventy-Five Mile Beach, the sense that they're at the ends of the earth. Pringles in red cylinders, drinking liters of bottled water, the same temperature as their tongues. They swim in lakes and creeks and they walk and skimboard and dive, their bodies doing what they're meant to, aching by the time the sun sinks behind the horizon. They sleep with one leg each tucked inside a shared nylon sleeping bag. They become obsessed with dingoes. They're dangerous. If you see a dingo, you're not to run. They'll chase you. When they finally see one, frozen, sitting in a sand dune the color of its beige coat, Caitlin presses the brakes gently. It blinks. She whispers. Maybe it sees them. It's so close they fantasize about patting it, even though they know they never could. When the dingo eventually darts away, its head close to the ground and tail between its legs, his eyes fall on her. Her skin radiates in the afternoon sun, her hair wavy from their morning swim.

"What?" she asks, smiling coyly.

"I didn't think it was possible to love someone this much," he replies.

For so many years, he'd imagined what it might be like to be in a relationship. He'd just wanted someone to hang out with all the time. To put his arms around for no reason. But this—what he had with her—had elevated his life to something so idyllic it felt like it had to belong to someone else. Here he was, with someone who knew him, really knew him, and loved him anyway.

They say they'll come back to Fraser Island. And they will. Once with friends. Another time, just them again. And it will always be paradise—the dunes, the sea, the darting fish and the birdlife, the clear mornings and the sunsets. But it's more than that. Paradise is them. Comfortable silence in the car. A touch on the arm in the middle of the night. A question. Playing. The kind of childlike play that you never meant to give up but did at some point. Paradise is her.

Ana

A MOMENT CAN FEEL LIKE A DAY AND THREE MONTHS CAN feel like a week and he would be here in an hour, which felt like a year away.

She knew what she had to do.

She had dropped the kids at school and Paul was at work. No one knew Rob was dropping by. There was no reason for them to know—in fact, telling them would make it an occasion when it wasn't. It was a cup of tea, that was all. Still, not telling them did make her feel like a liar. But Paul hadn't asked and it hadn't come up, so she'd simply failed to mention it. Because it was not a big deal.

Though she and Paul had known he was back—for Sebastian's funeral. Such a tragedy. He'd only been twenty-two. Rob's sister, Colleen, had found her son in the back shed after searching for hours. So Rob was here to bury his nephew and hold his sister upright as they did.

Ana had been the first person he'd told after Jenny. In a brief text message with not many words. She'd phoned him immediately and, to her embarrassment, found herself crying on the phone to him. She'd never met Sebastian. But she knew that Rob loved him. That he'd recognized the battle with depression, that he understood why Seb had done what he did in a way most people couldn't. Rob had said he was scared. But it wasn't death that he feared. It was how long we all have to live. And what we do with it. Ana also knew that Jenny wasn't with him. Apparently she'd had elective surgery booked that she hadn't wanted to postpone. Jenny's gallbladder, or its removal, Rob had said, a new bitterness in his voice, had spared her the trip.

After that night in Sri Lanka, Ana had felt like she was watching her life from above. A trailing eagle rather than a willing participant. She'd sent Rob a message at dawn, after having lain on her side for hours, sleepless, her mind doing somersaults. She'd apologized. "It was a mistake. It shouldn't have happened."

Three dots had appeared within seconds. "No, that was me," he'd replied. "I'm sorry I got carried away." She'd wondered whether he was sorry for kissing her or sorry that she was married.

The next morning, his body had felt different when she'd reached her arms around his neck, leaving a "See you soon" in his left ear. It had felt both more familiar and more forbidden, like a drawer she'd been told not to open. As she sat in the back of the taxi, the coastline slowly escaping, she'd felt like a moth that had been circling a light. But now the light had been switched off and she didn't know where she was or what she was looking for.

After that, their messages had changed. They'd become a thrilling secret shame buried in her back pocket. "You must've known," Rob wrote to her early one morning. "You must've known how I felt when I sat beside you on that train, every morning and afternoon for eighteen months, asking what you'd had for lunch and if you'd slept well and if you and Paul were doing anything that weekend."

She typed that she remembered how she'd fallen asleep on his shoulder one evening, after having hardly slept the night before. She remembered waking with a jolt, a drip of saliva at the side of her mouth, wiping it away quickly as Rob had murmured "It's nearly our stop" into her hair.

Back then, her friends had all said it. Do you see the way he looks at you? You must know. He searches for you, his eyebrows raised, his neck craned, when he walks into the Durnham Hotel on a Friday night. He sulks when you're not there. He talks about you, placing you in conversations where you don't belong. But she hadn't known. Because she'd always had Paul, and Rob had never sat too close or touched her arm for too long or said anything that had made her stop and wonder.

There had been one moment when perhaps she should've wondered. She'd been twenty-three. It was a week or so after Paul proposed. She remembers a summer barbecue. Rob was sitting on the grass beside the pool, on the fringe of a group of people. She bounded over to him, her cheeks aching from how much she'd been smiling. Rob was quiet. Cheersed her.

"Congratulations," he'd said, looking at her as though he knew something she didn't.

"Do you want to see the ring?" she'd asked, holding her hand up to him. She remembers how it had gleamed in the sunlight and that Rob had made a joke about it blinding him.

Then he'd said, "Don't marry him, Ana." He'd taken a sip of beer, swallowed it deeply, as if concentrating. "Marry me instead."

She'd just giggled and rolled her eyes and then Paul had walked over and that's where the memory ends.

He'd been imagining that kiss for twenty-five years, he'd confessed late one Tuesday afternoon. She'd stopped, halfway down an aisle in Woolworths, her phone in her right hand, the other on the handle of a full trolley. "Not every day," he'd clarified. Not on the day he'd married his wife. Sometimes, years went by when it seemed he'd outgrown it. But there were periods throughout their friendship when his mind would become stuck on the longest love affair he'd never had.

After Seb died, the rest unraveled. He'd realized that he had to leave Jenny. Not immediately. And he wouldn't be leaving because of Ana, he'd said. He wouldn't come knocking on her door, begging for something she couldn't give him. It was because happily married men didn't kiss other women, he'd said. *Funny*, she'd thought. *I'm a happily married woman who just kissed another man.*

He knocks softly on the front door and she puts one more thing in the dishwasher to give her space for a final deep breath. She knows nothing can happen. Not because she has any faith in her self-control. Quite the opposite. Nothing can happen because she hasn't showered today. And she would never let a man touch her when she hasn't showered. An effective chastity belt.

She'd known she couldn't trust herself in a room with Rob, with him sitting on one seat and her on the other. No kids to interrupt, no husband asleep in the next room. But she could trust the Ana of last night, who'd not only made a choice but formulated a strategy. And now she was wearing her armor.

She walks to the front door, calling out "Coming" in a strange singsong voice that makes her wince. Opening it, she sees Rob in the doorway, taller than he exists in her mind, smiling at her with eyes that remember every message she's sent since April.

At the sight of him, she instantly curses herself for not at least putting on some tinted moisturizer. Or something to brighten up her lips. She's wearing a T-shirt, an old sports bra that's become her everyday bra, gym shorts, and ankle socks, her hair pulled back into a tight ponytail. If he was still attracted to her, this should challenge the last of it. And then the decision will be taken out of her hands.

"How are you?" she asks, her arms pulling his neck in toward her. He returns the hug, then walks down the dark hallway into the sun-filled living area and drops wearily onto the modular suite. He drapes his arms across the back cushions, as though there are two people either side of him and he's reaching around their shoulders. Exhausted, his head falls backward, his Adam's apple protruding.

He tells her it's all fucked. All he dreams about is Seb. His sister hasn't eaten in days. Seb's best mate spoke at the funeral to a church that was overflowing. There were even people out in the street and across the road, unable to hear a word, but standing there silently anyway. She sits with a leg tucked beneath her thigh, asking questions as he speaks. By the time the kettle has finished boiling and she's poured them both a cup of tea, Rob says he doesn't want to talk about it anymore.

"Tell me something that will cheer me up," he says.

"Billy discovered a supermarket chocolate cake in the pantry the other day," she tells him, "and ate the whole thing in one go." Rachael had found him with the lid hanging from his nose, stuck with icing.

Rob laughs while rubbing Billy's belly with his foot and asks, "Isn't chocolate meant to be bad for dogs?"

She agrees, yes it is. But Billy has a stomach of steel and didn't so much as burp while he licked his lips and paws for hours, savoring the taste of his very own cake. Paul had joked that if Billy did drop dead, then it was just evolution taking its course, she tells Rob. And then she pauses. Aware that she's brought up Paul and death in the same sentence—probably the last two things he wants to hear about right now.

They talk about the kids and Sri Lanka and Rob's work and how much exercise he's doing, and all she feels like doing is curling up on his lap, asking him to run his fingers through her hair. Soon, he has to go. He's going to his mum's before he leaves tomorrow morning. He tells her he doesn't know when he'll be back next. But hopefully it's under better circumstances.

She walks him to the front door and they both just stand there for a moment, rain beginning to sprinkle lightly behind him. It smells fresh. The gray specks in his blue eyes match the sky, a wash of clouds that look like they're about to burst. She says she'll miss him and he says the same and they hug for longer than friends do.

"You mean so much to me," he whispers in her ear, as though it's a secret someone else might hear.

"You too," she says, loving the way her body feels wrapped in his. As her chin rests on his shoulder, she wonders how long they could stand there, breathing each other in.

When he eventually pulls away and turns and walks toward the front fence, she doesn't know how she's going to get through the afternoon. And then the night. And then tomorrow. How do you live your life in a perpetual state of waiting? And then even once the waiting is over and he's here in the flesh, her fingers on his skin, he's still out of reach.

She calls out, right before he pulls the gate open, the gate that Paul made with his own two hands on a long, humid Sunday afternoon, "Hey, text me, okay?"

Claire

✿

Maggie comes to claire's flat most nights a week now. She usually arrives with a plastic shopping bag of food hanging from her wrist and kisses Claire on the cheek before walking straight to the kitchen and dropping it on the bench. Maggie then cooks them dinner in the galley kitchen while Claire sits on the round white dining table, feet on the seat beneath her, impersonating the most ridiculous complaint she received that day.

The flat is in Dalston, in East London—it's one of the areas she can afford the rent. Despite its flaws, it does seem to be a magical suburb that's somehow twenty minutes' walking distance to everywhere, and most weekends she meets friends at a bar three streets over. It's busy and loud and everything costs twice as much as she expects it to.

Sometimes she trains with Maggie at her gym. She hates the idea of it and, if she's honest, she doesn't really enjoy the sessions but always feels better afterward. They see plays no one has heard of at tiny theaters and go to bars where they drink too much and forget to eat dinner.

At first, Maggie stays over one or two nights a week. And then a second toothbrush appears in her bathroom and bras that don't belong to Claire appear in the washing basket. Her pillows begin to smell like Maggie's shampoo and soy milk materializes in the fridge. Every time she sees traces of Maggie in her home, Claire grins and then admonishes herself. *You've known this person for a few months and you're already designing your whole life around her.* But Claire is like an addict with a drug at her fingertips—every time she uses, she feels euphoric. There are no side effects. No hangovers. Every second of it is pleasure. Pleasure being injected directly into her veins.

She thinks about her when she showers and when she looks out the window on the bus and sees a couple with their fingers interlaced. She thinks about her when she fields another complaint at work and knows it's a story Maggie will enjoy.

"And what did you say?" Maggie will ask, turning around from the stove to give Claire her full attention. Nothing in her life is significant on its own. It is made significant by the fact that it will later be heard by Maggie.

Claire calls Yazmin to tell her one rainy Friday afternoon. Not because she especially wants to, but because of a message she received from her earlier that week that suggested she already knew. Yazmin's voice is cold when she answers.

"So you know about Maggie?" Claire asks, rubbing her eyes.

"Yeah. Well, I do now. When were you going to tell me?"

"I don't know," she mumbles. "I thought you'd be pissed off. You've never been that keen on Maggie and I didn't want it to become this big deal. I just don't want to fight with you about it."

She hates this. She just wants to fast-forward six months to a time when they drink too much sangria and laugh about their stupid argument over Maggie.

"I don't get it. I told you . . . there's something not right there. She's fine when we're out and there's a bunch of us. But, Claire, this isn't a good idea. I know her better than you do. She comes from a messed-up family. She's struggled with drugs and mental health stuff. I've seen a different side to her . . ."

"Yeah, I know. We've been over this. But that was years ago and she's changed. You've also seen that firsthand. Do you seriously not trust me to make my own decisions?"

She doesn't wait for an answer. She doesn't want to hear it.

"Anyway, I didn't call to ask your permission." Her words are clipped. "I just thought I'd let you know that, yes, we're in a relationship and, yes, it's serious. This is the happiest I've ever been. And I guess it was ridiculous to think that you might just support me."

Yazmin scoffs. "And let me guess, she's about to move in?"

She swallows. "No, but so what if she was?" Claire couldn't deny that she'd thought about it. "We're living in the most expensive city in the world, Yazmin," she adds through gritted teeth. "Would it really be that bad an idea?"

"You're such a lesbian cliché."

They're both silent for a moment and just as Claire goes to speak, Yazmin interrupts.

"Well, I'm glad I went to the trouble of introducing you to

someone, only to be completely cast aside the second you're in a relationship. I just really hope she's worth it."

And Yazmin hangs up the phone.

Claire's left standing there, on the street, her umbrella barely protecting her from the shards of rain cutting at her skin. The sky is gray and the pavement is gray and puddles on the street are filling with gray water. She's known Yazmin since before they could write their own names. The two quiet kids at Toowoomba State School. They'd barely exchanged a word for most of preschool, but it was understood they were friends. That they were each other's person. And that Elizabeth, who made a fuss and sat up too straight and laughed too hard at the teacher's jokes, was the enemy. The first time she'd seen Yazmin in London was the first time any of this had felt like home.

If Claire's honest, she's angry with herself. Angry that she hasn't so much as sent Yazmin a text message in two months. Angry that she's forgotten to call her back more than once. *But she's the one making me feel like shit,* she reasons, stomping toward her dark-brick building. *Doesn't she know this is all I've ever wanted?* Claire wonders whether Yazmin would ever understand that feeling that before she'd even met Maggie, she was waiting for her. That there had been an emptiness that could only ever be filled by being with Maggie. That she hadn't ever really known what happiness felt like before Maggie. Did Yazmin want her to be sad? Is that what she truly wanted?

Her phone rings again. It's Maggie. For a moment she's worried she is being tricked—that Yazmin is truth and Maggie is lies and how embarrassing this whole thing will be if it blows up in her face. Is this person, these six letters on a phone screen, really worth losing Yazmin for? Where is her line? What would she sacrifice for Maggie, and what would be too much? She knows, of course, before she even asks the question. Everything. She would sacrifice everything for the sound of Maggie's voice. And so she closes her stinging eyes and answers.

THEY HAVEN'T EVEN been dating three months when Maggie tells her in bed one night that her lease is up. Her housemates are moving back north, she says, lying flat on her back, Claire clutching at her like a koala does a tree.

She could find some new housemates, she mumbles, but before she finishes her sentence, Claire tells her that doesn't make sense when she's here all the time anyway. She hasn't been home in three nights and usually only ever returns to pack her bag with some clean clothes.

Claire's been thinking about it. Her flatmate, Abbie, is rarely home but when she is, she does make the odd comment. Last night, when Maggie had been in the shower and Abbie was unstacking the dishwasher, made up primarily of Claire's and Maggie's dishes, she'd looked her in the eye and said, nodding toward the bathroom door, "Bitch better start paying rent."

And so, Claire convinces Maggie to move in with her in Dalston. It's the first time she's lived with a partner, and she gives it less thought than she does the prospect of having a second coffee on a Friday afternoon. Nothing with Maggie is complicated. She is warm feet on a cold day and reading a book in the local park, the weak sun tickling her face. She is lazy mornings and watching TV and laughing so hard no sound comes out. She is color and life and sex. She is late nights when the world has fallen silent and it's just the two of them in the dim living room, talking about how time speeds up the longer you live.

Sometimes, when Maggie sleeps beside her, Claire looks over at her upturned nose, her slightly parted lips, and thinks she loves her so much she can't stand it. Do other people feel this too? It can't be possible. She concludes that no one else in the world could feel like this right now, because they're not lying next to Maggie. They're in bed, next to an ordinary person, someone they think they love because it's the best they've ever known. But it doesn't make sense that everyone loves equally. We can't know how other people feel love or how fiercely they experience it. All Claire knows is that there is nothing more than what she feels for Maggie. And she pities everyone else on earth, stuck living something different.

Ana

She's on her back, head cocked to one side, panting from her chest. He rolls over and kisses her gently on the cheek, before lifting himself out of bed, the momentum forcing a grunt.

She hears the stream of his urine in the toilet bowl gradually fade to a trickle. He comes back to bed and lies back down with his back to her, wriggling to get comfortable. He pulls at the blanket so she has a little less.

"Night," she whispers, and he mutters a half word back. She

stares at his back. Hairier than he knows. Odd-shaped moles that need checking. She knows his body better than he does.

She remembers the first time they had sex. She must've been about eighteen. He'd pulled her shirt off and then fiddled with her bra clasp for a little too long until she took over. He'd taken her in. Stared at her. Then she'd undressed him. Just like in the movies. He was golden and his skin was soft and smooth over his muscles. She'd run her hands down his chest, bare and silky.

If she scrunches her eyes closed tight enough, she can still just remember the feeling. The thrill. The ecstasy. The way he felt too big when he slid himself into her and she whimpered because it hurt, but made it sound like a cry of pleasure. He'd worn a condom, so there'd been no mess when they'd finished. It had been nice, it had felt like she'd thought it was supposed to.

He doesn't bother taking her shirt off anymore. It stays on. Why go to the fuss of taking it off when you'll just have to put it back on all over again? He's seen what's underneath. It's as familiar to him as his own weathered form. She can't recall when it had started. They only needed the bottom half anyway. She knows it doesn't sound great—makes it sound like the sex is bad. But it's not. It's satisfying and simple and they both know where to put their hand next. No one had ever made her orgasm before Paul. A few boys had tried but she doesn't even consider what they'd done at that age "sex." It had felt more like a gynecological exam.

Paul is sex and sex is Paul and for her entire marriage, she's finished almost every time. Unless she's been drinking, in which case she pats him on the hand in a signal that means never mind. He knows how to make her orgasm more quickly and more intensely than she can make herself orgasm. He knows what to say and when to change his rhythm. Her body is his body and his body is her body.

But looking at each other without clothes on is as arousing as watching people change out of their dripping swimmers in the change room of a public pool, their skin white and crawling with spider veins. Or as erotic as looking at the dining table they'd owned for years. Marks from stains they'd never wiped down properly. Scratches from when Oliver had run a toy car across it, over and over again. Their bodies had become part of the furniture. Sometimes, she forgets his is even there.

But now, as she stares at his shoulders, broad and leathery from too many years in the sun, she knows she loves him. She married a good man. A brilliant father. She smiles as she thinks about the lady next door, who she often jokes he's having an affair with. She's ninety-one, and her husband died last year. And every few days, Paul knocks on the door and asks her how she's doing. If there's anything that needs fixing. If she'd like him to mow her lawn on the weekend.

Moisture pools in the corner of her right eye as she thinks about the nights he'd tell Rachael to jump in the car and they'd drive around for hours, listening to music, and he'd be asking about the girls in her year, giving her a hard time. Telling her that no matter what, he'd be her best friend. It was the kind of thing that would make you cringe at fourteen but smile at twenty-four. The way he played with the boys and showed them by example how to be a good man. There is no better dad than Paul. No better man than Paul. She has never once questioned his loyalty. He goes to work, having grown a business from nothing, provides for his family, and loves his wife. That's enough for him. It will always be enough for him.

But it's not for her.

When they have sex—and guilt will drive you to have more sex, not less—she clutches at his sides, trying to stifle a sob. She worships this man. He makes her better. As he touches her, sweat gathering behind her knees, she closes her eyes. She feels the pleasure so much more intensely, deep inside herself. And suddenly it's not Paul's fingers stroking her, but Rob's. Firmly. Quickly. It's building and building and it's Rob's face. His lips. His mouth between her legs. His words. "I love watching you come. Come for me." And she releases. Her legs shake. She's silent because that way she can't say the wrong name. It does something to you. Sharing only a select portion of yourself with a person who lives inside you. You have to start lying to yourself.

And then you learn to believe it.

THE FIRST TIME they had sex, she expected to feel self-conscious. Not just nude, but naked. She'd imagined having his eyes on her. His gaze moving from her neck to her breasts, sitting lower than they ever had, her nipples a dark pink. He'd pause on the scar just above her pubic bone, a sickly purple.

Rob was back to visit his mother, who had suffered a stroke. It wasn't life-threatening, but he'd wanted to be at the hospital. It had only been three or so months since he last sat across from Ana on a rainy afternoon, leaving an indentation in the family sofa. And now he was back, his silhouette visible through the glass paneling on the front door.

When they touch, his black shirt warm from the morning sun, she does not want to let go. As she pulls away, her heels returning to the ground, he steps through the door and slams it shut. There, he kisses her deeply on the mouth, his palms on her cheeks. In that moment, it's the thought of what's happening, rather than the action itself, that consumes her.

She pulls him into her bedroom—their bedroom—and it's not at all like she's imagined it would be. Any sense of vulnerability or self-consciousness evaporates as they tear at each other's clothing. This isn't like the sex she had at fourteen or fifteen. It shouldn't even go by the same name.

He kisses her firmly, breathing urgently. They stop and stare at each other for a moment, as though wondering if they can stop this from happening. But they can't. His hands move under her clothes, cupping and squeezing her, pressing his hardness into her hip bone. She barely recognizes her own voice as she lets out a moan. She pulls off her top and then her bra, and the look in his eye is one of a man who is seeing something that matters. It's like he can't wait, desire spilling out of him like boiling water on a stovetop. No matter how hard she kisses him, it doesn't feel like enough. Closer. Closer. Her body keeps begging. She wants to bite and tear and squeeze. They are overcome by instinct, he's guiding her to his belt and then his zipper and then past an elastic waistband and inside cotton. She lets out an indescribable sound at the feeling of it in her hand. It's warm and rigid, as hard as the bedside table beside them. As she wraps her fingers around it, she realizes she doesn't know what to do. This isn't Paul. It's a different man who wants different things. Her breathing quickens and she takes in his smell—mandarin and cedarwood and sharp cologne. It smells like a desire that has been buried within her since she was a child, forgotten until now.

Redness grows on her chest and pinkness surrounds her lips, not used to being kissed so hard. When he pulls down her underwear, black cotton, another half attempt at a chastity belt, she doesn't tense. She feels more herself than ever in her life. Holding her, he shifts her to the edge of the bed. Sweat has begun to crawl along her hairline. He groans at the sight of her, his breath fast and desperate. He pauses and whispers in her ear, his lips wet.

When he finally enters her, she moans so loud she worries the dog will panic. Her legs shake and his eyes are half-closed, as though he can't bear to see her and feel her at the same time. "I've been waiting so long for this," he says in a low voice. She thinks of the dreams she's had. The fantasies. How when her phone buzzes, she often feels herself getting wet, which has become some sort of Pavlovian response to his messages. "I'm so close," he growls. Her body pulsates as she feels him clutch on to her, his head over her shoulder. His screams are muffled by a pillow. Paul's pillow.

For a moment they say nothing. Their bodies have said everything. Communicated things they couldn't with words. When Rob moves off her and onto his side, sweat has made his hair two shades darker. The whole room smells different. Perspiration and sex have overpowered his cologne and the air feels damp. Heavy. He runs a fingertip down her ribs to her waist. Her skin feels like satin sheets, he says. The softest skin he's ever touched.

As Rob puts his head back on her husband's pillows, his sweat imprinting itself on their marital bed, she tries to tell herself she feels guilty. But she doesn't. She feels a lot of things. Exhilarated and alive. Vulnerable. Sexy. Astounded it has actually happened. But guilt is nowhere to be found. She is in this bed, with this man, thinking about nothing beyond it. And that's the truth.

HE COMES BACK again the next day. And the one after that. And she meets him the night after that, telling Paul and the kids she's going for dinner with Amber. "Tell her I said hi," Paul calls out over his shoulder from the couch, remote in his hand. His elbows are nestled into the same pillows that Rob had sat on as she'd straddled him only hours before.

The days and then a week pass in a whirl of secret meetings and lies, of gasps and groans, clutches and kisses. They are together in his rental car and in his hotel and then again in the hotel shower. Three nights in a week. And during the day. She is constantly aware of the time and of how every moment with him is one taken from her children, from Paul. It's with a mix of elation, self-disgust, and sadness that she drags herself from him each night and heads home, unlocking the front door and trudging down the hallway, her shoes clicking on the floorboards.

The lights are usually already off by the time she gets in. There are always signs of life—a blanket hanging off the sofa, half a glass of juice on the dining table, an exercise book laid open—but there are no conversations or questions. Everyone is asleep. A bulge grows in her throat as she accepts she's missed another night with her children that she won't ever get back.

Friday is his last day before returning to Sri Lanka. He'll be back again just after Christmas—Jenny will be coming too. He doesn't want her to, he's explained to Ana. But how do you tell your wife of nine years you'd rather she stay home? He was going to end it, he repeated to her, as though living in the same house as his wife was an act of infidelity. But after Christmas. When his mother wasn't recovering from a stroke.

It's Paul who suggests the holiday house. She swallows. And then nods. A week in Byron Bay. The five of them, and Rob and Jenny. He and Rob could play golf in the mornings and surf with the kids in the long afternoons. All she says in response is, "Leave me with Jenny all day and I'll never forgive you," and they laugh and end up googling narcissistic personality disorder and diagnosing her on the spot.

"Well, she obviously makes him happy and that's all that matters," Paul says, swinging off the couch to grab himself another beer.

"Yeah," Ana replies, trying to sound natural. "Yeah, she must."

Patrick

⁂

THREE YEARS LATER

*I*T'S BEEN THIRTY-FIVE MINUTES.

He knows because he's been watching the numbers turn over on the dashboard. Eleven-fifty p.m. He lets his eyes close and rubs his eyelids, working out what time he will need to set his alarm tonight to make it to tennis tomorrow morning. Every Sunday, he meets Sam at the courts at seven and they play three sets while hardly exchanging a word.

But instead of being in bed where he ought to be, he is sitting alone in his car. Light rain falls on the windscreen and pools on the ledge of his driver's-seat window. The road is black, reflecting the moon and streetlights. Francesca's house is visible in his rearview mirror, the front room illuminated. Occasionally, he sees people leave, lifting jackets over their heads and scurrying toward a car waiting for them out the front. At one point he sees Josh, a friend of Francesca's whom he has met a few times. But so far, no Caitlin.

His phone lights up in the center console.

"Sorry coming," the message says. The muscles around his jaw ache and he can't sit still. She's been drinking. And when she drinks, she rambles. Or cries. Accuses him of being rude to her. Mostly because he is being rude to her. She barely makes sense.

"I've been out here for more than half an hour." It's the last in a series of messages throughout the night. He rubs his forehead and takes a deep breath in.

The image of her squealing her goodbyes for another half an hour flashes in his mind and he wants to storm in, grab her by the wrist, and yank her out. The selfishness. If he wanted to be up at midnight, he'd have said yes to the house party at Francesca's too. But he hadn't wanted to. And yet here he is.

Ever since they'd moved to Sydney, it felt like Caitlin had taken her list of priorities and reshuffled them. At the end of last year, they'd both been accepted into the graduate program at Fabled, one of the country's largest software development companies. It was the best-case scenario—one they'd barely let themselves hope for. But when they'd started at the beginning of January, it had become clear this job meant something different for Caitlin than it did for him. He wasn't sure if she was better at it because she worked hard, or whether she worked hard because she knew she was better at it—

either way, she was in a different league from everyone else in their team.

Work was her first priority. And her second priority is the reason she's at this overcrowded house party on a rainy Saturday night. They'd come here knowing a handful of people who had also moved over from Perth, and that had suited him perfectly fine. He had Caitlin. Sam, whom he'd grown up with. In Perth, Caitlin had had an almost comically large group of girlfriends she'd met at uni. Here, she had a few guys from work whom they got drinks with on a Friday night. And there was Francesca, who worked in admin, whom he wasn't even convinced Caitlin liked that much. For years, he'd felt like the thing that mattered most to her. In Sydney, he wasn't.

The light of the front veranda blinks in the darkness and he sees her silhouette waving at someone in a dim hallway. She walks like her legs don't trust her feet and he holds his breath as she wobbles down the uneven walkway to the footpath. When she looks up, she spots the car and wanders toward it, as though her mind is on something else. Pulling the door handle, she discovers it's locked, so pulls harder, throwing her arms up like she's asking a question. He grits his teeth. He's been sitting here for nearly forty minutes now, in a back street in Redfern. Several dark figures have passed by his car, edging unnecessarily close to the passenger door. He'd have been thoughtless not to lock it.

He fumbles to unlock it, but she keeps pulling it just as he clicks the button.

"Stop pulling!" he shouts, and she steps back from the car.

Sliding into the passenger seat, hair damp, she groans in frustration. "Why didn't you unlock the door when you saw me coming?"

"It wasn't locked forty minutes ago."

"Look. I'm sorry. They wouldn't let me leave." She's pissed off, speaking as though he is refusing to accept an apology she's barely even offered. She leans on the window and sighs.

"What the fuck do you have to be pissed off about?" he demands.

She's silent. Looking at her hands. His heart is pounding, knuckles white on the steering wheel. He whacks the indicator down and it feels good for a second. *How dare she.* He imagines punching the wheel. The sound the horn would make. The world on the outside matching how he feels on the inside.

The car parked in front of him is closer than he remembered. He has to reverse first.

"Please don't speak to me like that," she whispers.

The muscles in his arm twitch and his breathing quickens. *How did this become about how I speak to her?* He stamps his foot on the accelerator and it takes a moment for his mind to catch up to what his eyes can see. The car jolts forward with all its force and the scene unfolds in slow motion. There's a crack, the breaking of glass, and the scraping of metal. His neck is whipped forward and then back again, as he sees the rear end of the white BMW mold itself into a new shape. It doesn't look like metal but melting plastic, the way it contorts, the back panel half falling off onto the road. Caitlin screams his name.

The next sound he hears is the slam of a car door, a man roaring at him. "What the fuck?" the man bellows through the window, shaking his head in disbelief.

Patrick gets out, apologizing, and surveys the damage. The back of the man's BMW now bears the shape of the front of Patrick's Toyota Yaris. It's clear the boot can't be opened, and the number plate is kinked and askew. One light is shattered and the bumper bar looks like a wobbly tooth that needs just another light tug to fully dislodge.

He apologizes again, working hard to contain his own anger

while also placating the other angry man. He assures the other driver that he hasn't been drinking. But they call the police anyway. They Breathalyze him. He cannot look in her direction. Her eyes are red from too much white wine. They exchange details. The police say something about a charge for negligent driving, which would mean a fine and demerit points. He isn't really listening. His mind has left his body and he isn't here anymore.

The Yaris is damaged but nothing compared to the BMW. The Yaris is still drivable. The police give him clearance to drive it home and get it fixed from there. When he sits back in the driver's seat, his whole body is hot. His vision is jolty, seeing only patches of what's in front of him, and his hands shake. The car is silent for the drive home. No one turns on the radio.

When he parks the car outside their apartment block in Enmore, they sit for a moment in the dark.

"Sorry." Her voice is so quiet he isn't immediately sure what she's said.

The rage in his body has built from his stomach to his chest and now it's falling out of his throat, and once he lets it go, there's no way to bring it back in. Words spill out of his mouth that he hardly recognizes. His body convinces him that he hates her and he calls her self-centered and mean. She made him sit outside like a taxi driver, as though he had nothing better to do than to wait on her to finish.

"Can you even see how selfish you are?" he shouts, smacking a hand down on the steering wheel. "How both our lives revolve completely around you?"

She gathers her bag and lets herself out of the car. He watches her walk to their front entrance and slowly let herself in, not looking back. His head rests on the wheel, which is tacky against his forehead, and he closes his eyes. The inside of his throat burns.

Eventually, he climbs out of the car and walks the three flights of stairs to their apartment. She's already asleep. He lies next to her, making sure their bodies don't touch.

HE HEARS HER wake early and by the way she shifts, he knows she's not speaking to him. For a while he tries to go back to sleep, but there's a knot in his stomach being pulled tighter with every passing minute. He rolls over and yanks his phone off its charger. There's a message from Sam. He says it's still raining and the courts will be too wet to play. Relief.

He needs to talk to Caitlin. They rarely fight like this. Maybe a handful of times in five years. He is flooded with the memory of last night. The vein protruding from the other driver's forehead pulsating as he shouted. He'd looked at Patrick in disbelief, like he couldn't understand how someone could be so stupid. Standing on the road beside him, he'd felt like a boy. A child being scolded. He'd wanted to be anywhere else in the world. And Caitlin. Shit. Caitlin.

When he gets up, he finds her sitting on their gray sofa, both hands clutching a mug of tea. Roxy is resting her head on Caitlin's lap, her eyelids dropping involuntarily. Whenever Roxy, their yellow Labrador, feels scared or nervous, she runs first to Caitlin. She also sits under Caitlin's feet when they're eating dinner, identifying the weakest link. Most nights, something happens to fall on the floor from her dinner plate. "Strange," he often says. That never happened before they got the dog.

He scratches Roxy on the top of her head, then smiles at Caitlin and gives her hair a ruffle too. Usually she says, "Ruff," and they laugh and it's stupid. But this morning, she just smiles back politely.

No teeth. He settles in at the other end of the couch, resting his hand on Roxy's back. He doesn't want to be the first to speak.

She asks him how he's feeling and he says, "Like shit." She nods slowly.

"Yeah," she says, staring at her black tea but not really looking at it. His body stiffens.

"How you acted last night..." She pauses. "I can't be around that."

"I was just angry..."

"You scared me," she says, looking up at him. He knows what she's going to say. She's wearing the look she always does right before she says it. He reminds her of her father. How his voice would rumble through their double-brick house, echoing off the slate floors and through the hallways. How he would turn in a second. His eyes would become small and focused, his lips thin. He'd throw things. A vase against a white wall. A full plate of food from the dinner table. So loud she'd jump.

"Seriously. You remind me of him. I feel like you're always a few bad minutes from blowing up."

"I'm not like him, though. You know I'm not. I hardly ever lose it..."

She shakes her head in disbelief. "Yes, you do, Pat. And I hate it. Last week, you lost it in the car on the M4. And after work on Thursday, when I was talking about what happened with Kim..."

He had snapped about Kim. It's just that Caitlin went round and round in circles with it. Kim is on their team at work. She arrives late and leaves early—whatever she's meant to be doing inevitably shifts to Caitlin's to-do list. Most weeknights, they sit across from each other at their dining table and he has to listen to Caitlin tell a story about Kim even though work is the last thing he wants to talk about. But there's always something—her tone in an email or how she groans every time she's asked to do anything or how their supervisor made a fuss over an idea that actually belonged to Caitlin, not Kim. It's not Caitlin's specific resentment of Kim that bothers him so much. He doesn't think it makes her a bad person. It's just that he can't see how these conversations—Caitlin thinking out loud—serve any purpose. If there's a problem, fix it. He'll grumble something like, "So why didn't you just say that was your idea?" and she'll go quiet and say that's not the point. *Then what is the point?* he wants to shout. On Thursday, he'd had enough. She says he yelled. But he merely raised his voice. "I can't talk about this anymore, it's driving me insane," he'd begged.

"I don't want to be in a relationship with someone who has a problem with anger." Her voice is quiet but assured, like the words had been rehearsed before they came out of her mouth.

He nods slowly. Looks at the fireplace that doesn't work in the corner of the room.

"Okay. Okay," he says, landing his gaze back on her. "I didn't mean to scare you. I won't do that again. I'm sorry." He pauses. "I'll work on it . . . I promise."

"Are you going to see someone?" It's not really a question. More of a proposition.

"I'll think about it," he says. But he thinks probably not.

He makes them fluffy scrambled eggs and after breakfast they walk Roxy in the park. As they edge closer to home, silence falls between them. He thinks about the promise he made. How it will make him better. Address something that, if he's honest, he's always hated about himself. It reminds him of men he doesn't like.

That's what a relationship is, he realizes. A hall of mirrors. Mirrors that sometimes distort and exaggerate, but also show the truth. When you look good, you can hardly recognize yourself. You keep catching glances of yourself, looking more closely every time. It's addictive. You fall in love with the other person first, but then you fall in love with the new part of yourself that the love has created. How you look to them. But when things turn bad, the mirror feels too close. Suffocating. It reflects every microscopic detail of your ego and your failures and your maddening habits.

But without it—without the relationship—you never truly see yourself. You can get through life with no one ever looking at you close enough to say that you're a little bit petty. Jealous. Or you're angry. Or you're impatient.

He puts his arm around Caitlin and kisses her on the side of her head, taking in the smell he fell in love with sitting on the stairs of the bandstand in the middle of Russell Square. What he means to say is thank you. Both of them want him to be better, because they know it's possible. And until that moment, maybe no one had ever really cared about him that much.

Claire

Claire

THEY'RE IN THE BATHROOM WHEN IT HAPPENS.

Claire is facing the mirror, a towel around her and tucked in above her chest. Another towel wraps her hair on top of her head. She is struck by how awful she looks. Purple circles are like shadows under her eyes. Her skin is translucent, veins clear on her eyelids. Her lips are chapped and dry and a breakout of pimples is climbing up her left cheek. She tells herself she must be looking too closely. Seeing things that aren't there. If she really looked like this, people would be repulsed by her. Maggie is in the shower, the exhaust fan doing little to prevent the small round mirror from fogging up. Claire has to keep wiping it down with the end of the towel attached to her head. Eventually, the towel falls off and she stares at herself, wet, knotty hair matted to either side of her head.

The sound of the shower stops and Maggie is singing to herself when she comes up behind her, drying herself off. She's humming as she untucks the white towel Claire is wrapped in and kisses her on the neck. Maggie turns her around, but all Claire can say is, "I can't." Her eyes go blurry and she picks her discarded towel up off the floor, tying it back around her body.

"What, what's wrong? Hey . . . are you okay?" Maggie pulls her in close, rubbing her back. "Tell me what's happened?" she murmurs, her brow creasing and her eyes searching for an answer. Claire doesn't have the words yet. Maggie leads her into their bedroom, puts an oversized cotton cardigan on her, and slips her legs into a pair of gray tracksuit pants. Claire can hardly keep her head upright. Her eyes have become vacant. Defeated. She feels nothing.

"Claire, babe. Talk to me. Did something happen at work? I didn't realize you were upset. If I did, I wouldn't have . . ." She covers her eyes with her fingertips. "Something is obviously wrong. Just talk to me."

After a few minutes of listening to her own breathing, Claire says, "It's not you, Maggie. I'm just sad. Actually, I wish I could even rise to the level of being sad. I feel muted. Like I'm trying to laugh at a joke that isn't funny. My whole life is this movie I have to pretend to enjoy but I'm not enjoying it. And I'm tired. All I want to do is fall asleep and not be watching the movie. I don't necessarily want the movie to end . . . I just don't want to be awake in the theater anymore. Does that make sense?"

Maggie is silent, looking down into her lap. She's picking at the threads of the towel. "Are you sure it isn't me, Claire?" she whispers. "Am I making you unhappy?"

"No," she says deliberately. "It would almost be easier if it were you. It's me. I just look at myself and I don't want to spend time with her. I don't want to hear her voice or her thoughts anymore. She's suffocating. And my body feels like someone else's. It's all gone cold. Like my sexuality has just been switched off and I want to switch it back on again but I don't know how to."

It's quiet again. She thinks back to when this all started, maybe two months ago. Around Christmas. She remembers the sluggishness. Twelve hours' sleep wasn't enough. She'd still need a nap in the afternoon. They went to a party on New Year's Eve and she had this sensation of wanting to plug herself in. Like her head was underwater and she couldn't see or hear properly. *Why can't I feel any of this?* she asked herself, watching people dance and light sparklers and count down from ten.

Her appetite was a mess. Her mouth always lonely and her body always empty, even when her stomach was full. Then nauseous from eating too much. And then there was the guilt. *You lazy piece of shit*, her mind whispered. *What the fuck is wrong with you? How can Maggie love you when you're like this? You're pathetic. Just get out of bed.*

And then it was one o'clock on a Saturday afternoon and the place was a mess and she felt like she was stuck in a bad dream where she was trying to open her eyes but couldn't. Outside was either pitch-black or dusk. She hadn't seen a blue sky in weeks. Going outside hurt, the way the cold air clung to her skin and turned her breath into fog. Nothing to look forward to. Life was just one endless night and she had stopped waiting for it to be morning.

"I think you probably need to see a doctor," Maggie says, still not looking at her. Maggie's always more honest when she doesn't have to look Claire in the eye.

"Yeah. I don't know. Maybe."

But by the following morning, Claire has an appointment. Maggie goes with her. The doctor has her fill out a questionnaire. Her jaw clenches.

"How often have you been bothered by feeling down, depressed, or hopeless?" *Wouldn't it be strange not to be "bothered" by being depressed?* she thinks to herself.

"How often have you been bothered by feeling bad about yourself, or that you are a failure, or have let yourself or your family down?" Of course she was bothered that she hated herself. That nothing had come of her life. That she was in a state of malaise, her feet stuck to the ground, unable to step forward. Who wouldn't be bothered by that? *For fuck's sake*, she thought. She could just circle anything.

For most of the questions, she stops herself from selecting the most extreme answer. She doesn't want to be rushed to hospital in a straitjacket. So she chooses "More than half the days" for the majority of her answers and then slides the A4 sheet of paper that looks like it's been photocopied too many times back over to Dr. Griffith.

"Mmm," he says, making markings on the paper, as though she's a simple equation to be worked out. He asks a few questions about where Claire is from. How long she's felt this way. What she does for work.

"I'm not a psychologist, so take this with a grain of salt, but in my opinion these are symptoms of seasonal affective disorder. You don't get real winters down in Australia, do you?"

She shakes her head and tries to offer a smile. She's heard of that. SAD. People in Alaska get it.

"Now," the doctor says, looking over his glasses and at his computer screen. "Do you have any history of anxiety or depression?"

"Yeah, probably. Never formally diagnosed. But I've always had periods like this. Just never this bad before."

The doctor nods. Uses two fingers to type on his clicky keyboard. By the time Claire leaves, they have a plan. She'll see a psychologist. Get her vitamin D levels checked. Try one of those light therapy lamps. And if none of those things work, they'll look at medication. She feels a twitch in her stomach. Hope, perhaps.

Patrick

&

*I*T'S EARLY OCTOBER WHEN THE RECEPTIONIST DROPS THE brown cardboard box on his desk.

"What did you order?" she asks, placing the largely empty package beside his mouse.

He delivers his prepared answer. "I wish it was more exciting. It's literally just a titanium screw for my bike . . ." The words have barely left his mouth before she's forgotten them, focused instead on what's in the remaining three parcels, hugged in close to the side of her body.

"Gemma," she shouts, lifting the next package from her pile. As the clip-clop of her heels against the floorboards fades into the distance, he swiftly places the box in his bottom drawer. The key that's hung out of it for as long as he's worked here is turned right and removed for the first time, then he buries it under a bunch of papers in the drawer above. Probably not the best hiding place for a key, but if he puts it anywhere else he'll lose it. When he looks back up at his computer, he runs his hands through his hair. Done.

Just after midday, he wanders over to Caitlin's desk and asks if she's ready for lunch. She's about to run into a meeting. He offers to grab her something while he's out and she thanks him over her shoulder as she shuffles into the boardroom, a laptop balancing on her forearm.

Most days Caitlin can't go out for lunch. She complains about it, but there's a falseness to her grumbling. Since they'd both started there, given the choice, she'd stay at the office late every evening, always work through her lunch break, and jump on her emails on a Friday night. He wasn't the only one who'd noticed. A few of the senior developers had too. He'd learned the better you were at a job, the more they would ask you to do. They both knew her workload was almost double his.

When their year in the graduate program had been coming to an end, she'd been called into a meeting and offered a position as a senior software engineer. He'd been asked whether he'd come on board as a software engineer—one big rung down the ladder from her role. Both had said yes. So now she sat on the other side of the office, with a team who barely spoke, their spines curled over keyboards.

Rick sees him heading toward the lift and shouts, "Are you going to the Salad Bar?"

"Yeah." He intended to call his mum and let her know the box had arrived.

"Hang on, just grabbing my wallet."

They stand in the lift, Patrick checking his phone.

"You and Caitlin coming to trivia on Thursday night?"

"I will," he says. "Not sure if Caitlin will make it. I'll ask her tonight."

Rick says Francesca will be there. Josh too. There's a group of them who go most Thursdays.

It's warm outside, the sun defrosting their air-conditioned skin. He crosses the road to the side of the street with less shade. Rick checks his phone and then asks, "Is it ever weird working with your girlfriend?"

"No," Patrick says, looking at the footpath. "We've been working together for ages now so it's pretty normal."

"Was it awkward when she got promoted, though? Isn't she kind of your boss?"

It's not the first time someone has asked him that question. Caitlin says that if it were the other way around, no one would even consider it. She's probably right. He remembers why he doesn't particularly enjoy getting lunch with Rick. He asks too many questions. You always come back to the office worried you've accidentally said too much.

"Nah, not really. We're not competitive. Her position is just different from mine. Not really what I want to do. And it's not like she gets to call me into her office and reprimand me for doing a shit job. Although . . ."

Rick laughs too hard, raising his eyebrows and whistling. He nods like he knew that would be the answer. What Patrick doesn't say is that when he sees Caitlin in the office, usually wearing a buttoned-up linen shirt and denim jeans, he feels proud. In awe. Fascinated by how differently her brain works than anyone else's. She's an arresting communicator. Her memory is infallible. Once when she rattled something off about the specs of a dev-ops tool their team had created eighteen months ago, he called her Rain Man. And then he did an incredibly offensive impersonation that no one other than her has ever been allowed to see. He's watched her at conferences, the only woman in the lineup. There's a thrill you get from being in the presence of someone doing what they do best. What they were put on this earth to do. Every feature on their face makes sense. Their body tells a story. Self-assurance radiates from every pore in their skin. You watch other people watching them. In that moment, the universe has conspired to make them utterly perfect.

When he returns to the office, he fidgets for the rest of the afternoon. Goes to the bathroom a few times. Makes himself a cup of tea he doesn't feel like. Compiles a list of things to do tomorrow. He's accepted nothing productive will be happening today. His mind is scattered, going over the conversation he knows he has to have tonight. Caitlin is on a deadline and so will be staying back late. It's the only time he can make the call without her getting suspicious.

He says goodbye to her on his way out, his backpack hanging off one shoulder. She says, "Love you," and immediately covers her mouth and laughs. They don't usually say that at work. He texts her as the lift doors shut. "Love you too x."

By the time he gets home, he's dizzy. His palms are damp and a wet patch has glued his shirt to his lower back. He'll have a shower first. Then he'll make the call. *No*, his brain barks back. *Just make the call*. He falls into the couch, is swallowed by the cushions, and stares at the home screen of his phone. Tells his thumb to find the number. To tap.

After two rings, there's a pause and then a "Hello?"

They speak for a few minutes. She asks how everything is down there in Sydney. How work is going. She tries to keep the curiosity out of her voice, but beneath all the questions is a hint of worry about why he would be calling her on a Monday night.

There's a gap in the conversation. A space for him to explain the reason for the call. He clears his throat. "So, the reason I'm calling," he says, carefully finding his words, "is that I just want to let you know that, um. You know how we're going to Canada next month?"

"Yes," Caitlin's mum says slowly.

"Well. When we're there, I think I'm going to propose. And I just wanted to let you know beforehand. Because I thought it was the right thing to do."

He's always liked Natalia. She treats him and Caitlin as though they're the most interesting people in the world. Whenever they stay with her in Brisbane, she sits across from them on the outdoor deck, hands under her chin, asking them about their friends and their apartment and whether they're still doing that indoor rock-climbing thing. Caitlin had told him that the first time Natalia had met him, she'd pulled Caitlin aside afterward and said, "Hold on to that one." Ever since then, he hasn't felt like he needed to try too hard. That's why he's surprised by how nervous he is.

There's a few beats of total silence. He holds his breath. Then a squeal. He can imagine the expression on her face from the sound of her voice. He breaks into a grin, more relieved than he'd expected to be. Between sniffles, she thanks him for telling her and says she couldn't have wished for anything more for Caitlin. They speak for a few minutes longer and his shoulders loosen. He tells her about the ring and she oohs and aahs before making him promise to take lots of pictures.

"Welcome to the family," she says. "And thank you. Thank you for making my Caitlin so happy."

When he hangs up, he closes his eyes and all he can see is the rose-gold band and the rose-cut gray diamond, surrounded by a half halo of white diamonds. He visualizes it sliding onto her thin finger, freckles scattered below her knuckle. He tries to imagine how she reacts.

Three weeks. Three weeks until Canada. He'd thought getting Natalia's blessing would calm him down. But his stomach churns and tingles run down his thighs. *Shit.* How will he sleep between now and then? How is he going to carry on as he normally does, lying next to her in bed, the exact words of his proposal running through his head? She can tell he's hungry before he even knows it. Can sense he's frustrated by the way his legs are crossed. Sometimes they look at each other, smile, and say the exact same thing at the exact same time. The idea of not telling Caitlin that he's about to propose to Caitlin seems ludicrous. She should be the first to know.

Three weeks. And then—for the first time in his life—it might feel as though everything has fallen into place.

Ana

❦

"*I* CAN'T EVEN REMEMBER THE LAST TIME WE HAD SEX,"
Jenny slurs at her, in a rare moment of vulnerability.

It's New Year's Eve and the kids have gone to light sparklers on
the beach, led by Paul and Rob. The Byron Bay wind has picked up,
the kind that flicks coarse grains of sand at your ankles. Ana has
stayed back at the house with Jenny, their full champagne glasses
demanding their attention. Jenny's eyelids have drooped and her
words are coming out in a jumble that doesn't make sense to Ana
but appears to make sense to Jenny. A thick strand of hair, coated

with salt and humidity, has fallen across Jenny's face, but she seems unbothered. She takes a large mouthful of warm champagne and speaks, looking toward an ocean of endless black.

"It's true . . . he hardly touches me, anywhere," she continues, as Oliver's laughter blows up toward them with the wind. Ana feels the discomfort of knowing someone is about to cry. And she doesn't know what to do. To hug Jenny would feel unnatural. Like a lie. She pretends she can't see the tears, glassy over doll-like brown eyes. The rest of her face doesn't match. *Well, that's what getting work done to your face does*, Ana thinks cynically. It means you can't sob. Only drip.

But before Ana can say anything, the wooden steps back to the house from the beach, scattered with splinters, begin to thud. Rachael's head emerges from the dark.

"It was too windy," she says, brushing her hair with her fingers.

"I got sand in my eyes," Louis whines, and Paul takes him inside to rinse it out.

"Sorry," Jenny mumbles. "Too much champagne."

Ana decides she doesn't like people who cry when they drink. It means they're unhinged. "We've all been there," she says anyway, like a middle-aged netball coach who has no time for anyone's bullshit. She considers offering her another drink, just as an excuse to be somewhere else for a while, but decides against it. The last sip Jenny had taken had barely made it to her mouth, droplets spilling on her leopard-print kaftan. Her mascara has smudged above her eyes, the steamy air turning everything wet. The silence hangs for a moment.

She thinks of how Rob had kissed her hard in the shadowy kitchen last night after she thought he'd gone to sleep. How her body had crumbled. He'd placed his hands either side of her face and said forcefully, "I love you," and silenced her lips with his before she could respond.

"I love you, I love you," she'd whispered back in the darkness. Then she went to bed and lay awake, counting down the hours until she could see him again.

A trace of contentment emerges on her face. Barely perceptible, the corners of her lips tilt upward. *He was telling the truth*, she thinks. For months, he's been telling her that he and Jenny don't have sex. He can't stand the thought of it. She'd thought that's what all men having affairs said. A way to pledge their fidelity, despite their blatant infidelity. They want you to think they'd be faithful, if only they were with the right woman. How torturous to be trapped in a loveless marriage—that's what they want you to think. The mistress ends up feeling sympathetic. The narrative rewritten to make *him* the victim. And his wife the perpetrator. But her affair isn't like other affairs. She used to think the world was so black-and-white. That a "cheater" was nothing more than a selfish cowardly psychopath.

That's what Ana had thought of Jenny when Rob had told her about her affair—the one she'd had with her colleague Kevin. It was so objectively wrong. An unforgivable transgression.

She'd always wondered how someone could lie in bed next to someone else and say "I love you" when they were betraying them. She'd probably said it out loud to Paul at some stage, when one of their friends had been revealed to be cheating on their wife. If you're unhappy, just leave, had been her philosophy. We are not at the mercy of our impulses. We are not animals. Every day we make a choice. And being married meant you'd already made your choice. Your husband.

But now she knew there was no such thing as a cheater. Only a person who cheated. And she couldn't leave. She'd entertained every possibility in her mind. Paul was, and always had been, the breadwinner. Starting off as an apprentice builder, he now owned his own business. It made money. Enough for them to get by. But that was it. There wasn't enough to send the boys to private school. Or go on a family holiday to Europe. So there wasn't enough to get a divorce. To live in two separate houses. With three bedrooms each.

And to leave Paul for Rob. That was just laughable. Sometimes she thought about it. The way you dare yourself to jump off when you stand on the edge of a steep cliff. *Imagine how much it would ruin my life.* She'd be disowned not only by Paul but by his family. Exiled. She'd traumatize her children, inflicting psychological damage they'd probably never recover from. They'd hate her. Not in the way Rachael says she hates her whenever Ana says no to sleepovers at Kylie's with no parents. But in a permanent way. The kind of hate that plants itself in your guts, its vines curling around every bone in your body, its leaves budding in your muscles, the power of it keeping you awake at night. The kind of hate that grows so fiercely that it's impossible to discern where you end and where it begins. It becomes you. Its tendrils claw their way through the chest and up through the throat until one day one of her children calls her a "slut" or a "whore." And it won't be in the heat of the moment. It will be born from that seed that's been festering for years. And it will be true.

Louis returns to the deck with the rest of them and she pulls him onto her lap, gives him a cuddle, kisses the side of his forehead. "Mum, can we go surfing with Uncle Rob tomorrow morning?" he asks, looking up at her with bloodshot eyes, the inflection in his words making him sound exactly like his father.

"Of course you can," she says.

THE HEAT IS suffocating. Her phone flashes on the rustic, off-white table beside her. It's not even seven thirty. She stretches her legs straight out in front of her, flexing her feet. They're clammy and warm. A slick of oil fused with sweat coats the skin on her forehead, dampening her hairline. She knows she can't go back to sleep. A skylight is piercing her eyes and the glaring sun scolds her through the transparent white curtains. She needs a shower.

Beside her, Paul breathes deeply. It's strange that at night he snores so loudly she half expects someone to emerge and shoosh him, but in the morning his body falls almost silent. He sleeps on his front, his head pointed toward her, his mouth hanging open. She thinks she would be quite content if she never crawled into bed next to this man again. Resentment. That's what she feels. And don't all those pop psychologists say there's no coming back from resentment? Or was that contempt? Either way, she feels both.

She turns back to her phone. A message. It's Rob. Would she like to go down to the beach before anyone else wakes up? Jenny will be in bed all morning after last night. She replies, "Meet you there in five," and throws on a blue sundress, the kind she'd rarely wear at home but lives in up here. The round neck sits just under her collarbones, the hem just above her knees. She finds a face wipe on the dresser and runs it over her forehead and cheeks, and then her armpits. Deodorant. Toothbrush in mouth. Hair up. Sunglasses. And then she tiptoes to the door and twists the knob silently.

He's at the base of the wooden steps, waiting for her. His fitted red T-shirt makes him look as though he belongs on *Baywatch*, granted a few decades too late. His hands rest on his hips, chest proud to the sun, watching the waves rhythmically roll into themselves. White water creates the illusion of a marble staircase. One wave over the top of another. And then another. The sky is a brilliant blue. The kind you only see in travel brochures. Not even a hint of a cloud. The sand below it is flat and dry, footsteps yet to disturb it.

"Hi," she says softly, stopping just beside him.

His toes are almost buried, the top of his foot brown from too many days outside. They walk toward the shoreline, sit down not far from it.

"I can't do this anymore," he announces after a few moments, his gaze everywhere but on her.

"What do you mean you can't do this anymore?" she asks, her voice sharper than she intended.

"This." He motions between them. "You're the woman I should've married. Should've had kids with. I'm completely in love with you. The idea of you with Paul every night is driving me crazy. It's fucked."

"You knew, though, Rob. You knew what we were entering into. I can't leave my kids. What do you expect me to—"

"I'd never want to upset your kids, Ana. But I need us to do this properly. It's done with Jenny. And you know it's done with Paul. Come on. You know it." His eyes are full of desperation, squinting from the glare. She wants to do this properly too. But there's also no such thing.

She asks about him and Paul. Is he prepared for that friendship to be destroyed? He's been close friends with Paul for almost as long as he's known her. They've gone on rugby trips together. Golfed and surfed and rotated sausages at too many barbecues to count. Stood shoulder to shoulder at a mate's funeral. Is he ready to be disowned by almost every group they belong to? Who will they have, other than each other?

He's determined, though—says he is certain that's enough for him. He wants her to move with him. To Sri Lanka. He can support her financially, he says eagerly. Give her everything she's ever wanted. Bring the kids with you, he suggests, knowing as the words fall out of his mouth how ridiculous they sound. She leans into this world, though. She can smell it. Taste it. The more he talks about it, the closer it feels. They're cooking together. In bed, watching a movie. Holding hands as they stroll into their local café. All the things they can't do now.

"I need you to give me twelve months," she says. "To sort things out. To work out what I'm going to do." Her hands claw at the sand behind her, holding up her body. She points and flexes her toes, one at a time.

"Do you promise?" he asks. His eyes, boyish and fervent, waiting for an answer.

"Yes." The waves become louder.

"I wish he'd just have an affair," she adds dryly, looking back toward the town in the distance.

Claire

When people ask about a proposal, that's not the detail you're meant to tell them. That you were in a bad mood or you were finding them particularly needy that day or you were wondering when their awful haircut was going to grow out. But the day you're proposed to is also just another day in a messy, ever-evolving relationship, perfect only from the outside.

She's on the bus home and her stomach rumbles. It's nearly eight.

Her phone rings again. Maggie. She feels like not answering, just to make a point. Maggie's not working today. She'd called at lunchtime to ask how Claire's day was going. Kept tagging her in posts on Facebook. Sent her a picture she found on the internet that was a little bit funny, but not funny enough to justify texting her at work. Then she'd called at a quarter to five to ask when she'd be finished and a half-distracted Claire had told her she'd be late tonight. She had a bunch of admin to do that she'd been putting off all week. And so she hung up and put her head down and by the time Janine came in and asked if she'd like to join them for a drink, it was almost seven. They'd already poured her a glass of something white. She sat up at one of the stools at the high lunch table in the communal kitchen and joined the conversation about everything that was wrong with Zahara, who also worked in the complaints team. Claire had nodded along to things she hadn't known and some she didn't even believe, because it was exhilarating to feel like she was a part of something, even if that meant sacrificing poor Zahara, who could be annoying but wasn't as bad as they all said. When she'd pressed the button for the lift, she'd been smiling, the light buzz from the two glasses of wine she'd drunk buoying her. But as she'd stepped into the lift, she'd felt a wave of guilt wash over her, like she'd been complicit in something kind of ugly.

She sees a bunch of missed calls from Maggie and a handful of texts, and so she messages back, "On my way home now, should I pick something up on the way or were you going to cook?"

And now she's on the bus, only half an hour from home, and Maggie is calling again. She tries not to sound pissed off as she answers. "Hey—nearly home, what's up?"

"Where have you been?"

"Just had a few drinks at work with some people. You're being very needy today," she says, laughing. Maggie laughs back. She knows it.

"I miss you. Get home, see you soon."

Six months ago, she'd have found all this sweet, but tonight the calls and the texts and the obligation to always be somewhere else feels suffocating. Sometimes it's as though she's in two places at once, straddling two worlds, never quite fully planted in her own life because she's living Maggie's too. A day is neither good nor bad, it's an amalgamation of both their fears and anxieties and how one of Maggie's clients spoke to her today and maybe Maggie didn't have a good night's sleep or she forgot her Oyster card. She wouldn't change it for anything, of course, but she dares herself to imagine for a moment what it would be like if she lived just one day at a time. Not two.

She walks up the stairs to their flat, aching to get out of her work clothes. As she reaches the door, she notices how dark it looks inside. Like their hallway light isn't on. Turning the doorknob, she calls out, "Maggie, why are all the lights off?"

She hears Maggie in the other room and stops herself from yelling out, "Why is it so dark in here and why are you ignoring me?" When she reaches the end of the hallway, her eyes meet Maggie's and she must look irritable. All she wants to do is change out of her clothes. Have some dinner. Climb into bed.

But Maggie smiles meekly at her and that's when she sees that the entire living area is covered in tea-light candles. As Claire's eyes are adjusting to the dozens of flickering flames dancing in the darkness, Maggie gets down on one knee in front of her, looks up, and says, "Claire, will you marry me?"

Maggie, with her ripped jeans, oversized white jumper, and short hair tucked behind her ears, has never looked so vulnerable.

Not necessarily because of the question she's asking, but because of the effort she's put in. She wants this to be A Moment.

"You didn't have to do this!" Claire can't help but exclaim. Maggie reaches up and slides the ring they'd both chosen onto Claire's finger.

"Yes, Maggie. I will marry you," Claire says softly.

They'd started talking about marriage a few months earlier. Claire's visa would run out at the beginning of next year and neither of them wanted her to go home. It made sense for them to go through with a civil partnership. They'd spent too many evenings in front of a laptop, choosing the rings they wanted and discussing what kind of ceremony they'd like. They'd settled on something small in London and, perhaps one day in the future, something bigger in Australia with Claire's family. Or maybe it wouldn't be too long until marriage—the real thing—would be available to them and they could save up and have a proper ceremony with lots of people. But for now, it would be at the Register Office on Harrow Road, with a few friends and hopefully their parents—if Claire's could make it. The discussions had been largely pragmatic. It was a step that made sense.

But as Maggie stands up in the candlelit room, it is clear that she wants this to be romantic too. They are entering into a civil partnership so that Claire can stay. But Claire is staying because she never wants to leave the person standing in front of her.

"I love you. Thank you for making this so special," she says.

They sit in the candlelit room for a while, deciding how they're going to tell people. Claire waits an appropriate time before saying that so many flames on a timber floor in an old London flat makes her nervous. Maggie shrugs and together they blow out all the candles. The warmth lingers in the room for hours.

Patrick

꧁

CAITLIN TUGS ON THE ARM OF HIS JACKET.

"You okay?"

"Yeah," he whispers back, his eyes wide so she knows he's serious.

Her Kathmandu jacket is zipped right up to her neck, a black scarf tucked tightly into it. Gloves that look like oven mitts tug at her beanie, drawing it further over her ears. He keeps thinking how small she looks under all her layers, a floating head wrapped in thermals and jumpers and thick socks and waterproof boots you'd never be able to buy in Australia. Her cheeks are flushed pink from the harsh wind.

The week before they arrived, the temperature had dropped to minus forty with wind chill. Their guide, Matthew, had told them that when it was that cold, you could barely stand outside. No skin on your body could be exposed. Not even your face. Your eyelashes become coated in frost. If your nose ran, it was only seconds before icicles began to hang from your lip. They were glad to have missed that.

The days are more bearable than the nights. This morning, their weather app had said the day would have a top temperature of zero degrees Celsius and Caitlin had exclaimed, "Balmy!" while pulling on a second jumper. Matthew keeps saying it's unseasonably warm and they tell him that in Australia an unseasonably warm winter means you can still go to the beach. And come home sunburnt.

"Is that a moose?" she asks, leaning her face against the high chicken-wire fence.

Matthew explains it's not. It's an elk. He tells them they shed their summer coat and replace it with a thick, woolen parka that keeps them five times warmer.

Patrick and Caitlin are silent, watching the elk slowly blink, the only indication it's alive. They study how its eyelashes fan outward, creating something so human about its expression. Delicate and beautiful. Snow has settled between the elk's wide-set eyes, and it gazes back at them.

"It looks like Roxy," she says at the exact moment he thinks it. The elk stands up, front legs first and then back. It shakes like a dog after a bath and then brings its back foot to just behind its ear, scratching an itchy spot. Once it's finished, it looks out into the distance, wondering what to do next. Eventually, it wanders over to a group of three other elk and settles.

Imagine if life were that simple. Eat when you're hungry. Find others when you're lonely. Sleep when you're tired. The day is spent acting on immediate impulse. Patrick feels a desire to switch places. To be given respite from his own thoughts for the afternoon. Elk aren't playing out the next twenty-four hours of their lives, trying to surface the best possible scenario while being dragged by their ankles toward the worst. He realizes what it is in their majestic, angular faces that reminds him of Roxy, their dog at home. Peace. Behind their eyes and deep in the joints of their jaws is a sense of peace. What is the opposite of peace? Agitation, perhaps. And he is filled with it.

All he can think about is tonight. Will it even happen? Will he even be able to get the words out? He's not himself today—that's why Caitlin keeps checking on him. He's not in the moment, instead his brain is fizzing through a thousand other ones. He's been trying not to ruminate on it, but he's worried she will say no. Of course, he wouldn't have bought the ring if he wasn't fairly certain the answer would be yes. It's not like they've never talked about marriage. But there was one condition. Something he was required to fix. He didn't know how long he had to prove he'd fixed it, though. He can't remember the last time he lost his temper. This year, he'd bought books. Read hundreds of articles. Meditated and journaled. If he felt that tug in his chest, his heartbeat accelerate, his thoughts spiral, he took himself off to be alone. Later, when he could manage it, he said things out loud—put what he felt into words.

The more he read, the more he realized where his anger had come from. In his family, nothing was ever expressed. You never said "I hate you" and you never said "I love you." His mother had never just given him a hug for no reason. The first time he tried to put a pen to paper and write down why he was so angry, he discovered he didn't have the words at his disposal. It was like they belonged to a language he'd never learned. Never even heard. Eventually, terms and phrases became the conduit to the outside world. He could articulate it to Caitlin. She still brought up the therapy thing. A gentle nudge. But the truth was, he didn't need it. He didn't need a stranger delving into his childhood, looking for things that were pretty fucking obvious. He knew he had a temper. But psychologists can't help a feeling. Just your response to it. His anger was a problem that needed fixing and he could find the solution on Google.

YouTube taught him how to breathe properly. He tried yoga. Mindfulness. He was sure they worked for some people but he'd stopped doing them almost as soon as he'd started. The breathing stuck. And the talking. Mostly, he felt he developed some self-awareness. Like when years ago a boss had told him turning up five minutes late to the morning meeting was a bad look, he'd started showing up on time. In the same way, when his anger had been pointed out to him, he became ashamed enough to control it.

Last time they'd spoken about getting married, Caitlin had said she needed to see where they were in twelve months. That was about eight months ago. Nearly nine. But if he waited for the full year, he couldn't have proposed here—in the middle of a Canadian winter.

"You sure you're okay?" She gives him a look.

He can't stand still. "Yeah, sorry. I'm just cold."

When they return to their hotel in downtown Whitehorse, which is small but cozy, an open fireplace welcomes them, giving the room an inviting glow. They shower and check their phones, and Caitlin posts a few photos of elk and moose on Facebook. It's too cold outside so they decide to eat at the restaurant inside the hotel. Neither of them drink over dinner—it would make them sleepy and tonight they'll be out late.

It's just before ten when the tour bus picks them up. Frost has settled on the outside of the bus windows. Matthew warned them yesterday at the briefing when they were given the clothes they hired that the icy wind will slap them in the face. The puffy snow jackets they expected. Same with the leggings, the thermals under pants, the long-sleeved tops and jumpers. But then came the thick waterproof overalls. They'd had to ask Matthew how to wear them. Sitting on the bus, Patrick can feel his body temperature rising. He takes off his beanie. Everything outside is black, so they can't see where they're going. It's giving him motion sickness.

It doesn't take long to get to the aurora viewing. As he takes the last step off the bus, he looks up, hoping to see the green lights swirling above him. What he sees instead is spectacular. Thousands of drops of light scattered across black, patterns and shapes unfamiliar to him. He can't remember the last time he looked—really looked—at stars. How they compete with the blanket of darkness, forcing their way through.

They all make their way into a heated cabin for a briefing. Matthew says there's about a sixty percent chance they'll see the aurora borealis tonight.

"That's the beautiful thing about nature," he says. "You never know what it's going to do." That's an easy thing for him to say. He sees the northern lights every time they descend because he's out here with a bunch of tourists. But for them—this trip took them a year to save for. They've come halfway around the world. This is at the top of their bucket list. It will not be beautiful of nature to give them the finger and stay dark while they stare at it for three hours every night. They could do that in outback Australia.

He isn't religious and doesn't know how you're meant to pray. But he says some words in his head, begging whoever is up there in the sky to give them the northern lights. This is part of the plan. If they don't come tonight, he has to wait another twenty-four hours. And if they don't come then, it will have to be the night after. And if they never come, he doesn't really have an alternative plan. Maybe it'd be a sign.

Matthew tells them that even scientists admit there are unanswered questions when it comes to the aurora borealis. They do know that the spectacular brightening of the sky with dancing, colorful light that we see is caused by electron and proton particles blasting out from the sun and colliding with the earth's atmosphere. He says if you're absolutely silent, you can hear them, a hissing, crackling sound, moving all around you. Some locals believe it's bad luck to look at the lights. Others understand them to be human spirits, swirling in the heavens.

Inside the cabin, they're given heavy steel tripods that can withstand the cold. Plastic ones will snap. Matthew directs them each to a different spot, each pair or individual spaced a few meters apart. As Patrick adjusts their tripod, his fingers barely functional under thick snow gloves, his heart races. The air burns as it pulls in through his nose and settles in his lungs. He notices his nostrils freeze with every inhale and defrost with every exhale. The camera settings offer a welcome distraction, as he experiments with exposure times and shutter speed. Eventually, it's all set up and they sit on the snow and wait. The sky is still dark, the glow of the stars making parts of it look electric blue.

There's a bit of chatter while they all wait, their bodies slowly adjusting to the cold. People ask Matthew questions and point out constellations. Frost gathers on their arms and legs. They wait. They accept that tonight might not be the night. They wait some more; they peer through their camera lenses, hoping to catch something not visible to the naked eye.

Then, a faint glow. Barely perceivable. It sits on the horizon like a gray misty cloud.

Someone points up at it. Asks Matthew if that's it.

"Looks like it could be," Matthew says, looking out in front of him, as though it is something he summoned.

They adjust their cameras, again experimenting with different settings. Patrick tries a shutter speed of five seconds, but the colors aren't bright or active enough yet. There's excited talk among their group, Matthew offering advice on how to capture the colors as clearly as possible.

Over the next hour, they watch as the misty gray light rises higher into the sky and hues of green and orange faintly dance above them. They look like shimmery ribbons being pulled by an invisible hand. Josie and Harrison, the couple set up next to Patrick and Caitlin, say they can hear the crackle. But he can't.

They sit watching the light being pulled across the sky in arches. For the most part, they're silent. He mumbles that this is incredible. She murmurs in agreement. *We're so small*, he thinks. *So insignificant.* The sky could fall on them any second—explode as a result of some cosmic reaction science hasn't even discovered yet. And they are specks. Grains of sand that will one day be washed away, buried at the bottom of the ocean. There's something liberating about knowing you don't matter. Not in the grand scheme of things. Not to whoever's hand is pulling these gargantuan ribbons across the night sky in Yukon. But his newfound perspective only lasts a few moments. He remembers that tonight might be the most significant of his life.

He puts his arm around her shoulders and she nestles her head into his neck. "I don't think I knew what happiness was before you," he says, kissing her on the side of the head.

They check the camera and the sky turns into swirls of green and pink and yellow behind the lens. It looks alive. It's whatever the opposite of apocalyptic is—heavenly? He has to do this. They might not have another night when the lights are so vivid.

They sit again and he can feel the cold of the snow finding its way into his socks.

"You're my person," he says. His hand reaches under his ski jacket and inside his overalls, searching for the box, buried deep inside his pocket. She's distracted, only half listening. His fingers find the shape, grasp it, and pull it out through the layers. He exhales through pursed lips. She looks up at him.

"Will you marry me?" The box is open, a ring barely visible inside it.

Her black glove reaches up to her mouth, hanging open. He can't read her eyes.

"No!" she bleats.

She drops her hand to her side and she's smiling. The light of the sky makes her eyes sparkle. She throws her arms around his neck, falling into him as she does. She kisses him and her lips are freezing, his numb.

"Caitlin," he says between kisses. "All you've said is no."

Whispering travels from behind him. Josie and Harrison have seen the proposal. He hears someone take their camera off the tripod.

She laughs and holds her hands up to her mouth. "Yes, you idiot. Obviously yes."

He fumbles to remove the glove from her left hand and awkwardly slides on the ring. It catches on her knuckle before settling on the base of her slim, white finger.

"How did you even pick this?" she asks, holding it up to the light. "It's just beautiful."

"Congratulations," Matthew shouts, and Patrick suddenly feels embarrassed. Exposed. Like there was something performative about what he just did.

For the rest of the night, though, the group falls into their own conversations. Caitlin wipes tears from her face. She says, "They feel good," and laughs. They're warm against her skin. Every muscle in his body relaxes, hints of a headache forming behind his eyes.

He puts his arm around her and she rests into his chest.

Can life really be this good? he thinks, looking up.

There is a faint voice, if he's honest with himself, that whispers in his ear. *No.*

Ana

❦

SHE HATES HIS MOUTH. IT MAKES HER FEEL SICK. HIS LIPS
are too thin and his chin is slack and dented. When he yawns, it
looks affected. Like he's pretending. He lets out an exaggerated huff,
his right hand resting by his side. He doesn't even bother to cover his
mouth. *Look inside my mouth,* he is saying. Look at my dry tongue
and red tonsils and black fillings. The color of tar.

They're sitting on the couch, watching some series she can't get
into. He likes it. Or he says he likes it and then he falls asleep halfway through every episode, his head sinking backward, bottom lip

hanging, like one of those clowns at a fair, begging you to throw a white ball in their mouth. *This is torture*, she thinks as she hears his big toe rub against his second toe. And then *flick*. A callus has formed, dry and round, just above the knuckle of his second toe. The hair has stopped growing. *Flick*. Only his right foot. It's only ever his right foot. *Flick*.

"Can you stop doing that?" she asks.

"What?" he asks, unbothered. Only briefly glancing away from the television screen. *Flick*.

Eight months. She repeats to herself. A mantra. Only eight more months of this. *Flick*.

"The toes. Stop with the toes." She lets out a halfhearted laugh. Padding. So her insult isn't so sharp.

"What?" he says again, chuckling. *Flick. Flick. Flick*. She rolls her eyes.

"Now, remember I'm away this weekend," she says, changing the subject before she snaps. "Kylie's mum is getting Rachael for netball on Saturday morning, but you'll have to get the boys to soccer. And I'll leave some dinner in the fridge," she says, her voice even and matter-of-fact.

He nods, not really listening.

Imagine if he knew, she thinks.

Just as Paul lets his eyes fall closed, she hears her phone vibrate on the granite benchtop where it's been left to charge. Him. Her skin tingles and her stomach wakes up, claws clutching at her from the inside. She waits a moment and then makes her way into the kitchen, the phone screen dark. In an instant she unlocks it, the picture of the kids at Easter she has as her background partially obscured by a message alert. Only it's not from Rob at all.

It's from Jenny.

Claire

❦

It started with a pair of shoes.

They've been married eight months. When friends ask Claire if they fight, she says, "No, not really," which she's always thought is a miracle for two Geminis. Mostly their relationship is peaceful. Considerate. Hanging towels up because not doing so would upset the other. Speaking to each other kindly. Except when they're running late and it's Maggie's fault, in which case Claire is shockingly rude for twenty minutes. And then they move on. If a comment is made over dinner with friends that upsets the other, there's silence rather than yelling. Sometimes they get sad. But never angry.

They've moved out of the flat they shared with Abbie and now rent a studio in Brixton. The area is full of energy and life and the guy downstairs goes to work in a dress and stilettos except when he feels like wearing a suit and tie. When winter rolled around, Claire dusted off her light therapy lamp and they ate better and shivered in the cool blue sun at Brockwell Park, looking out at the London skyline. At Christmas, they'd visited her family in Australia, staying three blissful weeks in scorching Queensland. But by the end, she almost missed being able to go to the bathroom without having already sweated through her underpants.

Maggie fell in love with Australia in a way Claire had not been expecting. She enjoyed walking along the wide, grassy streets at dusk, barefoot and smelling of hours-old sunscreen. She adored the weekend they spent on the Gold Coast, diving into the ocean one morning and refusing to get out for hours. She loved the food and how people spoke to each other, like the guy at the corner shop who said, "G'dayhowareya," all one word, as though he was playing a part in a movie. In Australia, everyone was always exercising outside. Doing pull-ups on a bar set up beside the beach. Jogging through the main streets. Public pools had been dropped into the middle of towns and people did laps outdoors, the sun massaging their backs as they went.

It made Claire see Australia through Maggie's eyes, almost as though she was experiencing it for the first time. You didn't have to lock your door and when you wandered down the main street after dark, you didn't have to hold your breath. It was everything London wasn't. For better and for worse.

A few weeks after they returned home, Maggie brought up

moving there. "It's the type of place you raise a family," she'd said. "You're happier when you're there, you know," she'd added. In bed that night, Claire had wondered whether she was more in love with the idea of London than with the place itself. Brixton was gritty and complicated. Overflowing with character. Toowoomba was none of those things. Simple to a fault. Ten years behind the rest of the world. But the truth was that Maggie was home now. She didn't care what city that landed them in.

And so the Australia idea lived in the back of their minds and they continued to work and save and go to plays and meet up with friends at the pub on the corner. Life had a comfortable flow. A peace that let Claire sleep at night. It felt warm, even when London was cold.

It's a Monday when Claire is promoted to a group sales role. She's had her eye on the position for months and when Janine resigns, she sees her knuckles rapping on the door of her manager, asking whether it would be appropriate to apply. The process is fast-tracked and a week later, Claire is back in her manager's office being told the role is hers. They offer her more money and even though she should probably negotiate, she just says yes right away. She'll move to the other end of the office but spend most of her week at external meetings. The first thought she has is, *I need a new pair of shoes.*

After work, she gets a bus to Oxford Circus and wanders around Topshop and Marks & Spencer and Zara. The clothes she's wearing feel cheap and itchy, so she buys a new knit and a maxi dress and a button-up blouse that's more indicative of the person she wants to be than the person she currently is. But the reason she's here is to visit Carnaby Street. Specifically, Irregular Choice. She's wanted to buy a pair of their shoes since she arrived in London. They're loud and sequined, some covered in glitter, others adorned with pom-poms.

Any tiredness she is feeling from the day subsides the moment she walks in. The carpet is a kaleidoscope of color and fake flowers and brightly colored teddy bears hanging from the ceiling. She's only been into Irregular Choice once before and had promised herself that she wouldn't step back in there until she could afford something. Everything is garish in the best possible way. There are shoes with *Star Wars* patterns and unicorn horns as a heel. There are cat prints and floral prints and watermelon prints and Union Jack prints. She tries on pair after pair, making small talk with the shop assistant, a woman about her age with a shaved head and tattoos up to her neck.

"They just make me smile," Claire says, tilting her head and looking at herself in the mirror. "You could never be in a bad mood with these on."

Eventually she settles on a pair with a round, pink glittery toe and a single red Mary Jane strap. The rest of the shoe is green and patterned with tiny frogs, and a huge flower adorns the back. You couldn't walk into a room and have people not notice them, but they're also not so obnoxious as to look unprofessional. The shop assistant calls them "fruity" and as Claire leaves with them boxed and bagged and swinging in her hand, she feels like a real adult.

On the way home, she keeps opening the box for another peek and even takes a photo and sends it to Maggie. "It's your worst nightmare," she types in, and smiles to herself. She doesn't receive a reply.

When she walks in the door, she tells Maggie to shut up and sit down because she has something to show her. She slips on the shoes and fastens the strap, before striking a variety of mock poses and demanding, "Are these not the most ridiculous, most fabulous things you've ever seen?"

But Maggie doesn't laugh. She doesn't even smile.

"What are you pissed off about?" Claire asks, suddenly feeling embarrassed.

"What am I pissed off about? You just walked in and told me to shut up . . ."

"Maggie. I was clearly joking."

Maggie walks into the kitchen and starts rinsing dishes that have been left in the sink.

"What's wrong? I was just excited. I told you I got a promotion today and so I thought I'd reward myself and buy these shoes I'd been looking at for years . . ." Her voice trails off.

Maggie looks up at her from the sink. "I wouldn't be caught dead with you wearing those shoes," she says.

Claire is silent. She feels as though she's standing in the nude in front of someone. Except she's not in the nude. She's wearing stupid shoes that she wants to kick off before Maggie says anything else.

All she can think of to say is, "Okay," and then she goes into the bathroom, feeling completely numb, and has a shower.

The first person she wanted to send a photo of the shoes to wasn't Maggie. It was Yazmin. That's who had first shown her the store when she'd arrived in London three years ago. "This is so you," she'd said, looking at the shoes as if they were works of art on tiled podiums. She'd said it with affection. Encouragement. When Claire had picked up the most outlandish pair, dinosaur-inspired boots that went halfway up the calf, Yazmin had simply said, "Oh my God. It's like your brain just vomited on a pair of shoes." Claire remembered thinking she'd finally found a place that understood her.

Sitting on the toilet seat in a towel, she sends a message to Yazmin. It just says, "Miss you." They've texted sporadically since their fight and they sometimes see each other at the pub or in a mutual friend's backyard on a Saturday afternoon. They're polite to each other now.

Too polite. Yazmin had messaged her "Congratulations" after she'd seen her engagement announcement on Instagram and Claire had found herself wishing she'd just be honest. Whatever that meant.

The next day, Claire gets the bus to Oxford Circus again after work. She walks to Carnaby Street and feels a twist in her stomach when she steps through the pink doorframe. The same woman with the shaved head smiles at her and says, "Back again?" Claire pushes the shoe bag across the counter and fumbles her words. She asks for a refund. They're not the right size. The woman asks if she'd like to exchange them for a pair that fits. "No," she says emphatically. No. Just the refund. And she walks out of the shop, this time with nothing swinging in her hands.

Ana

ॐ

ANOTHER RED LIGHT. SHE PLAYS GAMES WITH HERSELF, counting down. Only six more seconds. Then green.

She needs this weekend. The timing isn't ideal. Rachael has exams and it's the boys' soccer semifinal. She needs to be at home. But she needs this more.

Four. Three. Two. Green. Her wheelie carry-on bag is in the boot. Packed inside are her swimmers, a simple linen dress that requires ironing, a book. She'd pulled the book out on the plane but had just found herself rereading the same paragraph over and over again, her eyes scanning the words but not registering them. Her thoughts had kept drifting—first to a white bedspread, thick and heavy. Then glass doors. Clear turquoise water. The kind that's so clear that your body casts a shadow as you swim. Orange skies and breezy mornings. The taste of water crackers with a thick slice of Camembert. The creaminess clinging to the top of her mouth. Rich and buttery.

Her sat nav tells her to take the next left. One hundred and fifty meters. You're there. A message comes through. It's Paul saying to enjoy it. To tell the girls he says hi. And also does she know where the boys' soccer socks are because they can't find them.

There's also lingerie tucked into her carry-on. Perfume. A sueded silk camisole she hasn't worn in years. It makes her skin look brighter and warmer than it is.

She slows down, her foot resting mildly on the brake. Two fingers find her lips, tapping against them as she searches, squinting under her sunglasses.

There he is. Looking for her. Brown Birkenstocks, holding his weight on one foot, the other jutted out at an angle. A black overnight bag is at his feet. He looks tall and slim and his hair has grown, messy at the front. He looks at his watch. Hasn't spotted her yet. *We did it*, she thinks.

She rolls down the window and calls out, "Rob!" waving her right hand out the car window and leaning out a little so he can see her. His face transforms. He breaks into a wide smile and she can see the twinkle in his eyes, even from here. He points toward the car park and signals that he'll meet her inside.

Jenny's message had been only three words long. "Rob left me."

Ana had called her immediately, making her way soundlessly out to the front steps and closing the front door behind her as the call connected.

"What happened?" she'd asked, as Jenny had said "Ana?" into the receiver.

Jenny had had questions, mostly. Had Ana known? Had Rob spoken to Ana? What should she do? Ana answered as if reading from a script. No, she hadn't known. And no, Rob hadn't spoken to her. "I'm so sorry," she'd said, almost meaning it.

Though they've spoken several times since that day, Rob still hasn't shared many details with her. Just that Jenny would be entitled to half of what they had. And that she'd be taking it.

Paul had been uncharacteristically shocked by the news. "He left her?" he'd exclaimed over dinner the following night, as the kids had leaned in, picking at their plates for longer than usual.

"I think she's pretty," Rachael had said, staring at her mashed potatoes, and Ana had been left feeling irrationally cross.

He doesn't wait for her to shower inside their Noosa hotel room. Her shirt and bra are torn off before she's even kicked off her shoes. There is an ache inside her. Desperate. Empty. A space opening for him.

"Fuck me," she begs, repeating it. He pushes her onto the bed, kissing her down her neck. She's weightless. Floating. He holds her close and finds his way into her. She feels it everywhere. She will die if it stops. When her muscles contract and release, her groin left throbbing, she wants to start over immediately. To feel the buildup all over again.

Later, in the shower, the water is too warm for him but not warm enough for her. They search each other, asking, *What are you thinking?* with their eyes.

"I've never had sex this good in my life," he says, looking up at the showerhead, taking a mouthful of water.

She says the same. Her orgasm came in waves, strong and then stronger until it couldn't get any stronger and then it did. She saw colors. Blue and pink and green flickering lights. Indescribable patterns, swirling around in her mind like van Gogh's *Starry Night*, yellow spots moving behind her eyelids.

The next two days are champagne, fish and chips, the taste of lemon and salt. Whispers in the bath, moans and hands gripping the bedsheets and clammy skin. Curly hair, sandy feet, and the coconutty smell of sunscreen. The kind that smells like childhood. The days pass too quickly, the sun drifting in the sky, high above them one moment and then nestled on the horizon the next.

They sit on the balcony, overlooking the almost empty beach, only a few surfers floating like leaves on waves. Her hair is wet from the shower, her face dewy from fresh foundation and creamy blush. A pinkness is developing on the thin bridge of her nose—just on the lower half, the part not protected by sunglasses or her wide-brimmed straw hat. She looks at him. He's holding a beer bottle, droplets of moisture sliding down its neck and then stopping. And then they jolt again. Sliding then stopping. She breathes in deeply and tries not to exhale for a moment. Maybe that will make time stop. She can hold on to it. But time is like a freight train, powering on, never even slowing. It continues on at the same speed, not even noticing her two hands, white knuckled, trying to grind it to a halt.

Sitting beside her, his hand resting on her thigh, is the right man. She studies him adoringly. His jawline is home to hundreds of hairs. She loves the way his cheeks indent when he smiles, changing the shape of his face. He looks at her—into her—and says, "You're beautiful," cocking his head to one side, like he's beholding a painting.

"So are you." She smiles, stroking the inside of his forearm. In the light, his eyes are the color of the ocean with a thunderstorm overhead. After the heat has reached its peak and the fruit has gone warm and your clothes feel starchy from dried sweat. It starts as a shadow and with it comes a breeze. Cool. Like someone blowing on the back of your neck. And then the clouds blanket the ocean and suddenly the world is a different color. Relief. His eyes are the color of relief.

There is something in his expression that tells her she will never know everything. Not like she knows Paul. The unknowing is where the desire lives. The gaps. Curiosities. A hole with no bottom. Peering into it evokes both terror and possibility. Like a pool that's too deep.

"Will we get sick of each other?" she asks softly.

He shrugs his shoulders. "We could," he says, as seagulls squawk in the distance. "We just have to work at it. Not make the same mistakes . . ." He pauses. "I think about it all the time, probably every day, about the life we're going to have. I work. A lot. I'm rarely home for dinner and I'm at the gym every morning. It's not like everything is going to be easy. We're going to have shit days. A bunch of them. But if you love someone enough, then you make it work. You make every second you spend together actually count. You just have to."

For a while they sit in silence and just listen to the ocean, the cracking of waves curling into themselves.

"I wonder if I had married you if things would've been different. Or if at forty-two, after being with someone for more than twenty-five years, it just becomes . . ." She searches for the words. "I don't know. It runs its course. There's nothing left to discover. Is that just what happens to everyone?"

"I don't think it happens to everyone," he says with conviction. "I've known you for just as long and never felt bored."

"You know, before this"—she gestures to both of them—"I never believed in soul mates. But I think I do now . . ."

He leans in and kisses her on the forehead, with the tenderness of someone who means it.

SHE CAN HEAR the clattering of dinnertime beyond the front door. Clinks, clangs, a chair scraping and the swash of a tap turned on too far, and Louis is laughing and she can hear the clicking of Billy's paws against floorboards, circling the dinner table like a shark circles its prey.

Standing just in front of the door, as though paralyzed, her sobs are silent. They'd started on the plane, with a trembling chest. Then warm tears had dropped onto her cheeks. Soon, she could taste them. She'd sniffled and wiped her face with her hands, hoping the woman beside her just thought she had a cold. She'd grabbed the book that had been poking out of her handbag and opened it on her lap, but the words had just been swirls of black. By the time the plane had landed, the page looked like it had been out in the rain.

The sobbing had continued on the train, three inhales to every exhale. "You always see people crying on trains," her mother had once whispered to her when she was a kid, when Ana had pointed to a woman who was crying at the other end of the carriage, her makeup running down her face like a watercolor painting left to drip. She'd almost smiled at the thought. The train meant you were returning to someone. Or that you'd left someone behind. Sometimes both. And she'd sobbed a little louder, thinking about the boy she got to know on the train all those years ago.

Her face had felt tight by the time she reached the taxi rank. The night air bit at her, tensing the muscles in her back. A gust of bitter wind dried her cheeks, blowing her hair, which still smelled like salt and sea, out of her face. In the taxi, her face had crumpled in the darkness of the backseat, the jerkiness of her breath drowned out by a voice on the radio, in a language she didn't understand.

And now she was at her own front door. But it didn't feel like home. Now home was forty-two thousand feet in the air, sitting in a business-class seat. A sob came out like a squeal. She felt light-headed, her body fatigued from splitting itself in two. It ached. Everything ached.

He'd begged her to go with him. To just pick up and move. "I just need more time," she'd told him. "To sort everything out. I need to do this properly." He'd cried while holding her in bed, one of those gutting cries where the whole body convulses and the shoulders shudder violently up and down. They'd made promises, bold and real, about where they would be this time next year. And then she'd left for the airport, feeling like she might be sick.

The time between her breaths, still trembling, are growing longer. Her eyes are closed, squeezing tears out onto her face, and she feels like there can only be so many left. *You're here for the kids*, she tells herself, nodding once in agreement with the voice inside her head. If it weren't for them, she'd have never come home.

She inhales and shakes her head impatiently. Her eyes look up to the veranda awning and she uses the insides of her index fingers to gently dab below her eyes. She blows air out through her mouth. Like she's blowing out a candle. She counts to three, then twists the doorknob and pushes her way inside.

The boys throw their arms around her and she brings them into her, kissing their heads and saying, "I missed you two!" Her voice is unsteady, but no one notices. She tells Rachael she has to hug her mother. They're the rules. Paul kisses her on the cheek. She wonders if he can taste tears.

"I love you all, but I'm not feeling a hundred percent," she says flatly. "I'm going to have a shower and have an early night. Can you lay your uniforms out for me tonight?" She rattles off a few more instructions. Gives orders. It makes her look like she's in control. Like she knows what she's doing.

She stumbles back down the hallway, her legs the weight of lead. Her face is expressionless. Eyes almost stunned. She feels like she hasn't slept in a week.

In the shower, she tries to cry. But the tears have run out. Her body can't produce anymore. Now she is just left with numbness, not a single thought circulating in her mind. She slackly dries herself with a towel and puts on her pajamas, her collarbones and back still wet. But it doesn't bother her. She turns off all the lights and falls into bed, lifeless and defeated. The tears creep back up on her and she buries her face in a pillow, stifling howls that in a masochistic way feel good. They feel true. She wants to lean into this, to be submerged in this feeling as long as possible. Every moment the feeling gets worse and she savors it. She doesn't want it to stop.

Patrick

THERE IS A SENSE IN THE AIR THAT SOMETHING IS HAP-
pening.

The office is quiet. Uncomfortably so. Necks twist and chairs
slide on their wheels. When he'd walked over to Caitlin's desk to ask
if she wanted lunch an hour ago, she hadn't been there.

He's sent her a message, but nothing. Then his phone starts
vibrating. Her name. He answers as he stands up from his desk, trying to find somewhere more private. All he can make out is her ask-

ing that he meet her downstairs, across the road at the park. "Yeah, of course. Is everything okay?" She hangs up.

He leaves as fast as he can without drawing attention to himself. When he gets to the footpath, he can see her diagonally across from the office, on a side street, standing under a purple jacaranda tree, her arms wrapped around her chest.

As he approaches, he sees that her eyes are pink and swollen, her lips a straight line. It's strange, he thinks, how when adults cry they look like children again. Smaller, somehow. When he reaches her, he instinctively pulls her close to him. She falls against his shirt and he asks gently what has happened.

"Kim made a complaint about me." She wipes her wet nose.

He knows better than to say it out loud, but he knows why. It will be because of the way Caitlin speaks to her. This isn't a surprise. To complain is petty. But it was only a matter of time.

"I got pulled into HR. They said they had to deal with it as a formal complaint because other people in the team had witnessed it . . ." Her cheeks are blotchy and strands of saliva join her top and bottom lip. She says it was over the team meeting they had yesterday, where Caitlin had called her out publicly.

"I'm going to quit. I nearly did it on the spot but I needed to get the words right. I can't do this anymore." The mascara on her top lashes is wet and every time she blinks a new black smudge appears on her eyelid. He knows she'll never quit, but knows better than to say so. "Aren't you going to say anything?"

"Yeah. Yeah, sorry." He looks at the chipped bark. Thinks it would hurt to walk on barefoot. He knows there are questions he is meant to ask. Things he is meant to say. A way he is supposed to touch her back. But nothing comes. In fact, the whole situation makes him feel tired. He just wants to go to sleep and for this problem to be sorted by the time he wakes up. The tears. The ruminating. The calling her mum about it. He wants to fast-forward through all of that.

"Maybe just say you won't talk to her like that again and then everyone can just move on," he mumbles.

He hears her exhale through her nose. "Yeah. Good point. I'll just sit and smile while she makes *me* look bad. And when management ask questions, I'll explain that I didn't want to make a fucking fuss . . ." Her jaw is locked tight, her voice catching over gritted teeth.

"That's not what I meant."

"You did, though. If I were a man, there's no way I'd be reprimanded by HR for being too blunt to a colleague who is completely incompetent. I'd probably be promoted. This has been turned into some bitchy thing that it isn't." She looks up at him, shaking her head. "You just don't get it."

She's right. He doesn't get it. If he heard that someone didn't like the way he spoke to them, he'd probably change the way he spoke to them. It seems fairly simple. But nothing is simple with Caitlin. She's right about Kim. Of course she's right. Kim has more sick days than anyone else in the business, and whenever Caitlin needs her she's not there. Getting a coffee. At an appointment. Waiting for a plumber. It's annoying, sure. But Caitlin gets an almost sick joy from reacting to it. He's heard the way Caitlin's pitch changes when she's addressing her. The complaint is probably fair.

At home that night, he's washing up after dinner when he notices the apartment has fallen silent. He walks over to their bedroom door, which has been left ajar, and sees her curled up, lying on the carpet. Roxy is lying next to her on her side, one eye half-open. There's nothing left to say, so he returns to the kitchen and finishes the dishes.

Ana

THERE IS BLOOD IN HER UNDERPANTS. RED AND BROWN and streaks of silver. A color she has never seen before.

She leans in closer, narrowing her eyes on the stringy tissue that doesn't belong. Like aluminum beside rusted metal.

Another wave hits. Pain she tells herself she doesn't recognize.

No one tells you about the physical pain. Probably because that's the part that passes. The part that doesn't live in your stomach until the day you die. But at this moment, all she can feel is someone tightening a wrench around the bottom of her spine, tighter and tighter until it's about to shatter. Then it moves to somewhere deep inside her stomach. And she swears she can feel fists twisting her from the inside. They twist, like they're wringing out a sopping wet towel, and then, for a moment, the hands loosen. The towel is left to drip. But it's not dry yet, so the fists twist again and again and harder and harder and *when will they let go*. She scrambles for the bin next to the toilet. She opens her mouth to throw up.

Air. She comes up for a breath. She sits up straight, remembering that her underpants are full of something that doesn't belong. There are blood clots. That, she can recognize. But the silver. It is definitely silver.

She senses the wave right before it takes her under again, but there's no chance to take a breath. With her teeth clamped shut and her forearms cradling her stomach, she rocks back and forth on the warm toilet seat, her bare feet on the cold white tiles. She lifts her head for a moment, small blue ceramic squares climb halfway up the walls. She looks at the off-white door. This room. This room is hell.

When the wave pulls her under again, she squeezes her eyes closed and grunts. She's in the en suite off their bedroom, but Paul has already left for work. The kids should still be asleep. Her cries shouldn't wake anyone.

The wave passes and for a moment the water is still again. She pulls her underpants half up her thighs and shuffles to the bedside table and snatches up her phone. She needs him for this.

Rob answers just as she senses the crest of a new wave overhead. Her lungs are empty and she doesn't have the strength to find the right words.

"I think," she says, flinching, "I'm having a miscarriage."

"Ana—I didn't know you were . . ." His voice shakes. "I'm so sorry. I'm so sorry this has happened. Tell me what I can do. I can get on the next plane. Let me come. I want to be there," he rambles, an affected calmness coating every word.

She shakes her head, as though he can hear it. "Just be here," she says quietly, "just stay with me on the phone." For a while they sit in silence.

By three o'clock, she knows for sure that today she lost a baby. They'll never know whether it was going to be a boy or a girl, short like her or tall like Rob. She misses the smell of a head she never sniffed, sweet milk and warm biscuits and a cleanness that reaches your throat. After leaving her doctor's surgery, she rests her head on the steering wheel and closes her eyes.

"I'm so sorry," she says, her eyes prickling against her eyelids like sandpaper. "I love you," she tells her little boy or little girl. She holds her arms protectively across her stomach, aware there is nothing, really, left to be protected. *How can you miss someone you've never met?* she asks herself. This time yesterday, she didn't even know her body was two people. Not one. She's grieving the loss of something she never even got to be happy for.

Her doctor had asked if she was on any kind of contraception. She'd explained that she had the Mirena and wasn't that meant to be ninety-nine percent effective? How had this happened? What had gone wrong?

"Have you experienced any breakthrough bleeding in the last few months?" the doctor had asked, addressing her computer rather than Ana.

"Yes, a little bit. Only for a few days at a time. I thought that was normal?" she'd said.

The doctor had scrolled on her computer, clicking away, until she said, "It says here that your Mirena is over five years old."

Ana had cocked her head to the side while she redid the maths.

Shit. It had been at least five years. She'd got it the year the boys had started kindergarten. It had hurt more than she'd been expecting and she'd had to pick them up after a half day, cramps grasping her insides and traveling down into her thighs. The boys were eleven. It had been more than five years. How could she have been so careless?

"But I'm forty-two . . ." she'd reasoned, staring at this doctor who knew so much about her but whose name she had suddenly gone blank on. *People don't get "accidentally" pregnant at forty-two, do they?* she'd thought. She had friends the same age who had given up by now after months if not years of trying, paying thousands for IVF, giving up alcohol and taking up F45, while downing a dozen vitamins a day—all while still crying silently into their pillows at night, cursing their bodies for working against them.

And here was Ana. A mother of three. Married to a man who loved her. Miscarrying a baby who had been conceived accidentally, despite a half-functioning Mirena. She knew it was Rob's. She hadn't slept with Paul in two months. Maybe more. His father had been in and out of hospital and on top of that, things had been tense. Sometimes she even wondered whether he knew. Six weeks ago, Rob had been back in Durnham to stay with his sister and they'd all gone out to dinner. Paul had been quieter than usual. He'd sat back in his seat at the local Italian restaurant like a spectator who didn't quite know why he was there. At one point, he'd asked Rob if he was seeing anyone.

"No, not really," Rob had answered quickly, his eyes refusing to meet anyone else's.

"That's unlike you, mate," Paul said, and laughed, his upward inflection signaling that buried within that remark was a question.

But Rob just shrugged his shoulders and helped himself to a slice of pizza. She watched his hands, delicate and beautiful, and thought about how they had felt touching her only hours before. She waited for the guilt to hit her but it didn't. There was only desire and disappointment. Disappointment that it wouldn't be Rob she went home with tonight. She would have to wait until tomorrow, when the house was quiet and still, and a voice rang out from the front door.

When she drives into her driveway that afternoon and looks at the house that she and Paul built, their children's shoes slackly tossed outside the front door, she feels a wave of something else. Relief. Maybe her body knew. Maybe it had protected her. She knows that if she had discovered that she was pregnant in a few weeks, she would've kept it. A decision would've been made for her.

She plays out the next few months in her head. She leaves her family. But where does she go? Sri Lanka? That's ridiculous. What are the hospitals even like there? She sees herself giving birth and it's Rob's hand she's squeezing. And she loves him so much. But there is no family to bring this baby back to. Rachael doesn't gently kiss its forehead while everyone is watching and then pinch its arm while their backs are turned like she did with the twins. This baby doesn't watch in awe as their older siblings do cartwheels in the front yard. She won't find them all in a fort on a Friday night, blankets draped over chairs, laughing so hard she can't help but smile. And when she lifts that fort, curious about what's so funny, she won't see Paul lying in there, a child sitting on his chest, pulling at the sides of his mouth, forcing funny faces.

All she sees is Rob. She sees his arms around her late at night. She feels his lips and his hands and the way their bodies interlace on the thick cushions of his gray couch. She sees his tears as their baby is born and hears the way he whispers to them both. This is all he's ever wanted. He looks at them—his eyes full of possibility and hope. It is the day he learns who he is.

There is a lot she sees. But there is more she doesn't see. There is no Rachael. No Oliver and no Louis. Billy isn't curled at her feet or bringing her a stranded sock as a gift. There is no Christmas Day at Kelly's. Or long afternoons with all her nieces and nephews that fall on Paul's side of the family. Her friends disappear—the ones who are really the wives of Paul's friends. Her life becomes so small. Like she's chosen her one person to live with on a desert island but has then been damned to live there for all of eternity.

Claire

⚮

THERE WAS NO ONE MOMENT THAT CLAIRE AND MAGGIE decided they would move to Queensland.

It was that night at Andy's Greek Taverna, when they'd been seated right beside the window. Outside, it had been pouring rain and the road had looked like an oil spill dancing on a black ocean. Claire had told a story about when she was a kid and she and the girl next door would run out onto the road every time it rained and try to swim in the overflowing gutters. That smell. Cool rain hitting hot bitumen. She'd return to the house covered in leaves and her dad would hose her off in the front yard. It didn't rain like that in London, she'd declared. You do not *play* in London weather. They'd talked about kids. Maggie would be thirty this year, Claire twelve months behind. "That's the childhood I want my kids to have," Maggie had said, and they'd both gazed out the bay window.

It was the afternoon when Maggie had sat at her laptop at the dining table, looking up flights and visa applications. A civil partnership in the UK wasn't recognized sixteen thousand kilometers away. Not like marriage.

It was the day Claire had been made redundant from Marshalls, a good job but one she'd outgrown. With it had come a payout that gave them freedom. The kind of money that demands you make a radical decision.

And so they'd thought and researched and Claire had messaged a few friends back home. When she would think about the future, it began to take the shape of Australia, stuffy corner shops and highways with dry paddocks as far as the eye can see. She could hear Australian accents and feel a cotton dress stuck to her sweaty back. Maggie was the same. Australia went from being hypothetical to a checklist. A plan. A date. A flight on a Sunday afternoon.

They're in a taxi on their way to Heathrow Airport when Claire feels her first wave of panic. The narrow brick houses with their identical brown rooftops and chimneys poking through flash past her, appearing and then disappearing. She thinks of all the families sitting inside them, reading or watching TV, not knowing how special their little lives are. She wants to grip the streetlights, unpack their overstuffed suitcases, and run back to their empty, echoey flat. This is where she's spent the best years of her life.

Maggie grips her knee instinctively. Does the thing where she massages it. Every memory Claire has of London—Nutella crepes at Christmastime, a fox hiding around a street corner, watching *Macbeth* at the Globe Theatre—are all Maggie memories too. She loves this city because it gave her Maggie. And now she's leaving, but she is taking the biggest, most magical piece of London with her.

Maggie has expressed no apprehension. She had resigned from her job at the gym and they'd had a big farewell for her, and then they'd gone out to dinner with friends, where Charlie had drunk too much red wine and cried. Maggie had just laughed and said, "We'll probably be back to visit in six months." Everyone promised to come to Australia, but even as they said it, they didn't mean it. Things got weird at the end, like they'd all known they'd never see one another again.

It's late at night when they arrive in Singapore with puffy ankles and dry mouths. They barely say a word to each other as they go through customs, explaining to the man at the counter that they're only here for two nights before they continue on to Australia. His face doesn't move as he stamps their passports. Maggie sends a message to Bridge and tells her they've landed safely and will meet her for breakfast as planned. Bridge replies back excitedly, saying something about all the activities she has planned for them, but they can't even muster up the energy to read it. Tomorrow.

The next day they wake early but have no desire to get out of bed. They have sex and then watch a television show they can't follow and then have sex again. In the shower they talk about how excited they are. They feel free. It's exhilarating. Like they're starting again. Planting seeds in different earth, waiting to see what will grow.

The day with Bridge is awkward at first. They haven't seen her in the year since she moved here with her girlfriend, but once they arrive at Gardens by the Bay, the three of them fall into step. Claire thinks it looks like something out of *Avatar*. They take photos of Supertree Grove and stand in silence, watching the indoor waterfall. The humid air clings to their skin as they wander for hours, through greenhouses and flower domes and around lily ponds. When Bridge walks them back to their hotel, the smell of rain has arrived.

"Okay—nap, and then dinner, then we'll head to the night zoo," she says, waving as they turn into the lobby. They'll meet at eight. "Maybe bring an umbrella," she calls over her shoulder.

After Claire lays her head on her pillow, the sky outside opening up through the window, she falls asleep quickly. She dreams of Australia. Of a toddler who looks like Maggie in gum boots, stomping her feet on pellets of rain as they hit a gravel road. The child is laughing, throwing her head back, clutching on to her full belly. Her eyes are big and brown. Maggie is standing on the front veranda of a house she knows is theirs, a golden-haired puppy sitting at her ankles. The rain falls on the tin roof and it soon turns into a waterfall, cascading onto the front lawn. It's the kind of rain you know will pass, and that when it does everything will be greener and fresher than it had been.

She wakes to Maggie turning on the shower and tries to clutch on to the dream as it fades away. She wants to live there just a little longer. Eventually she rolls out of bed, feeling hungover even though she's had nothing to drink, and pulls on a dress, a denim jacket, and some new sandals she'd bought on sale in London just before she left. Neither of them have an umbrella.

They set off down the street toward the restaurant Bridge has picked out and immediately Claire nearly slips over. The pavement is glassy and the rain pours into her sandals. She walks slowly, pulling her jacket overhead and squinting through the thick, droning rain. Thunder cracks in the sky and she yells out to Maggie a few steps in front of her, "Hey, be careful, it's super slippery," and by the time Maggie turns around to ask her what she'd said, Claire has fallen sideways onto her right ankle, hearing a crack just like thunder on her way down. At first she doesn't know what's happening. A sound escapes from her mouth, but once she's on the ground, she knows she's not going to be able to stand up again.

"It's broken, Maggie. It's broken," she says, scrunching her eyes closed, wishing she was in any moment but this one.

"Oh, come on, it's not broken." Maggie tries to help her up.

Eventually, she gets her in a taxi and Claire feels nauseous. Clammy. It hurts. It hurts so much she thinks she might pass out. Ten minutes later, they're at the hospital, and when cold hands touch the outside of her ankle, she flinches. She's wheeled off to get an X-ray and is then returned to the waiting room. She cries and then Maggie asks what she was calling out to her on the street anyway and when she tells her, they laugh. After a while, they are taken into a treatment room to see a doctor, who tells her that her ankle is fractured and that it will need to be in a plaster cast for six weeks once she gets back to Australia. He can't plaster it right before a long-haul flight. He instructs her to lie her leg flat on the hospital bed and she holds her breath while he bandages under her foot, all the way to her calf. The only thing that cheers her up is Maggie shaking her head, trying to suppress a smile.

They never make it to the night zoo. Once they are back at the hotel, Maggie finds a plastic bag, puts it around Claire's bandages, and secures it with an elastic band. She helps her into the shower and back out. She rearranges the pillows for her before she lies down in bed and lets her choose what to watch on television. She doesn't even complain when she has to pack both of their suitcases.

Bridge hugs them goodbye outside their hotel the following morning, Claire hunched over on her crutches, which have already started to bruise her armpits. Her foot under the bandage feels itchy and she fights the impulse all morning to scratch it. She thinks about how when she lands in Queensland, she won't be able to swim at the local pool or walk up to the shops. She can't drive. Have a bath. Get a job at the pub or the theater. Do pretty much anything on her own. She will be in Toowoomba, just about unable to leave the house.

In a split-second slip, she realizes, she has managed to ruin everything.

Patrick

❧

YOU THINK THAT ON THE DAY THE WORLD FALLS APART, the color of the sky will change. But it doesn't. It stays blue, and your phone continues to vibrate, and you take the dog for a walk, just like any other day.

The first sign something is wrong is a phone call just before six in the evening. She's boarding her plane and will be at Sydney Airport in a few hours. She says she'll see him at home.

"Do you want me to come get you?" he asks, mouth half-full of spaghetti Bolognese.

"No, it's fine," she says. "I'll just get the train."

In six years, she's never chosen the train over a lift. She has a big overnight bag and she sounds tired. The train isn't even that quick.

In hindsight, he probably should have known then. She'd rather be in a dark carriage surrounded by strangers than in a car with him. And maybe he did. Maybe the thought crossed his mind and then he shooed it away, like a fly coming too close to your mouth. But what difference would it have made if his stomach had sunk then or a few hours later? It would hurt all the same.

He half expects her to change her mind when she lands at Sydney Airport. The train might have felt noble back in Brisbane, but surely when she walks through the terminal, tantalized by the prospect of dinner and the couch, she'll call. He has his phone next to him while he watches *Mindhunter*. On loud. Just in case she needs him. But his phone stays black, even when her plane is due to land. He double-checks the flight's still running on time. But it only confirms it: she had arrived in Sydney twenty-five minutes ago and not even sent him a message. Her phone must be out of battery.

Dinner is sitting on the bench, looking more uninviting by the minute. The spaghetti has turned hard. He puts it in the microwave for thirty seconds so it's warm when she walks in—she should be here any minute. She'll be hungry. And when she sees it, she'll say "Yesssss" and roll her eyes back into her head and scramble for a fork before eating it right at the bench. She'll tell him about the trip. It was good, she'll say, pausing while she swallows. She'll tell him how she saw Dani, will complain that Dani's still seeing Max, whom they both can't stand. And then she'll say "I missed you" and look sad for a moment, before kissing him quickly, keen to get back to the rest of her dinner.

But when she arrives home, she's a storm cloud. Cold and dark.

The energy in the room shifts. She drops her bag onto the hardwood floor and when he looks at her properly, her cheeks are wet and red.

"Hey, what's wrong?" he asks, imagining that something bad—he doesn't know what—happened on the train.

Sobs. Then silence.

"Was the train okay?"

"I didn't get the train," she says. "I got an Uber."

His mind is running down a thousand avenues all at once. Why would she get an Uber from the airport when he offered to pick her up? What a waste of money. And why did she say she was getting the train when she wasn't? Why does this person in front of him look different? It's like she's not the same person who left. She wears the same body but something has shifted and whoever is inside isn't Caitlin.

"I can't be in this anymore."

And then he falls very quickly out of the sky. There is no coherent thought. No response that makes sense. All his mind registers is that it is falling very fast and trying to maintain consciousness.

A voice from somewhere asks, "What?" He feels the blood rush from his face. His tongue goes dry.

Who is this person inside their home? She's wearing her engagement ring. But this isn't the woman he proposed to. What about their promises? Wasn't there an agreement that they wouldn't do this to each other? A pact? *You're not allowed to do this.*

She isn't the only stranger in the room. He's one too. His sentences aren't really making sense and there are thoughts floating around in his mind but they aren't associated with words. Where is he and what the fuck is happening? This cannot be happening.

He will later understand that this was the worst moment of his life. But for now, it's just another moment, followed by the one where the spaghetti Bolognese was in the microwave and he thought he knew how this moment was meant to go and some part of him wants to ask if she would like her spaghetti Bolognese because he'd already prepared it for her and it's just over there. He can smell it. It smells like Sunday nights and Sunday nights are Caitlin and so is every other night of the week.

In this tiny living room, they have somehow gone from agreeing they would love each other until they died to her deciding they would stop loving each other now. She says she had always wanted children. That was how she saw her life. And then, in the last year or so, she'd stopped seeing them. Like they were erased from her future. And at first, she'd just thought she'd changed her mind. But then she realized she hadn't. It was just that she didn't see herself having children with him. He wasn't the father who belonged in the family she imagined.

He must be asking more questions because she keeps explaining.

This wasn't just a trip to see her family, she says. It was to get away to think after the camping trip the other week.

"Everything is always so busy," she tells him. "I'm doing three or four things at once and work finishes late and then I eat and then I go to bed, and I never actually get to ask myself if I'm happy or if things are good. And I'm just floating. Floating through my life but I'm not actually in it. And then I went camping and all the noise stopped and I could hear myself again."

But he's thinking about her family. They knew before he did.

He still doesn't understand. Sure, this might be a problem. But they've had problems in the past. Problems can be fixed, they just have to talk about it. His head keeps trying to catch up to the last thing she said but it can't. He's looking at a scene that doesn't make sense. A scene that doesn't belong in his life. This is someone else's story. Not his.

Part of the scene is that they're both crying and no one is being consoled. If this were any other day of their relationship, she'd be at his side, cursing the person who hurt him and telling him how they were going to make this better. What do you do when the person responsible for your pain is the one who is meant to fix it? There's only one person he really speaks to who would care about any of this. And it's her. The person telling him what he did wrong. How he failed at the one thing that ever meant anything to him.

"I was on the brink of a breakdown," she says. "And you couldn't understand. All I needed was for you to listen but I was yelling into this empty void. I wanted you to give a shit and I couldn't make you."

He insists that he did care, he just didn't know how to fix it. But that's not what she ever wanted. To try to fix it was to suggest that her pain wasn't valid. That she was just a problem that required a solution. When she struggled, she felt like a burden that was just thrown onto his to-do list: "Sort out Caitlin." He needed her to hurry along. Recover. Be *normal* again. And that meant she couldn't be herself.

Time is suspended as they stand in that living room. He doesn't want to leave because he knows it will be the last time this place is theirs. They were the ones who made it a home. The whole greater than the sum of its parts. Even as she speaks, the paint on the walls peels. The imprints their bodies have made in the couches disappear. Their sheets become tainted and their pillows haunted. A light place becomes a dark place.

And when Patrick leaves the apartment he has lived in for four years of his life that night, it will be the last time it ever feels like home. Because home was never the carpet or the roof or the front window shaped like a sunrise. It was the woman standing inside it.

Ana

It had been almost three months since she'd been with Rob. The
end of the year was full of school functions and Christmas parties
and catch-ups with girlfriends who used Christmas as some sort of
arbitrary deadline to have dinner and complain about how busy
they were.

Her days were filled with longing—but not the sad kind. The
kind that gave her a flutter in the stomach in the late afternoon,
knowing there were only a few more hours until she got to see his

face and relay back to him a day that sounded far more exciting than it actually was. Her insides dropped every time he emerged on her screen. Some nights they said things and other nights they did things. Sometimes just watching him—the way his hand moved, hearing the sounds he made, the shallow panting, was enough to make her feel like she was on the brink of orgasm. The thought of him kept her perpetually aroused. She slept less and exercised more. Every now and then, she'd catch glimpses of herself in the mirror and be struck by the smooth curve of her hips or the way her breasts looked and feel proud. It was as though she were wearing someone else's body—one she could appreciate from afar. She wasn't inside it anymore but outside of it, and when she touched herself for him, she felt how much he wanted her and her hands became his hands.

But some nights, he pressed her. Twelve months. She'd promised. And now they were nearly there. She'd rub her eyes and hold her heavy head up with her hands and insist she was working on it. She was going to leave, she just had to work out how. That's what you were saying this time last year, he'd reply, exasperated. Were they really any closer?

It's Boxing Day night and everyone is finally in bed. He's called a few times but she hasn't been able to answer, as Paul had still been up watching an Adam Sandler movie with the kids. She's trying to be present. Not let Rob take moments that don't belong to him. The night is warm and all the doors are open, ready for a breeze that never comes. When she sits on the back step to return his call, she hangs on to the traces of pine and cedar, sharp and sweet, lingering from the Christmas tree in the corner of the living room.

He answers the video call and everything is dim inside his house, even though it's late afternoon there. He asks about the kids. Did they like their presents? And he smiles as she tells him, but his eyes don't crease at the edges. He doesn't show any teeth.

He'd spent Christmas Day with some friends but had spent the night alone. There was no wrapping paper strewn around his house. She doesn't have to ask to know that there is no tree or fairy lights or bushy wreath hanging on his front door.

"It's not just Christmas," he almost whispers, his head nestling into the sofa cushion behind him.

"It's every weekend. I am alone every weekend. I'm just waiting. Do you understand that I'm just waiting for you?"

"I'm sorry," she says quietly.

"I can't just sit in my house waiting for you to leave. It's not fair on me. I'm forty-three. Forty-fucking-three. I wanted kids . . ."

"You know I can't give you kids, though, Rob. If you want kids, you need to find someone else. I don't want to be the one who deprives you of that," she says. They've had this conversation. They're always having the same conversation.

There's silence. She rests her head on her knuckles and they stare at each other for a moment, waiting for the other to pretend they have a solution.

"Maybe that's what I need to do," he says.

He doesn't think she's going to leave Paul, he tells her. At one point, she wanted to. He believes that. But she can't. And if he sits here and waits, he will turn fifty while loving a woman who sleeps in the same bed as someone else on the other side of the world. And they will be years he will never get back.

She tries to argue with him. "Wait for me," she begs. But when she tries to make the promise to him she did a year ago, she can't. She's surprised to find her lips refuse. Instead, she changes tack.

"How can we make this work?" she asks him. "There has to be a way to make this work."

But he looks resigned. Tired. Keeps rubbing his face with the heel of his hand. "I never want to spend a Christmas like that again, Ana."

"So come here. Live here."

He scoffs. "I've spent my whole life getting away from Durnham. I've built my career here, I can't just pick up and move it over to Australia. You *know* that."

They look at each other. She's sitting under the stars on the edge of a town she's never wanted to leave. He's thousands of kilometers away, the sun yet to set.

"I love you," she says.

He says that sometimes loving someone isn't enough.

She realizes that all along she'd thought it was. That a life could be designed around a feeling. That it must be. But perhaps a relationship is when love meets circumstance, two variables as important as each other.

Claire

⚬

I T'S THE LAST DAY OF SUMMER WHEN SHE MEETS TIFF FOR
the first time.

Her house is dark and smells like stale food. It's late afternoon
and everyone is outside, drinking ciders and vodka sodas around a
glass table that is streaky from the last time it had been wiped down
with Ajax. She doesn't know anyone. Except Maggie, of course, who
stands up as soon as she walks in and puts her arm around her.

"Everyone, this is Claire. Claire, this is everyone," she says, before
finding her a cider in the outside fridge.

"And Claire, this is Bella." Maggie crouches on the cement and puts her forehead up against the face of a chocolate brown and tan kelpie. "You're always smiling, aren't you?" she says, scratching the dog behind the ears.

"You are a beautiful dog." Claire sits beside her and wishes she didn't have to stand up and speak to the human people who are a lot more complicated than this dog asking to be scratched on its belly is.

Once she sits at the table, in between who she assumes is Tiff and someone she's never heard of, she feels relief that people can't read her mind. While she nods at Tiff and tells her she has a lovely home, she thinks how easily this could have been her. Living in a yellow weatherboard house that gets too hot in the summer and too cold in the winter, with a poorly designed 1970s kitchen and curtains that smell of the ghost of some stranger's grandfather. She doesn't know much about Tiff, only what Maggie has told her, but she bets she's never left Toowoomba. The worst part is she's probably never wanted to. She probably went to school, met someone she didn't mind, and then married him. Maggie has mentioned she has a three-year-old son. So she's stuck. Stuck inside this one-story home, with cigarette stains on the gray carpet and scuffs on the white walls. She wonders whether Maggie gets it now. Why she had to get out of Toowoomba.

"How long have you been going to the gym?" she asks Tiff, her face a darker color than her chest.

"Gawd. Too long. Maybe four or five years?" she asks, as if Claire knows the answer.

As Tiff talks about her training and working with Maggie, Claire realizes she doesn't like her very much. Her eyes are dark, a muddy brown, her hair bleached yellow. She should be attractive. Her features—a small nose, straight teeth, plump lips, big eyes—

should add up to someone beautiful, but they don't. She smiles with the corners of her mouth and not with her eyes and when she laughs it's loud and distracting, but only ever lasts a few seconds. She appears unsettled. Uncomfortable. Like someone who doesn't know who they're meant to be today.

A gold crucifix hangs from a chain around her neck and she plays with it as she speaks. It reminds Claire of what else Maggie had said about her. She's a Christian. Grew up in a conservative home with a father who's a pastor. "Should she really be hanging out with you then?" Claire had joked, and Maggie had pulled a guilty face before admitting, "I think it's best if she keeps me a secret."

Tiff looks anywhere but in Claire's eye—at the sky, at Claire's shoes, at the ashtray in the center of the table. It gives the impression that she's waiting for this conversation to finish and a more inter- esting one to start—like there's something better going on behind Claire's right shoulder.

They talk about her son, Travis, and she finds a photo on her phone, which she taps at with long, acrylic French-tipped nails. He has her eyes. But Claire doesn't say that. She just pretends she thinks he's cute, even though his eyebrows just about meet in the middle and it looks like he's got half a jar of gel in his hair. *Why did Mag- gie have to choose this person?* she finds herself thinking. *Go out and make friends, by all means, but these are not our people.*

Everyone at the table picks at the bowl of Red Rock Deli chips on the table, while Tiff announces she doesn't eat them. Maggie makes a joke about how they should make a chicken and broccoli flavor and then she'd scoff them down, and Claire catches her eye as she laughs. She feels a moment of tenderness for her. How she can make fun of people—even people who take themselves too seriously—without upsetting them. Before Maggie, she used to walk into every social interaction racked with anxiety, playing out possible conversations and questions to ask. But now she has a security blanket. A hand on the leg that no one else can see. Someone to finish her story if she runs out of energy or to save her if she fucks up a punch line. She feels looked after. Like when her mum would drop her off at a birthday party and decide to stay on with the other parents, sitting just in the room next door.

There are periods in a long-term relationship when you fall in love all over again, deeper than you thought was possible. That's how Claire had felt while she sat at home, her leg resting on the ottoman in front of her, for six weeks. Maybe it was because she was so helpless. She'd never relied on anyone so much before. Maggie would come home from work, smelling of the outside world, with a bottle of wine or a block of chocolate for them to share later, and it would fill Claire with an odd sense of pride. This woman—funny and warm and generous and beautiful—who could be anywhere, doing anything, was choosing to be with her. Perhaps it was because she felt more vulnerable than usual, but she'd become hopelessly aware of how lucky she was. She was indebted to Maggie.

But with that came a shift that Claire couldn't quite explain. Those six weeks had also been the most frustrating of their relationship. The plan had been to live with Claire's parents at first, to get jobs and earn some money. Then they would work out where they wanted to move to. Brisbane, maybe. The Gold Coast. Maggie would apply for permanent residency, which she could do given her relationship with Claire. Perhaps they'd discover they hated it and move back to London—but whatever happened, they wanted to try somewhere new.

But then Claire hadn't been able to work. Money was spent

and not saved. They had gone from having total independence in London to living under the same roof as Claire's mum and dad—both in their midsixties and who insisted on recounting in detail the plot of the new Australian drama broadcasting on the ABC. As days blurred into weeks, Claire had felt the fog descending again, her thoughts becoming more hateful and critical. She'd dream she was trying to run and her legs wouldn't move and she'd sense someone was chasing her but still her body couldn't find the momentum to just run.

As hard as it had been for Claire, she worried it was even worse for Maggie. She was living with someone else's parents, in a town where there was nothing to do. Some mornings, Maggie would disappear for hours—she'd just walk around the streets—coming back with a sunburnt hue. After a while, she'd just gone quiet. Read a lot. Went to bed early. But about a month in, she landed a job at the gym on Ruthven Street. She met Jamie, Nic, and Steph, who were all trainers there, and Tiff, her first client. They'd occasionally grab dinner after work and Tiff sometimes had people over for Saturday afternoon drinks. Claire hadn't been able to come until now and no one is who she'd imagined.

As the sun goes down, Claire looks on as Maggie flicks through Tiff's Tinder, doing impersonations of the men she comes across. There are men holding five-foot-long fish. Or standing shirtless on yachts in Croatia. Or surrounded by groups of people, clearly not wanting the viewer to know which one they are. While she watches Maggie, with her soft hands and flushed cheeks, she feels relief. She doesn't miss men. Their rough faces. Their broad shoulders. The aggressiveness of what hangs between their legs.

"Imagine being straight, Claire," Maggie says, as if reading her mind. "And having to accept . . . that." She holds up a picture of a man looking at his reflection in a grubby mirror, a towel hanging from his groin, black hair dotted all over his body. He's holding his chin, as though he's thinking, and a caption below reads: "Looking for someone to be naughty with." Claire's whole body shivers in revulsion.

Three days later, it's a muggy afternoon and Maggie is pulling on some denim shorts she bought a few years ago from Topshop. Claire is towel-drying her hair, half watching Maggie as she tugs at the faded denim caught on her hips.

She's been short with Claire since she got home from work. When Claire had told her she had a job interview tomorrow, she'd just grunted, said "Cool," checked her phone, and then had a shower.

She pulls at the shorts some more and Claire resists the urge to tell her to stop yanking them. They're not going to fit. The waistband is caught under the widest point of her hips.

Maggie grunts, grits her teeth, and says, "You've made me fat."

The words, mumbled as though she didn't really want to say them, hang in the air. For a few seconds Claire's not sure she heard them right. The way she said the word "fat," the *f* smacking off her bottom lip, sounded like it was coming from someone else's mouth.

"What?" She stops and looks over at her.

"I said you've made me *fat*," she scoffs. Pulls off the shorts that no longer fit and throws them in the bottom of their wardrobe. Finds some gym shorts with an elastic waist she's been wearing almost every day for months and pulls them on and up over her stomach.

"You're not fat." She doesn't know why her first instinct is to protect Maggie's feelings. Maggie's always been at least four dress sizes smaller than her, and weight is something they've barely talked about. When she looks down, she notices that her arms are clutched over her own stomach.

"I'm fat for me. All we do is eat shit food and lie in bed. You—this relationship—are making me fat. You're always ordering take-away and so that's what I eat. I don't even fucking want it. When was the last time we even ate a vegetable?"

Claire's face goes red. Her chest blotches. She can feel her thighs resting against each other. Creases in her sides. Her bra pressing into her back, skin bulging beneath it. She wants to find a butcher's knife and saw at it. Pull it from her bones and cut it off, sewing what skin is left back together.

"You should have just said so." Her voice is soft. "I'm sorry. Okay. I'm sorry."

"I just want us to eat like normal people."

"I know I've not been good lately. I could barely move . . ."

"But you've always eaten like this!"

"Okay, I said I'm sorry? I've been going through a shitty time. I've got this job interview tomorrow and then I'll be out of the house again with a routine . . ."

"Yep." As Maggie goes to leave the room, she catches her reflection in the mirror again and mutters, "Shit, I can't even look at myself," before shutting the door behind her.

Claire sits on the bed and looks at her hands. She can't go to Tiff's tonight, with all those trainers and clients who talk about food as "fuel" and dart their eyes down her body every time she stands up. Have they said something to Maggie? Is that what they talk about? A lump grows in her throat.

Maggie pokes her head through the door and says, "Seriously, Claire, we've got to get going."

"Maggie, I can't."

"Don't be ridiculous. We're going." And then she waits in the passenger seat of the Ford Fiesta until Claire silently climbs in behind the steering wheel.

SHE LOOKS AT her phone again. Ten past nine.

No message. No phone call. Hunger pulls at her stomach.

At nine thirty, she decides not to wait any longer and heats up some leftover lasagna from the fridge. She eats it alone at the kitchen bench, her right hand scrolling through Instagram.

She wouldn't ordinarily mind if Maggie was late home. It's just that today is their wedding anniversary. Four years. Before Maggie left for work this morning, she'd kissed Claire on the forehead and told her she'd be home by eight—she was finishing at seven thirty and would get a lift home. But now it's edging closer to ten and Maggie hasn't been picking up her phone. It's ringing out, so the battery hasn't died.

Claire sits on the sofa beside her mum, who is watching an old *Graham Norton* episode with Madonna on it. "Madonna isn't making any sense," her mum says, but Claire doesn't respond. Her throat feels tight.

She takes herself quietly off to bed and lies in the dark, listening to her erratic breathing, which has taken on a life of its own. She whimpers under the weight of an invisible pressure on her chest and then sits up and googles the symptoms of a heart attack. Shortness of breath. Yes. Light-headedness. Yes. Pain or discomfort in one or both arms. No. But discomfort in stomach, yes. A sense of impending doom. Yes. Yes. Yes.

"Something is wrong with me," she sobs out loud to no one, then holds her right hand in her left, so she doesn't feel so alone.

Her thoughts are still attached to Maggie. *She wants to get away from you*, they hiss, like witches spitting into a cauldron. *You're her old wife who cut her hair short on a whim and then never grew it long again. You're fat and you're disgusting and she doesn't want to touch you. She'd rather be anywhere than in this room, with you and this contagious sadness that poisons anyone who gets too close.*

Her mind sees flashes of evidence. Most nights Maggie doesn't come straight home after work. She trains for an hour. Or eats with Nic or Tiff. Someone drops her out the front late and she doesn't say much before they crawl into bed and watch a show they're not really following and then fall asleep. A few times, she's asked if Claire wants to come out with a bunch of work people on a Friday night, but Claire always says no and now she has stopped asking.

She tries not to talk too much about what she's thinking. Maggie just groans. Or says, "I can't take this on." It feels like she's living with an illness where all her senses have been stolen. All the touch points that would allow her to experience the world have been muted. When people describe depression, they talk about the sadness. But they don't tell you that what's worse is the madness. Not knowing whether you can trust your instincts because your instincts are sick. Your instincts are leading you down a steady plank to a kind of death. Those instincts tell you to sleep. Don't move. Don't speak to anyone. Extricate yourself, like a cat that disappears before it dies. It's a feeling that lives in your skin and flows through your blood. With it comes the knowledge that it's not the world that's bad. It's *you* that's bad. And the world, really, is no more than two eyes and the light that lives behind them.

Last week, Maggie came home and said Tiff's dog had been hit by a car. Its hip was broken. A neighbor had knocked on the door and Tiff had rushed Bella to the vet. She would need surgery. It would cost more than Tiff had in savings.

"So I'm going to give her five hundred dollars," Maggie had said.

"What?"

"The dog will die without it. I'm going to give her the money," she'd explained, like she was spelling something out to a toddler.

"But that's our money, Maggie. We have to talk about these things."

"No. That's *my* money," she said emphatically. "And I get to decide how I spend my money."

"I'm sorry, I don't understand. Are you talking about loaning her the money? Is she going to pay us back?" The pitch of Claire's voice was rising.

"No—I'm not going to ask her to pay me back. It's mine. I earned it. And if I want to give it to a friend to keep her dog alive, I'm going to do it." She looked down at her phone, as though their conversation was of no consequence.

"So, just to be clear, my wage is *our* money but your wage is *your* money. Is that how this works?" Their money had always been shared. There had been her redundancy payout. She hadn't worked for a few months, but now she'd found something—her wage, apparently—going to a dog she'd met once.

Maggie rolled her eyes. "If you want to do something with your money, do it. I don't care. But for me, the whole point of earning money is so that if someone in my life needs something, I can help them. Why have it otherwise?" And then she stood up and walked away.

She's thinking about the money when she hears a rustle out the front. Maggie finding the spare key under the doormat. The lock clicks and footsteps thump down the hall. A light flicks on. It stings.

"Babe, sorry I'm late. Ended up eating with people at work, Tiff ordered dumplings." She unlaces her shoes and sits at the edge of the bed.

"How come you didn't let me know?" She hates how her voice sounds. It shakes.

"I didn't think it mattered? We're going out to dinner tomorrow night, aren't we?"

"Yeah. But tonight's our actual anniversary."

"I know that. But we're celebrating it tomorrow." She's confused. "We didn't have plans tonight?"

"I just thought you might want to hang out."

Maggie looks at Claire lying on her back, in flannelette pajama pants and a white top, mascara smudged around her eyes. She raises her eyebrows. Purses her lips.

"Who were you with?" Claire asks, trying but failing to keep her voice light.

"The same person I'm always with, Claire." Maggie massages her temples. Closes her eyes. "I only have like two friends here. You know who I was with." She turns her back on her.

Tears spring into Claire's eyes and she rolls over and lets her pillow absorb them. She tries to take deep breaths. When she rolls back, she sees Maggie pick up her phone, texting. She feels invisible. Images of them five years ago flash through her mind, like a slide show. How Maggie couldn't wait to be back at her front door, a bag of groceries hanging from her wrist. How she'd always made sure she got the express bus because the other bus had too many stops and she couldn't stand to wait an extra fifteen minutes to see her.

She feels the searing pain that comes with the realization that the person you're with doesn't love you the same way they once did. Like they're relaxing their grip.

After several silent minutes, she speaks. "You don't want to spend time with me." She wipes her cheeks with her palms.

"Fucking hell, Claire. You wonder why I don't want to come home? I don't want to take this shit on. You're like . . . a dragon. Breathing out negativity onto me. I had dinner with a friend and now you're in tears. For Christ's sake."

"Is something going on with you and Tiff?" She'd always imagined that when you accused your wife of cheating on you, you'd yell it. The words would burn coming out. They would shatter windows. But her words are barely a whisper. It turns out it's hard to yell a question you don't really want to know the answer to.

Maggie's face reddens. "Are you fucking serious?"

Claire doesn't answer.

"Of course not. You've actually lost it, Claire. You're acting like a fucking crazy bitch. Your paranoia and anxiety and possessiveness is ruining us. It will ruin us. These panic attacks and episodes. You're not in control anymore. To accuse me of something like that when I have never given you a reason not to trust me. Can you hear yourself?"

Claire curls up into a ball while Maggie's in the shower. She hits her forehead with the heel of her hand. She's so needy. And desperate. She swallows down the salty taste in her mouth and uses a towel from the floor to wipe the smudged makeup from under her eyes.

When Maggie returns, Claire says sorry. Sorry for being pathetic. She says, "I love you. I love you too much and it hurts."

Maggie says it back. "I love you more than anything, Claire. Trust me." But she sounds like an actor reciting a line.

They cuddle in bed and she circles her fingertips along Maggie's stomach. She wants to touch her. To feel Maggie become hers. To need her. She finds the elastic of her underwear and pushes her hand inside, watching the way Maggie's face changes. They don't speak while she finds a rhythm, listening to Maggie's breath, her hips moving up and down. She wants to whisper, "Sorry," but doesn't. She wants to whisper, "Remember this?" When she clutches on to her, finding her lips, it feels like them again. Maggie lets out a high-pitched cry. Limbs intertwined, her head resting on Maggie's chest, she feels safe. Home. Her heartbeat slows and her eyes fall shut. There is no better feeling than this.

Patrick

❦

WHEN HE WAKES UP, IT TAKES HIM A MOMENT TO WORK
out where he is. The wall isn't where it's meant to be and light is
flooding in from the wrong direction. His eyes stumble over the coffee table in front of him.

Then he sinks. Through the beige couch and on through the
cream, scuffed-up carpet. The ground that's meant to catch him
doesn't. Everything has disappeared. When he thinks he can't fall
any further, he does, and how does this happen? It's the feeling that
hits him first. Everything is wrong. He shouldn't be here. Why isn't

he at home, one arm wrapped around her waist, moaning as he pulls her in tighter?

The first thing he does is reach for his phone. She's going to have messaged. Called. This has all been an awful mistake and a night apart will surely have shown her that. Her foot would have searched for his leg in the night and found the sheets cold. Unslept on. As he presses the home button, he holds his breath. Please. Give him the name that's appeared across his screen thousands of times. Let her be feeling even a fraction of this.

Nothing.

His phone background smiles back at him, a picture of them just after he proposed, her left hand pressed up against her face. He taps on his messages. Maybe he just didn't get a notification. But the last message from her was yesterday afternoon. "Should be home around nine." Was there a clue he'd missed? Had her tone changed and he was just too oblivious to pick it up?

He scrolls through their messages from the last few weeks. Two days ago, she'd written, "I love you too." There were pictures of her dog splayed out on his dog bed in her home in Brisbane. Details about going out to dinner with her mum. There was a coolness now that he read them back. But she was always like that in messages. They were always short, straight to the point, and with perfect punctuation.

He thought back to a little over a week ago when she'd returned from a long-planned camping trip with her school friends. Had she been quieter than usual? Not really. That night they'd watched a documentary about genetically modified food on Netflix and committed to cleaning the cupboard out. She'd jumped in the shower with him that Sunday night and asked what he'd done, who he'd seen, if he'd missed her. He'd said yes, it's boring when you're not around. She'd kissed him and said, "I missed you too."

The timeline doesn't make sense. She told him last night that while she was camping she'd made up her mind. How could one weekend change everything? A few quiet hours? And they'd been happy when she returned. The next day she'd said she wanted to go to Brisbane for the week. She missed her family. And work had been trying to make her take some annual leave. He said that sounded like a great idea, even if he was quietly disappointed that it meant a few nights alone, their apartment still.

He hears the front door slam and long strides make their way down the hallway.

"Hey, didn't know if you'd be awake yet," Sam says, poking his head into the living room. He's bought them both a coffee, and hands one to Patrick as if to say, *Cheer up, mate, this should do it.*

Last night, the final question Caitlin had asked was, "Do you want me to go somewhere? Or do you want to?"

He'd been horrified. Before that, he hadn't even considered where he was going to sleep. The thought of staying inside that apartment, laying his head on a pillow that smelled like her shampoo and showering beside her body wash, had been too much to bear.

"I'll go," he'd said definitively, assuming she would interrupt him while he packed and insist he stay. Tears rolled onto his lips while he stuffed some clothes and a pair of underpants into his gym bag, Roxy wagging her tail, convinced she was going for a walk.

"I'm sorry," Caitlin had mumbled, wiping her nose. "Sam is expecting one of us . . . I told him you'd probably need to stay . . ."

Holy shit, Sam knew before I did, he thought. He stared at her, mouth agape. This had been meticulously planned. She could not stand to spend one more night with him. He ordered an Uber, snatched up his toothbrush, and five minutes later he was in the back of a Toyota Corolla, so stunned he could barely blink.

He hadn't spoken to Sam much when he'd arrived. There was just a hug, which was awkward and stiff, and then Sam had said, "Sorry, dude," before offering him a beer. The thought of alcohol made his stomach churn. He shook his head no. Not long after, Patrick had set himself up on the couch and Sam had taken the hint.

It took hours to get to sleep. He cried silently, mouth contorting into unpleasant shapes he didn't want anyone else to ever see. He squeezed his eyes tight, wishing away the world beyond them. The clock in the corner of the room ticked too loudly and his thoughts were so busy it felt as though dozens of voices were trying to talk to him all at once. By the early hours of the morning, he'd reasoned that Caitlin had panicked. It might take twenty-four hours or a few days or a few weeks, but eventually she would realize how wrong all this was. Sometimes you've got to blow your life up to work out what's worth keeping. They were each other's light and everything else was dark. He had to stay rational. There was no future in which they didn't do life together.

After a few hours' sleep—a bridge he'd hoped would fast-forward him to a phone call from Caitlin, apologizing and regretting everything—he'd woken up significantly less hopeful.

"So, how are you feeling this morning?" Sam asks, hand flat against the wall, ankles crossed over each other.

"Not good." He leans forward, staring at nothing.

"Yeah, this was me last year. After Amelia left. It will get better, even though that probably doesn't help to hear now. In three months, you'll be like a new person." Sam takes a sip of his coffee, eyeing Patrick's untouched one balancing on the arm of the couch.

Patrick doesn't know how to say that this isn't like Amelia at all. They'd been together two years, if that, and they weren't engaged.

There had always been issues with Amelia. She'd hated Sydney when they moved from Perth. Whenever they hung out, she'd make fun of Sam, impersonating how hard he was trying with his friends. One night, she'd stood with a hand on her hip and said, "Stop trying to be funny," and the room had fallen silent. The fact that Sam would even try to compare them feels ridiculous.

"The thing I did learn from Amelia, though, was that they don't want to do this either. It hurts them too . . . having to end it." He pauses. "Not meant to be, I guess."

A moment passes in silence. Patrick has nothing to say. Sam is extrapolating the rules of the universe and applying them to Patrick and Caitlin's relationship. But they don't fit. Their relationship was, or *is*, so private. No one else could know the promises they'd made and how sure they both were that this was it. He feels a little embarrassed for Sam, knowing that in a few days he'll call him and let him know that he and Caitlin are back together. That it was all just a bit of a mix-up. A hurdle they might joke about in their wedding speeches. And then Sam will have to retract all the stupid things he's saying now. This conversation is utterly pointless.

"So, what do you think went wrong?" Sam asks, moving the coffee to the table and perching himself on the armrest of the couch.

"I don't know." His voice is devoid of tone. He tells Sam what happened last night. How blindsided he'd been. He's not looking for advice, he's just filling the silence.

"Pretty brutal, the way she did it," Sam says, shaking his head. "So out of the blue, and to not even give you the opportunity to work on things . . ." He knows Sam is trying to make him feel better, but it's having the opposite effect. The last thing he feels right now is anger. In fact, hearing Sam speak about Caitlin like that makes him feel defensive. "It wasn't brutal," he wants to snap back, even though he knows it was and his insides feel like poison is leaking through his whole body. Stinging. Burning.

"See," he wants to tell Caitlin, "I will never stop defending you, even when you hurt me."

Claire

⁊

It has not been a good morning.

When her alarm had gone off at seven thirty, she couldn't get out of bed. She'd snoozed. Then snoozed again. And then it was eight fifteen and she hadn't had time for a shower.

She'd landed at her desk five minutes late and her phone was already ringing, Renee staring at it from the next desk over. When she'd answered, it had been a customer who called her a thief who ought to be ashamed of herself and she'd found herself scrambling through her drawers for the yellow stress ball they'd each been given on R U OK? Day. She'd been polite and had followed the script, say-ing, "I understand," but she'd known it was only going to get worse when the woman said that this was her third call in as many days and that no one had called her back like they'd said they would. The problem was that the woman was right. Someone at another desk had messed up. She'd apologized and tried to "de-escalate the situ-ation," as the manual put it—but once someone is enraged, they're too far gone. She'd wiped eighty dollars off her fees (that she never should have been charged anyway) and suggested they open a new account that had a different fee structure. The call had gone for forty-two minutes. And she hadn't even had a coffee yet.

They'd warned her at the job interview about the customers. "People hate banks," the HR director had said, shrugging her shoul-ders. At the induction, they'd talked as much about mental health resources as they did about day-to-day operations, which she prob-ably should have paid more attention to. Telling someone not to take it personally was about as useful as telling a footballer who'd broken his leg to just walk it off. She'd been called a monkey. A thief was common. Evil. A cunt. And it was her job to calmly respond, "I can hear you're very upset. Would you mind telling me exactly what happened so I can help you sort this out?"

The mental health advice was to take a break after a particularly bad phone call, but that wasn't possible when they had targets to hit. It was one after the other in their busy gray office, where the air-conditioning was always a few degrees too cold and most people ate frozen meals for lunch.

As she walks around the block at lunchtime, she notices her hands are shaking. She has this awful sense that she's forgotten something. Or that something isn't right. It tosses in the pit of her stomach all afternoon as she ruminates on how Maggie had spoken to her last night. How spit had flung from her mouth when she'd said, "You wonder why I don't want to come home?" But then she recalls Maggie's arm finding her in the night. And how she'd said "Love you" as she ran out the door to work. Things were normal. Weren't they?

By four o'clock she is sitting on a closed toilet seat, clutching her shaking hands together, repeating *It's okay, it's okay, it's okay* in her head. Her mind is spinning and spinning and spinning and she's begging it to stop but it only gets faster. As she spins, she sees flashes of Maggie leaving. Of Maggie with Tiff. Of Maggie dropping dead. She feels like a rabbit who has heard a thud out in the dark and is frozen, contemplating all the things it might be. *But where is the thud coming from?* She can't hear it. She can feel it. But the thing about feeling something in your chest and your stomach and your hands is that you're not sure whether you can trust it. She knows she's losing her mind. But is this sensation part of the sane mind she still has left? Or is it part of what's lost? How do you trust your own mind when it's playing tricks on you? When it's half-mad and half-sane?

When she sits back down at her desk, Renee asks about her plans for the weekend.

"Maggie and I are going to Encores at the Empire tonight." She sees Renee's expression. "Wedding anniversary."

"I've always wanted to go. Very jealous. And congratulations, by the way. You're welcome to have a drink at the pub with us before you go?"

"Oh, no. That's lovely but I'm going to head home and get changed first. Fix up this situation." She gestures to what she's wearing.

In the car on the way home, she relaxes. She wants a glass of prosecco. And the passion fruit brûlée everyone talks about. She thinks about the red dress with the round collar she plans to wear. When was the last time she even got dressed up? Put on lipstick? And eye shadow? She wants Maggie to tell her she looks beautiful. All tension will dissipate once they're seated, surrounded by other couples plagued by silence, and Maggie will say, "Sorry for calling you a crazy bitch last night," and she'll respond, "Well, in your defense, I am a crazy bitch," and then they'll laugh and maybe order cocktails. It will be like in London, when it was well past closing time and the waiter kept circling their table, waiting for a moment to interject with the bill. They need a night like that.

She has a shower and checks the time. Maggie is due home any minute. She turns on the speakers in their bedroom and does her makeup. Her parents are out. The house is theirs.

At six thirty, she calls Maggie, who'd said she'd be home half an hour ago. It's not a big deal. They don't have to leave just yet. But she just wants to make sure there isn't a holdup. It rings out. She rings again. And again. Checks Maggie's message again. She had said six.

And so she waits. On the bed. And then at the dining table. And then on the front fence. She watches as the time on her phone turns from six fifty-nine to seven o'clock. Swallows. The tears fall again, but she barely feels them. Her phone buzzes on the fence beside her. It's her mum sending a picture. She doesn't open it. The sun falls behind the trees and the sky turns purple. Then electric blue. Then black. Mosquitoes start to bite so she goes back inside. That's when Maggie calls.

"Maggie?" Her voice sounds like a child's.

"Hey, just saw your missed calls . . ."

"Maggie, where are you? Are we going for dinner?"

"Ah, sorry, I already ate here."

The line falls silent.

"It's . . . it's our wedding anniversary. We said last night—"

"I'm aware. This thing just popped up here at the gym and everyone was eating and I accidentally ate." Someone laughs in the background.

"I'm going to go." Claire hangs up and stares at the front door, waiting for Maggie to call her back. To message and say sorry. She does neither.

She doesn't know what she's meant to do, and then she realizes she hasn't eaten since midday. So she collects her keys and drives wherever her car takes her. She doesn't turn the radio on.

When she returns home an hour later with a container of fried rice from the local Chinese place, she notices that the bedroom light is on. She stands outside for a while and wonders what she might say. Nothing comes to her.

She's in the kitchen when Maggie emerges from their room with her lips clamped shut. She rests on the doorframe, arms crossed, shoes on, which is unusual.

Claire looks down at her food, waiting for the apology to come. She's already trying to formulate her response. Maggie must feel terrible.

But Maggie's voice is sharp. "I can't do this anymore. I need some space."

Fifteen minutes later, Claire is in the front yard, vomiting into her mother's rosebush.

Ana

❧

SHE CAN TELL BY THE WAY HER PHONE VIBRATES THAT IT'S
Paul. By the way it feels in her back pocket, she knows exactly what
it says. But she ignores it. It's not important.

Trees made up of greens and browns and yellows are suddenly
reduced to silhouettes, and she blinks for a few seconds, hoping her
eyes will adjust. If she gazes at the sky, she can see the color darken,
shade by shade, like someone is slowly dimming the lights with a
twist.

The cicadas are deafening. Pounding. Their clicking sets a pace she isn't comfortable with. She can't see them but it feels like they're crawling all over her, making her legs itch.

She makes out his narrow hips and broad shoulders in the distance, his feet pointing slightly outward with each step toward her. His hands are in his pockets, but she can tell by the angle of his stiff elbows that they aren't placed there by accident.

"It's me," she wants to say, gripping him by the tops of his arms and shaking him loose. She wants to find in his eyes the part that still loves her. "It's just me."

He catches sight of her in the distance—she can tell—and then looks back down at his feet, hardly lifting them as he trudges along the damp soccer field. As he comes closer, she notices that his jaw is tight and his brow is creased, dark half-moons stamped under his clouded eyes.

They didn't mean to meet this late. But Paul had got held up at work. The moment he'd arrived home, she'd collected her car keys and headed to the front door, passing him in the hallway, mumbling something about going out. She slid into the driver's seat and the clock on the dashboard told her it was already after seven. She fetched her phone from her back pocket and quickly typed out a message. She'd be at Kings Park in ten minutes.

They finally meet. The wind bites at her bare arms as she puts them around his neck. She feels his head tremble as it rests on her shoulder and she can feel his warm tears through her navy T-shirt. All she can say is, "I love you. I love you. I love you."

She notices he can barely stand upright, his legs are shaking so much. They can't do this to each other anymore. It isn't fair.

They'd agreed this would be the last time he came here—to Durnham—for her. He was staying with his sister and had come around last night for dinner with Paul and the kids. She'd watched as the twins hovered around the door half an hour before he arrived, picking fights with each other to pass the time. And then she'd gone to the bathroom and looked up at the ceiling, trying to force the tears back where they came from.

She would remember the days between Boxing Day and New Year's Eve by the way beads of sticky sweat trickled down the insides of her arms. Not because she was hot, but because she was tortured. She'd been the one who'd said the words. Once she'd said them, she realized she'd known all along. "I can't leave" was all it had taken for the life they'd built in their imaginations to fade, like a photograph left out in the sun.

He'd cried and then shouted, using language she'd never heard him use. Then she'd turned mean. And she'd learned she could be really mean. She'd accused him of trapping her, of making her feel like her children were disposable. He was selfish and materialistic and immature and didn't know what it was to be responsible for people. He'd called her a liar who had used him, and the hotness that ran through her veins distracted her from the sadness that was settling in her bones. As long as they fought, they were still connected, like two dogs howling at each other late into the night. The energy between them mutated, and now instead of sex there was fury, one as addictive as the other.

That night and the ones that followed, tears had fallen sideways onto her pillow, her mouth clamped shut so Paul couldn't hear her uneven breathing. During the day, they had exchanged thousands of words over text and had then spoken thousands more in the evening when it had been safe to talk. She'd told Paul and the kids she wasn't feeling well.

When the house was empty, she'd cried tears that tasted different—like guilt and resentment. She hated him. He had made her a terrible mother. She'd shouted at Rachael so loudly, it had felt as if the walls shook. She now sat on the back step alone with her phone rather than on the sofa, her boys nestled in her lap. She became plagued by the knowledge that she was bad.

But when you're fighting with someone, your chest pounding and fingers shaking, you don't get to miss them. Some alcoholics will drink methylated spirits before being deprived of alcohol altogether. Even though it was toxic and it burned, a life with him was the only one she wanted. And so she'd drunk, and she drank the pain in, barely able to stand how it felt on the way down.

He'd said they needed a break from contacting each other and she'd reluctantly agreed, desperate for air. And then two days later, he'd backflipped and said he needed to see her. To say goodbye properly. And so they'd made a plan.

Now he's standing in front of her and she sees a boy, vulnerable and anguished, dressed in the body of a man. They say "I love you" and "I'll miss you" and she says that when he moves home one day, they will be together again. When he kisses her, his lips taste metallic, dry, and sad. She expected to cry but doesn't. Instead, she holds him and assures him it will be all right. If she's honest with herself, she doesn't think this is the end. It can't be. Two people can't love each other this much and it just evaporates. If her life were a movie, there would still be another third to go. There is still time for this to end the way she hoped it would.

One of her instincts is correct. This is not the end.

Her phone vibrates in her pocket again. Harder this time. She knows it's Paul. She needs to go home.

Patrick

⁊

HE HEARS HER VOICE AND ALREADY IT SOUNDS DIFFER-
ent. Older, maybe. More measured.

It's been three nights since she ended it. With every minute that
passes, things get worse. It's like his body is splitting down the middle, muscles tearing, ribs being ripped open. It's giving way to a pit
of emptiness. The same dread you feel when you're swimming in the
ocean and can't see the bottom. The unknown spans too far. Terror. You shouldn't be here alone. His stomach hurts and his chest
is stomped and sometimes he thinks he would do anything just to

make the pain go away. *It hurts*, he whimpers to himself at night. When darkness falls, his thoughts get louder. He hyperventilates. She was his access to happiness, this thing he could see and touch and speak to. And now she is gone.

The curl of words coming from her mouth gives him relief. She is here. This isn't the first time they've spoken. He'd called her the day after, soon realizing he had nothing to say. Maybe he was hoping she did. She apologized and was gentle in a way that made him feel pathetic. That night he'd gone to bed sure she'd outgrown him. This was the end of the best relationship he could have ever hoped for— she would do extraordinary things, and meet someone extraordinary who fit. He was bound for neither.

This afternoon, he'd called her with a question. One that had crept up on him. As awful as it was, the question had at least given him a sense of purpose. An excuse to call her. And when she'd picked up after the fourth ring, the pain didn't feel so bad.

"Are you interested in someone else?" He'd realized as he said it that he could not handle the answer. But he'd convinced himself she was. It's the only scenario that makes sense.

She had sighed and he'd known the exact facial expression she was making. He'd wondered where she was. What she'd eaten for breakfast and whether she'd slept okay. He knew she had an important meeting today and he'd do anything to hear her talk about it, to tell him how it went. He hasn't been to work all week. On Monday morning, he'd called his supervisor and let him know what had happened. Take as long as you need, he'd been told. So he'd decided to go back to Perth. Sleep in a bed that had once belonged to him and give her the space she needed to change her mind.

"No. Honestly, I'm not," she'd answered, and even though it's the answer he'd wanted, he's left unsatisfied.

"Then why, Caitlin? Please just explain to me why."

He could hear her thinking. For the last sixty hours or so, each of which he has felt deeply, he has clung with one hand to hope. It has made him impatient, desperate to get to the next morning. At times, it even gave him surges of energy. *I need to make myself good enough for Caitlin*, he'd thought, more than once. He'd considered his options. He needed a new job. One he was actually passionate about. He had to become the kind of person she deserved. He had to find real fulfillment outside of Caitlin, so that Caitlin will want him back.

"I don't know how else to say this. I just don't love you anymore. I don't . . ."

He lies there, on the bed they'd shared last time they visited his family in Perth, and feels the words settle into his bones. The words had felt wrong—impossible—coming out of her mouth. *Who was this person?* He'd mumbled a goodbye, thanking her for the closure, a lie they both pretend to believe. When she'd hung up, it had taken everything he had not to throw his phone across the room.

He picks up the pillow from under his head and holds it against his open mouth, shouting into it. His brain is a kaleidoscope of images of Fraser Island and Canada and the way she wore her hair at uni and Sundays spent napping beside each other and the day they brought Roxy home and the way she always looked at him after they'd had sex and how she squeezed his hand when they were out in public because she knew he was shy and it was all the happiest he had ever been. He had been shown a picture of his perfect life and now he is watching it burn. *Where does all the love go*, he asks himself, *when there's nowhere to put it?* He hears his mother's footsteps edge toward his bedroom door, but just when he expects to hear the door handle twist, the footsteps set off in the opposite direction.

Claire

❧

Claire is sitting in the shower.

No one can hear her sobs over the sound of the water pummeling the tiles. She can barely see the bathroom cabinet through the steam. Her skin is red and her hands and feet are pruned. *The water must be hot*, she thinks.

Maggie has gone to stay at Tiff's. She has a spare room. Part of Claire was relieved that Maggie had somewhere safe to go. Had someone else in Toowoomba who cared about her. But after she'd left, Claire had what Dr. Salim would call a panic attack. She's been seeing her for a few months now, ever since things got bad. Dr. Salim says to think of the attacks as a wave. You'll feel them coming on. The sweaty palms and dry mouth. And then it will reach a crest. You might think you're going to die. Or have a heart attack. Or you'll stop breathing. But your body can't sustain that level of adrenaline for very long, she says. Sit with the feelings. And they will pass.

But that's not how her panic attack after Maggie had been. She'd vomited. She'd screamed. She'd cried. For hours she was caught up in the wave—tossed and tumbled and dragged down, lashed with jagged rocks and choked by salt water. There was no coming up for air. To navigate the crest, you need to know which way is up. But she was drowning in the darkness of deep water.

It hadn't passed by the next morning. She'd called her mother, barely making sense. She must've been able to say "Maggie's gone," because two hours later her parents had cut their weekend away short and come home, overnight bags being hauled out of the boot. At her mother's urging, she'd taken a Valium and for a few hours she had fallen into a dreamless sleep.

As Claire hunches on the shower tiles, she blows her nose with her hand. She thinks about London and *Glee*. About weekends up north with Maggie's family. About falling asleep on her lap on a plane trip back from Croatia and how it felt when she woke up and Maggie was stroking her hair. She latches on to moments she didn't know she had memories of. And a future she's drawn over years and years. She didn't realize she'd already played out next Monday in her head, and the Monday after that, and Christmas, and Maggie at forty and fifty and sixty. She cried hardest for the things that had never happened. For the children they were meant to have. What she felt was not just the pain of losing a person, but of lost hope. A future stolen by the same hand that promised it. The person she loved was also the person she most hated. A thief. A con artist. A murderer.

But her most visceral hatred is reserved for herself. She knows it's her fault. That anyone who gets too close will always leave. She plays a game of *If I hadn't* . . . If she hadn't accused her of cheating. A person who had never so much as looked at another woman in their five-year relationship. If she hadn't begged Maggie to spend more time with her. If she hadn't cried and demanded and picked fights. If she'd put in more effort with how she looked. If she hadn't taken her for granted. If she hadn't cut her hair short and started wearing less makeup. If she'd exercised. If she'd been less herself and more the person Maggie fell in love with, then everything wouldn't be ruined.

The hot water begins to turn cold and she climbs out of the shower. When she leaves this room, where will she go? What will she do? She's been dropped in the desert with no compass. A place she never wanted to go.

When she opens the bathroom door, she hears the ringing. Slicing through the air. On her bed, the screen is lit up. Maggie.

"Hello?"

"Claire?"

She quietens the voice that is telling her, *You don't know this person anymore.*

They are silent.

"How are you?" Maggie asks.

"How do you think I am?" Her tone is flat. A moment passes. "How are you?"

"I can't do this, Claire. I'm so sorry. I miss you. I really miss you. I don't want this to end."

Maggie says she had felt like she was losing her. Why had it become so hard? Claire thinks how strange it is not to know exactly where Maggie is. Exactly what she's doing. The words coming out of this person's mouth will decide her fate, the rest of her life. To Claire, Maggie is the most powerful person in the world.

There are apologies and they speak in a way they haven't in months. They laugh. They recount the last twenty-four hours of their lives, with details only someone who loves you would care about.

"So, what does this mean?" Claire eventually asks.

Maggie sighs. "I can't come back yet. I'm not ready. I think we both need some space . . . just for a little while. But I know I love you. You're the person I want to spend the rest of my life with. We just need some time. To sort ourselves out."

She says she understands, even though she doesn't. She asks how Tiff's is. Fine, Maggie says. Not as good as living with you. "Then why don't you come back now?" she wants to ask. But she's trying on someone else for a while. Someone who says less. Feels less.

When Maggie says she'd better go, she wants to ask why. Where to. They both say "I love you," and it feels different. Loaded with a meaning it didn't have a week ago. Claire feels like the color of her life has changed in an hour, from the blueness of the bathroom to the yellow warmth of her bedroom. She wants to continue listening to the tune of Maggie's voice. When they hang up, she looks in the mirror and there's a different person standing there than there'd been this morning. Every good quality she guesses she might have is confirmed by Maggie's eyes looking in her direction. She stands differently. Breathes differently. She is a person good enough for Maggie. This morning she had been empty. A body stuffed with cotton wool. No thoughts or beliefs. Broken and deformed. Ugly and unlovable.

But the good feelings pass not long after she's hung up. She checks her phone again. Thinks about calling her back. Whatever ground Maggie just paved feels unstable. Like quicksand. But she holds steady. It's all she has.

SHE DOESN'T KNOW what makes her think of it.

It's Monday night and she's scrolling through Facebook on her phone. She looks up. Bites the nail of her forefinger. Would she still be logged in?

She opens up Safari on her laptop and goes to Facebook. A newsfeed that isn't hers appears. Pictures of people she doesn't recognize. A red notification sits on the messenger icon. *Shit*. She can't check it. Or else Maggie will know. Will she, though? Or will she dismiss it and imagine she checked it herself and forgot? It doesn't matter. She's already clicked and an inbox full of messages appear.

Tiff Baker is the third from the top. Her thumb instinctively opens it.

The last message says, "See you soon x," and it was sent four hours ago. She scrolls. Doesn't know where to start. Wants to read them in order, not the other way around. She flicks back a few days. Photos. Lots of them. What? Is that Maggie's hand? Whose body is that? Her eyes are drawn to bare breasts reflected in a full-length mirror. White lacy underwear that sits low on narrow hips. A flat stomach. Blond hair over one shoulder. And a face she recognizes. Tiff. Brown dead eyes. Her bottom lip pouting.

Maggie asks for more. "I want to see you from behind. Touch yourself. Think of how it would feel if I tasted you." Tiff in a G-string. With nothing else on. "You're so bad!" Then, "You make me bad." She looks at the date stamp. The time. She would've been asleep beside Maggie.

But there's one photo that makes her gasp. She brings her hand to her mouth. This photo isn't of Tiff. It's of her. Claire. Curled up in bed, in flannelette pajama pants, facing the other way. The photo had been taken from the opposite corner of the room.

"She's fucking crying again," the message reads.

"How come?" says the next.

"Literally have no idea."

She remembers, though. She was crying because Maggie called her crazy. Told her she was ruining their relationship. Right after she'd asked if she was cheating on her. With Tiff.

She swallows and tries to scroll further but her hands won't stop shaking. Her breathing becomes shallow. Can't catch air for long enough. She runs to the bathroom and dry retches into the toilet bowl. Sweat stings her hairline and soaks the back of her neck. Her thoughts. Won't let. Finish. Tiff. But Tiff's straight, isn't she? Breasts. Maggie's words. Her own hunched back. The bottoms of her socks in the photo. Dirty. Black. Unmade bed. Dark. Dull. Weeks. Months. How long had this been happening? How had she not known?

She calls Maggie. Panting.

"Are you sleeping with Tiff?" she asks before she says anything.

"What? Claire, we've already been through this. Seriously? No. We're just friends. I can't . . ."

"I've never had a friend," she raises her voice, "I've never told a friend to touch herself for me and imagine me tasting her."

"You read my messages."

"Yep. I read all of them. I saw what you—"

But she's interrupted by the sound of a line that's gone dead.

Patrick

❧

THE CAFÉ IS ALIVE WITH CLINKS AND CHAIRS SCRAPING and indecipherable chatter. A waitress delivers his small flat white and he looks up to thank her. Her eyes are a fantastic blue and her nose and cheeks are peppered with brown freckles, so perfect they look almost drawn on. She is objectively beautiful. As she turns away, he gazes at her black skinny jeans, waiting to see if he can feel anything. But his insides are mute. All he sees is a person who is not Caitlin, but who is wearing the same black Vans with the white stripe that she owns. He takes a sip of his coffee and it makes him feel nauseous, filtering into a stomach that's been empty for days.

It was his mum's suggestion that he get out of the house, even if just to a café for a few hours. He's been there for a full week and is yet to change out of his navy tracksuit pants, which are fraying at the ankles. So he's brought his laptop and is flicking through Flatmate Finders, trying to find a new place to live. He can't bring himself to inquire yet—he finds something wrong with every house he clicks on. Shared bathroom. No air-conditioning. Too far north. Too far south. But really, the whole thing just feels like a betrayal. The Caitlin of two years ago would be horrified he's even considering a future without her.

He keeps replaying one particular night, like it's a puzzle his mind wants him to solve. It's the night when she'd come home from work upset and curled up on their bedroom floor. What must've been going through her head? What must it have felt like to learn there'd been a complaint made against her, after everything she'd sacrificed? He hadn't seen it before. But before that complaint, she couldn't have worked any harder. There were nights when she must not have eaten dinner. When everyone else—including him—spilled out on a Friday afternoon to have a drink at the pub across the road, she wouldn't even look up. They'd stopped asking her. Why had she done that to herself, he wonders. What was she trying to prove? She used to say that work kept her mother going after her dad left. And her grandmother after her husband died. Was that how she felt? That work was the only thing that never left you?

And then, he supposes, that day work had betrayed her. He sees himself standing in the doorway and tries to change the memory. He wills his foot to take a step forward. To walk over to her and ask a question. Any question. But his memory is stubborn. It won't deliver something that didn't happen.

As he clicks on a room for $350 a week, he hears the hum of a song he immediately recognizes. It brings back her smile and flashes of her shoulders, the light catching her collarbones. They're dancing at their friends' wedding and she's laughing, a strand of hair falling into her face. Longing pulls at him and this song is her. "Dreams," Fleetwood Mac. Everything good that has happened to him in the last six years can be traced right back to her and the maths is simple. Without her, there is no good. There hadn't been before and there wouldn't be now. He doesn't want to be in this café in Perth, suffocated by the smell of sourdough toast and scrambled eggs, looking at pictures of a run-down share house with no windows and a bedroom with only enough room for a single bed.

How did my life turn into the opposite of what I wanted? he asks himself, pressing his palms into his eyes. The future he was promised has been stolen and he wants to tell her that she can't do that. She was a source of endless small joys breaking up the mundane. He tries to remember the last time he felt happiness about something that had nothing at all to do with Caitlin. He can't.

It dawns on him that Caitlin got to know him—the real him that no one else got to see—and she couldn't stand it. She saw Patrick for everything he was—his thoughts and his fears and his beliefs and his family and his dreams—and she'd said, "No. This isn't what I want. Having nothing would be better than this."

He packs away his computer and nearly forgets to pay for his coffee at the counter. As he taps his card, he looks at his phone. His background is now a picture he took of the northern lights, a green halo dancing on the horizon. But it's obscured by a gray notification. A missed call. It's her.

Claire

❦

SHE CAN'T FOLLOW THE CONVERSATION.

Lauren and Pia are talking about another girl they'd gone to
school with. She has three kids by three different dads. One of the
guys is now in jail. Tried to stab someone. Maybe her. Or her sister.
She squints her eyes and tries to concentrate. Her eyes are drawn to
the couple behind Lauren's right shoulder. How he puts his hand
over her hand as he lifts his wineglass to his mouth. He leans in
when she speaks. Pushes his phone to the side when it rings. It's her,
though, she can't keep her eyes off. Long caramel hair that shines

under the dim lights. She's petite, fragile wrists and a sharp jawline, but she eats everything on her plate. *He'd love that*, she thinks. A girl who eats and never puts on weight.

Imagine being *that* girl. Who's likely never experienced rejection in her life. Her biggest problem would be deciding whom to choose. She has a black leather handbag resting on her chair leg, with a silver laptop poking out the top. She must've just come from work. Probably something creative. An agency. Clever. Late nights and early mornings.

Her boyfriend's eyes widen whenever she tells a story. Laughs. Shakes his head. He is in awe of her. *Maggie felt like that about me once*, she thinks.

"How've you been with everything?" Pia asks, her hands resting on the table. They already know what happened. She'd told them via a series of messages last week. But she starts from the beginning, because speaking about herself is the only thing she can focus on right now.

They'd met Maggie a handful of times, in the year or so since they'd been back. She got the sense they didn't really understand Maggie—she was distant. Quiet. Had suggested they leave early. Claire hadn't minded. She preferred Maggie's company over anyone else's.

Pia rolls her eyes. "You were always too good for her. You're creative and open and funny . . . and I got the sense she sort of dulled you. She was so . . ." She searches for the word.

"Basic," Lauren says.

"Yeah, that's it. Basic. You went to London to find yourself, but when you came back, you'd just found Maggie."

She pushes away the thought that says, *Yazmin was right*. So right Claire knows she can never speak to her again. She pictures Yazmin shrugging when she finds out they broke up. How her eyes will feign sympathy when they're full of vindication. She'd known it could never last. Inside Maggie had been a darkness. A tendency to self-serve. That's why Yazmin had warned her never to get too close to someone like that. Maggie wasn't sure enough in her own identity to offer stability to anyone else. Perhaps she never would be.

Lauren nods. Offers her a tissue. Three weeks and she's still crying in public. Memories flood every moment. Street signs remind her of Maggie. Her shampoo. The passenger seat. The underwear she always liked. Any notification on her phone.

"So, have you spoken to her since?" Lauren asks.

"No," she scoffs. "I don't pick up her calls." From the tone of her voice, she almost believes her own lie.

"Good! That's what you need. No contact."

She looks out onto the street and imagines Maggie walking past. Maggie seeing her, sitting at a table with friends, throwing her head back in laughter. *She's not thinking about me at all*, Maggie would think, and then she'd notice the new boots Claire is wearing and how she's straightened her hair so it looks longer. Claire will look up at that moment and smile at her, unaffected, and excuse herself for a moment. And Maggie will smell her perfume and see something in her eye she recognizes as the person she loved. Maybe then tonight would be worth something. Washing her hair and having conversations that are meaningless because she can no longer relay them to Maggie.

Lauren starts talking about some guy she's seeing. They met at work. Pia oohs and aahs in the right places and asks questions she can't possibly care about the answers to. He works hard. Just bought his own house. Has a sister and a rescue dog who's missing a toe. She wants to hiss that none of those things are personality traits but instead she tries to make her face feign interest. Moves the corners of her mouth. Widens her eyes. She feels like she's not herself but is watching herself—the director of a play shouting instructions at an actor. *Nod. Ask. Say mmm.*

Listening to Lauren speak about this person, whose name might be Mike (you tend not to remember things you don't care about), she thinks it's quite similar to listening to someone recount a holiday they've just returned from. She had the same experience when she first met up with friends after London and tried to recount a night out in Portugal or Paris or a spring day in Camden. You learn that the details mean nothing to anyone else. What you're trying to do is communicate a feeling. An attachment. An affection. For a place or a thing or a moment. And it's untranslatable. There's a frustration associated with it. *Why can't you feel what I'm feeling?* Eventually you accept—as everyone does after travel—that a common language does not exist. And so you give up. Soon, she thinks, Lauren will give up trying to make us feel for Mike what she does.

She goes to the bathroom and checks her phone. Blank. No message or missed calls waiting for her. It feels lighter when Maggie isn't inside it. A device that serves no purpose. She closes her eyes and imagines what Maggie might be doing. She must be thinking about her. It's a Saturday night. She should be nestled up in the crook of Maggie's neck watching a stand-up special on her laptop. She checks Instagram. She's blocked Maggie but she checks Tiff's profile dozens of times a day. It's public. And she posts a lot. A picture. Shared an hour ago. It's them. Their smiling faces, eyes behind sunglasses. It looks like they're walking around the parklands. Maggie's hair has grown a little and she's pulling her photo face. The sunglasses on the bridge of her nose are Ray-Bans. A gift Claire had bought Maggie for her birthday last year. To see them so close to Tiff's skin feels like an illicit betrayal.

The gold crucifix resting on Tiff's collarbone makes her want to kick the bathroom door. If this were a movie, she thinks, she would send the screenshots of Tiff's messages to her father. She's thought about what she'd write.

"Good evening, Pastor. This is what your good Christian daughter is doing while you're not looking. Just thought I'd let you know that God is very, very pissed off."

But she doesn't do that because her life is not a movie. It's sadder and there's less redemption. There's no justice waiting for her or a profound character arc. She doesn't get her ninety-second montage where she loses ten kilos and buys a new wardrobe and dyes her hair the color it should have been all along. There's been no night out with her girlfriends where she had one too many cocktails and came to some realization that they're all she'll ever need. If you sat in a theater and watched her story play out on-screen, you'd walk out shaking your head, saying to the person next to you, "I just didn't get the point of it."

In bed that night, she sends a message to her manager. She won't be in next week. She must've just about run out of sick leave. Everyone must hate her. She'd hate her. A response comes through. "Got it. I'll give you a call in the morning. Let's have a chat." She can already see herself watching the call ring out. The notification telling her she has a voicemail. She feels nothing.

The rest of the week is showers where she uses no soap and wets but doesn't wash her hair, picking at food but never a full meal, scrolling and then tapping and scrolling and clenching her jaw so much it gives her a headache. The sun outside her bedroom window taunts her, dancing across the trees, guilting her for not basking in it. It screams at her the word "should" and she rolls in the opposite direction, refusing to walk or swim or sit in the yard. When the skies open up on Thursday afternoon and rain taps on her window, she feels a moment of relief. Finally outside looks as it should.

There are phone calls with Maggie. Her heart rate quickens when she sees her name appear or when she gives herself permission to call her. Her fingers shake. They are the only moments of her day that matter. Maggie stopped answering her questions about Tiff a while ago, except to say there was never an affair. Nothing ever happened. They are friends and she is staying on Tiff's couch because she has nowhere else to go. Her words inject hope into Claire's veins—words and promises she needs to hear in order to get through another night. "I just need some time to be on my own," Maggie tells her. "To work out what I want. But I love you, Claire. And I miss you. Just be patient."

When Maggie has to go, Claire tries to think of another thing to say. To keep her on the line for even just another second. It is the only peace she feels and it takes everything she has not to beg, "Please, Maggie. Just stay. We don't even have to talk. Just don't hang up the phone."

Maggie calls her at lunchtime on the following Tuesday. Claire decides not to tell her about work. She quit. Couldn't even draft a resignation letter so told her manager in a text message. She can't remember exactly what it said. Once she'd sent it, she never looked at it again, deleting the message thread and the contact. It wasn't something she wanted to do, but she couldn't even walk around the block without having a panic attack. When she wasn't sitting on the edge of her bed hyperventilating, she was anticipating when she would be next, tiptoeing around her own emotions, terrified they'll hear her. Dr. Salim thinks they should have more regular appointments. Twice a week if possible. Her mother is spending more and more time at home, which she's starting to think isn't a coincidence. She knocks on Claire's bedroom door every hour or so and has taken to only speaking to her in a singsong soft voice, like she's a host on *Play School*.

Maggie says she has news.

"Guess who just had their visa approved?"

In all the chaos, she'd nearly forgotten about Maggie's permanent residency. They'd spent so much time and money on the application, needing to provide their civil partnership paperwork and photos and ceremony invitations and bank statements and text messages. Claire had joked that they should send screenshots of their nudes. Perhaps the videos they'd once sent each other would prove they were in a genuine relationship. Hours were spent writing about how they first met, their plans for the future, how housework was shared and how they spent their time. It was the strangest thing, to collect all this evidence to prove that love existed. As though any amount of documentation could attest to a feeling. The essence of their relationship didn't live on Facebook or in bank transactions, but through the words they exchanged when the lights were off and they were just disembodied voices in the dark.

"Oh my God. Congratulations! Took long enough."

Maggie laughs and starts doing her best Australian accent. She's in a good mood.

"Well, we have to celebrate somehow," Claire says, her smile traveling down the phone line.

They decide to go to Picnic Point Lookout. Claire says she'll bring champagne. This is what they need. She flicks on the shower, wondering if she should book somewhere for dinner afterward, struck by a sense of having woken from a bad dream. A voice tells her what perhaps she's known all along: *Everything is going to be okay. It will work out.* The past few weeks have almost been worth it. They both learned what they were taking for granted. She would be foolish to throw away a five-year relationship, the person she'd committed to for life, because of a few dirty pictures.

That trust could be built back. She is sure of it.

Ana

She can't go back out there. She knows she can't.

When was the last time she ate? Yesterday? At some point, she'd eaten half a Kit Kat and then thrown the rest in the bin. It had tasted like cardboard. Last night, she'd had a glass of wine and had then gone to the bathroom, thinking she might faint. Instead, she'd sat on the floor of the toilet cubicle, the tiles cold and bright white. She couldn't cry, so she'd just stared at the fly on her jeans for fifteen minutes. Or maybe it was half an hour. When she came back out, no one had noticed she was gone. "I'm going to head back to the hotel," she told Paul, and then she cried herself to sleep.

Now she's in a new toilet. It smells like expensive perfume and rose air freshener. There's deodorant in a wicker basket for anyone to use and she sprays some even though she doesn't need it. She retreats to a cubicle and she's breathing in through her nose for three, and out through her mouth for five. She can't remember if they're the right numbers but she just needs something to focus on and this will do.

Shrieks and giggles interrupt her rhythm and she loses count. The smell of bold, fresh perfume rises from under the toilet door and even she wants to kiss it. A word here and there emerges, unmuffled. A high-pitched voice chortles as instructions are given on how to lift up her tulle skirt, the heels of at least three women clomping on the echoey tiles. A steady stream slaps the toilet water and she holds her breath, hoping no one will notice she's there. Someone with a harsh American accent says that today must have been one of the most beautiful ceremonies she's ever been to. A voice that she recognizes as belonging to Charlotte agrees.

"It was beautiful, wasn't it?"

Her voice is stunning. It tells you she was born and raised in London by parents who lived in a two-story white-brick home with a fireplace. It tells you she has no brothers or sisters, just two doting parents who believe she is the most lovable thing on the planet. A self-fulfilling prophecy, because now she is.

Her skin is supple, as skin is when you're not even thirty-five, and is such that a moment in the sun will turn it from ivory to olive, evenly spread across her shins and her shoulders. She looks like she belongs on television, her wavy brown hair framing her face, with big brown doe eyes that demand you stare into them.

Is there anything else you'd like to know about her? Because Ana could tell you. She's explored every pocket of her social media profiles and scanned the profiles of her friends. She knows that she can dance because of a candid video her friend Lily uploaded a few weeks back of them at a bar dancing to a Kanye West song she now has perpetually stuck in her head. She knows she can't cook—but in an endearing way. She knows she can do a headstand and has done Pilates for more than ten years. Ana spends a portion of every day wondering whether she's had a boob job. She oscillates from being absolutely sure to thinking perhaps she's just genetically blessed.

There are some women you meet in life who just aren't the same kind of woman as you. They're a different species. Charlotte makes everyone around her feel ugly. And fat. Not because of anything she ever says. But simply by virtue of existing. The worst part is that she's also one of the loveliest women Ana has ever met. "Sweet" would be the word. Does she know how she makes other women feel? Can she see that every woman around her rounds her shoulders when she comes close and makes mental notes to eat less and exercise more and try that particular shade of red lipstick, because maybe then she'll be beautiful too? When Ana finds herself across from her, listening to her speak about boarding school in London or what she studied at university, she knows she cannot compete. Whatever the competition—this woman wins. And the rest of the participants are invisible.

It was a Friday night only a few months ago when she saw Charlotte for the first time. A photo popped up on Instagram. She was wearing a hat and sitting in the back of a golf buggy. The photo was captioned: "Not a bad caddie." The photo belonged to Rob.

She'd remained very still. Then she'd blinked a few times, not trusting her eyes. The room had begun to move and her stomach had sunk.

It felt like the moment that picture had appeared on her screen, the world around her was replaced with a new one. Things looked the same but felt entirely different. Colors were duller and smell had no meaning and everything good was someplace else. But even worse than that moment was the knowledge of how many bad moments were to follow it, each unbearable in its own unique way. That day, it was like a sound system had gone haywire and the music was turned up too loud. It made her eardrums shake. Every time she'd been sure the sound couldn't go up any further, it did. It got to be so loud that she couldn't even hear her own thoughts anymore.

After the picture came confirmation from Rob that they were seeing each other. "You'd like her, Ana," he'd said, which made it even worse. His energy had changed, as though he'd withdrawn it from her and was investing it in this new thing. He was calm. Curt. And the most terrifying thing was not that he no longer hated her—he didn't really care. When you're angry with someone, there's passion. And where there's passion, there's love. There is no love in indifference.

She'd tried to pull him closer. Just so he would remember. And he'd told her that for three weeks after returning from Australia he hadn't left his house other than to go to work. He'd barely eaten. He couldn't exercise. And now he couldn't live in purgatory anymore. She had put him in a cage and only let him out when it suited her and he was restless. There were things he wanted that she couldn't give him.

"We'll never have the connection I had with you," he'd finally admitted, but he wanted a normal life with dinners and sex and companionship. But even his admission hadn't made it hurt less. He could never go back to her after Charlotte. She was thirty, for fuck's sake. And so Ana had become obsessed—she almost wanted her to upload another picture with Rob, cuddled up on the sofa watching a show together. It would give her something to look at and cry about and she would ask Rob if they could both have more respect and then he would say, "Ana, you're married."

If you try to contemplate how big the universe is, you can't. Your mind reaches a brick wall and you can't see beyond it because some part of you knows you can't handle it. The very knowledge would send you insane. The same happens when she tries to contemplate what she has lost—the scale of it, the weight of it, the magnitude of it. She just can't. Her mind does not have the capacity.

Over the past two months, she's quietly and privately lost her mind. She doesn't sleep for more than a few hours a night and when she wakes up it takes a while for her brain to piece together the puzzle and then she's sinking again. When the kids are home, she does what's required, like a puppet being mastered by someone else. Dinner gets cooked and the floor gets vacuumed but she can't remember doing any of it. She's going through the motions of a life she's barely attached to. When they go to school, she cries and she crawls back into a bed that still reminds her of him. She grieves her life as she is living it. Every day she cries. And it makes her so tired. Sometimes, she enjoys how it runs through her, the pain of it all. Because deep down, she knows she deserves this. She deserves to live like this for the rest of her life. Sometimes she cannot believe what she did. She's a bad, deceitful, selfish person, who ought to bare her back for one thousand lashes a day. In punishment, she finds relief.

But this punishment, this situation that has sent her crouching in a toilet cubicle, is too much. Her wounds are open and wet with blood and the lashes are hitting the same spot as yesterday and the day before. She can't stand upright anymore. She's defeated.

Once Charlotte has left, she takes a deep breath. Finally, she leaves the stall. Makeup is fixed in the mirror, but no amount of foundation covers the lines that betray her age. She is an old woman. Sad and old. The door swings on its hinge and she automatically smiles too hard at the woman who enters. She recognizes her from the ceremony.

"Hi," the woman says. She looks thirty. If that.

Ana greets her back and loves her for not being Charlotte.

"And what's your connection?" the woman asks, unpacking half a dozen products from her black leather purse.

"Oh, I'm an old friend of Rob's," she says quickly, wondering if this person might have assumed she was Charlotte's aunty or something. How humiliating.

"Ah! That explains the accent." She smiles, reapplying lipstick.

Ana laughs self-consciously and throws the wet paper towel in the bin, desperate to get out of there.

"I'm friends with the bride," the woman says, running a brush under her cheekbones in a circular motion.

"Well, she looks beautiful," she remarks convincingly, probably because it's true.

"Always does," the woman says, leaning back from the mirror. "But I've never seen her this happy before," she adds, and Ana bookmarks that comment for later, for when she needs to cry and the tears refuse to come.

It's then that her phone vibrates and she glances at it as she pushes through the bathroom door.

"I'm sorry," it says.

Patrick

⁊

*W*HEN SHE PICKS UP, SHE'S PANTING, THE MUFFLED SOUNDS of passing traffic in the background.

"Sorry, just out for a walk," she says, as though they're old friends having an ordinary conversation.

"That's okay." He pauses. Hang on, she called him. "Just saw your missed call?"

"Yeah. So I've got to speak to you about something." He imagines her stopping, maybe glancing at the tan marks that have imprinted her engagement ring on her bony finger. Is she about to change her mind? Tell him this has all been an awful mistake? There's something in her voice he can't read.

She sighs. "There's no right way for me to tell you this. And I don't want to speak to you about it but I have to, out of respect."

"Okay?" He's impatient.

"I—I do have feelings for someone. It's new, obviously, and things didn't overlap but I thought you should be the first to know."

The sign above the café begins to spin and he has every thought and no thought all at once. He massages his forehead with his fingertips, confusion emerging on his face.

"What? Since when? Who is it?"

Another sigh. Almost a groan. A sound that tells him what he needs to know. He wishes he could be the type of person to hang up right then and never think about her again. But he knows he isn't and he waits like a dog preparing to be kicked in the guts.

"Josh. It's Josh."

It takes him a second to sift through the fogginess in his brain and make the connection. Josh. Tall. Thick, dark hair. Francesca's friend. The one who comes to trivia on Thursday nights. He *likes* Josh. They'd all gone up the coast and stayed in a holiday house together two months ago. A big group of them. Was he good-looking? Patrick had never thought about it, but of course he was. When people spoke, they looked at him, wanting him to laugh or nod. A few years older too. How long had she . . . ?

"How long have you felt like this?" He swallows. Shifts his weight to the other foot.

"Only since we broke up, I swear to you. You were in Perth and I went for a drink after work with people, which you know I never do, and we just got talking . . ."

"Hang on." His throat feels tight. "Does he know how you feel about him?"

It's been eight fucking days. He's not even changed his pants. Last night he woke up at four and couldn't go back to sleep. She's a ghost who lives with him, following wherever he goes. He could get on a plane to Paris tomorrow and she'd still be there, just over his shoulder, whispering to him while he's trying to forget her.

"He does. We . . . we've spoken about it."

He's going to be sick. Josh's hands on her hips. Stroking her head. Behind her while she sleeps. He rubs his mouth. Then runs his hand through his hair.

"Does he feel the same way?"

He knows the answer. Who can blame another person for wanting her? She confirms it. Nothing has happened yet, she tells him. He's not sure whether he believes her but what does it matter. There's nothing he can do. And if it's not happened yet, it's about to.

Across the road from the café, outside a little supermarket, a toddler starts crying. Her mother is picking up a gray stuffed monkey that the girl has dropped on the footpath. She's stomping her feet and screwing up her face, turning her cheeks from a sweet pink to purple. Her hand is reaching up, only getting as far as her mother's hip.

"Mine!" she demands, thrusting her head forward and backward, pulling at the pocket of her mum's jeans. He's heard people say that, usually, if you look close enough, there are no tears running down the face of a crying toddler. But this little girl's face is wet, her eyes glassy.

"Patrick? Are you okay?"

All he can think to say is, "But you're mine . . ."

And then he hangs up.

Claire

&

A STRONG BREEZE BLOWS HER HAIR OFF HER FACE AND her dress between her thighs. On her right shoulder is a handbag containing a bottle of Moët, two plastic glasses buried underneath. She looks out over the canopy of trees—green, brown, yellow, and specks of red, clouds casting odd-shaped shadows as far as the eye can see. It's quieter up here during the week, the chirping of birds louder than the footsteps of people.

It occurs to her, as she stares aimlessly at a sign about Blakely's red gum trees, that Maggie might not come. It doesn't take much for her to recall the sensation of waiting for her the night of their anniversary. How she had paced around the house, holding her breath, pleading to hear the roll of tires pulling up. She was meant to be here ten minutes ago and she hadn't texted saying otherwise.

But then, out of the corner of her eye, she sees a body she knows to be Maggie's. She can tell from the way she walks. Hands in pockets. Shoulders high. Broad strides. She glances at the family standing near her. Do they feel that too? How the air, over all these hundreds of acres, just shifted?

Maggie feels stiff when Claire puts her arms around her. She laughs nervously. "Look, your hair," she says, and Claire doesn't know what that means so just replies, "Yeah."

They find a spot to sit on the grass behind them and Claire is hit by a wave of embarrassment. While she fishes the bottle and glasses out of her bag, she notices that Maggie brought nothing. Her arms are crossed over her black hoodie and her legs are placed awkwardly in front of her.

In contrast, Claire is wearing a patchwork dress that cinches in at the waist, with brown leather sandals. She's wearing makeup and has spent too long on her hair and she feels that pang that comes with realizing you've misjudged the formality of the occasion.

They cheers and Maggie looks down at the grass. Claire asks how she's been. If work's busy. If she's heard much from her family. It feels like she's stuck on a desert island, hacking at a coconut with a blunt hatchet, desperate to crack it open and find what is inside. Maggie begins to soften, asking her how things have been at home. She takes a sip of Moët.

"Maggie. Come home." Claire's eyes are begging.

Maggie looks back down at the grass again.

"Please. Just come home."

"You know I can't do that." Maggie brings her eyes to meet Claire's.

"But you said, Maggie. How much longer do we have to wait? My life is on hold . . ."

"You and I are done, Claire. Just let go of it."

The way she says it. Like Claire can't understand why she has to wear a seat belt and her mother is carefully explaining, barely containing her irritation. Like it is the most obvious thing in the world and everyone can see it but her.

She doesn't remember how she gets home, but she does.

Doesn't remember how she finds her way into bed, but she does.

And she plans to stay there until her body stops bothering to wake up.

Ana

§

PAUL THINKS SHE HAD FOOD POISONING DURING ROB'S wedding in Sri Lanka.

They don't know what from, but she was so sick she nearly missed the wedding, he tells people.

She likes it when he says that the wedding was a bit weird. They'd only known each other for two months and now they're married. "That'll end well," he chuckles. He acknowledges that she's beautiful, "but not really my type," is how he puts it. She knows he's just trying to make his old wife feel better.

"Seems nice enough, though," he says passively.

From the day she saw that photo of Rob with Charlotte, she expected the crying. But it's the little everyday moments—the smaller sadnesses—that still come as a shock. Wanting to message Rob when one of the kids says something funny. Or when she gets a haircut. Paul notices—but does he care? Does he care in the same way Rob cared?

The other thing she didn't expect was an absence of fear. When she's not sobbing on the edge of her bed, she's sedated. Nothing scares her anymore because nothing at all could be worse than this. The days are now empty boxes, looking the same from the outside, but meaningless inside. There are some days when she shakes her head, certain she's living in a nightmare. This must be her punishment. Nights home alone with Paul are still the hardest. She tries to focus on what she does have—a beautiful home, a husband who loves her, and three kids whom she wouldn't give up for anything in the world. His clothes, his skin, his morning coffee, it all smells like home. But she'd be lying if she didn't admit that sometimes she wonders if home is where she most wants to be.

They still message sometimes, but with a forced formality that makes their conversations stiff. He asks about the kids. She asks about Charlotte, who she's convinced will be pregnant in no time. He says things are good. He misses Australia. Charlotte knows what happened between them, he tells her late one night. Apparently, she had a feeling. She isn't so comfortable with their friendship anymore. They won't be having dinner with her and Paul during their next trip to Australia. It wouldn't be appropriate.

She realizes that while she loved being in love, she hated being in an affair. It made her bad. It made Rob's life small and lonely. They both resented who they had become. That's not how love is meant to be, is it?

She's disgusted with herself, trapped in dirty skin she wishes she could tear off. Rob must be left with the most awful images of her, the dents on her thighs and the surgical scar on her soft, round stomach. He must laugh at how revolting she was, how her skin creped around her neck. And then he must turn to Charlotte, who always smells fresh and expensive, and marvel at her perfect body.

Most people move on from heartbreak by finding someone new to love—or at least leaning into the possibility. But there's no excitement or discovery waiting for Ana. She doesn't get to dream about a man who looks at her the way Rob once did. She doesn't get to long for the butterflies, or wonder what new parts of herself she'll find. The end of her relationship with Rob feels like going backward rather than forward.

And it's not just the Rob she loved she finds herself mourning. She misses the Rob she liked. The best friend of thirty years who was like an uncle to her kids and sent her funny pictures he found on the internet. She misses the simplicity and purity of it. With every interaction they have, their friendship fades away a little more. She knows she'll never get that back.

Sometimes she wonders if she would have been enough for Rob. A man who always wanted more. Who moved to Sri Lanka because Australia wasn't enough and who spends most of his time with people richer than he is. Who are more powerful than he is. As though he's trying to leave something behind. Paul isn't perfect. He's a man who has been happy with moderate success, who has done practically everything that was expected of him but nothing more, but he is home. And she will always be enough for him.

She stares at him across the dinner table—a white fleck of potato is hanging from his bottom lip—and she realizes you can love two people at once. In two different ways. They don't tell you that in novels. They don't warn you that sometimes the story ends partway through chapter fifteen, with loose ends and plot holes and characters unredeemed. Sometimes you end up with the wrong man and you work to make him the right one. And while you do, your heart does not slowly mend itself but breaks a little more in every moment of every day.

This man—the best parts of which run through the veins of their children—is good. Too good to hurt. He doesn't deserve what she did to him, and no part of her is compelled to confess. Her conscience does not deserve to be cleared. She is not worthy of forgiveness. This way, Paul never needs to know. There are moments when she can convince herself it never happened.

As she looks up at Paul, trying not to think of Rob, she dares to ask herself if it is possible to talk oneself out of a feeling. To reason with a feeling.

And two years after that first kiss, she loves Rob as much as she always did.

She loves him when she watches a movie. She loves him when she listens to music, so she doesn't listen to music anymore. She loves him in her sleep and she loves him when it rains. She loves him when she sees train tracks. She loves him when she drives past Hyatt House or Kings Park. She loves him when she sits on an airplane. She loves him when she smells the salt of the beach or hears the song he danced to at his wedding. She loves him when the house is empty and she loves him when her phone rings. She loves him even when she tries to hate him.

Every day she finds him in places she doesn't expect and wonders if there is anywhere he isn't.

At night, she feels like she's suffocating. All that love has nowhere to go. And so she wipes her eyes and rolls over to the person she has. She shuffles over and puts her arm around him, kisses his bare shoulder.

"Love you," he mumbles, grasping her hand.

"I love you too, Paul," she says, and tonight, like every night to come, she means it.

Patrick

❧

I'T'S EARLY MAY, AND TODAY BROUGHT WITH IT THE FIRST
hint that winter is around the corner. There was no warm tickle to
the wind. As they'd walked around the bay, he had felt the coolness
biting at his bones, drying out his lungs with every breath.

Now they're back at his place in Erskineville. It was renovated
right before he moved in, so the kitchen is brand-new with a marble
benchtop and high steel taps. A gas heater sits in the corner of the
living room, but it takes a solid hour to warm up just downstairs.
Her head is resting on his lap, a thick woolen blanket covering the

rest of her body. His two roommates are out tonight at a gig on King Street, so it's just them, watching a documentary that he's pretending to be more interested in than he is.

He looks down at the side of her face, eyes focused on the flat screen in front of them. Whatever he feels, he can't name it. With her here, the loneliness has abated. There's comfort. He doesn't think so much or cry into his pillow late at night. But there's also something not quite right. Looking at her feels like discovering the picture on the wall is hung slightly crooked. He tries to readjust the frame. Tilt his head to the left. But nothing does the trick.

She wriggles onto her back and smiles up at him. Her brown hair falls back off her face—if he saw a picture of this person he'd immediately think she was beautiful. Hot. Sexy, even. But the scene feels wrong.

"What are you thinking about?" She rests her hand under her head and her mouth draws into a straight line. He knows that look.

"You." It's half-true.

She sits up and kisses him. His body responds like it should. He wants her so badly. A hand finds the outline of his erection and strokes it, before pushing itself into his pants. At first it's a little uncomfortable. "Slow down," he whispers, and when she does it feels good. Really good. They move upstairs into his bedroom and she sits on top of him. He groans her name.

"Sophie."

When he finishes, he lies back and has a desperate urge to fall asleep. He can't, though. That would be rude. She curls up to him and it's suffocating. He should probably ask if she came. She acted like she did, but it all felt a bit performed. A bit quick. She probably didn't. He closes his eyes and hopes she will sleep. Or leave.

"That was amazing." She's panting. Why do they have to talk

about the sex every time they have it? There's not much to say. Sex is sex and now he's tired. Her cheek shifts and he knows she's looking up at him. He kisses the top of her head. Maybe that will give her the hint that he doesn't feel like talking.

He hears her tongue click in a way that tells him she's preparing to say something. "Sorry for being weird . . . but just thought I'd ask. How long were you with your ex-girlfriend—your fiancée—for?"

He tries not to flinch. They've not spoken about Caitlin. She must've seen her on Instagram or Facebook or something. It's clear she's been sitting on this question for a few weeks, if not the whole two months they've been dating. He scratches his head and tells her about six years. Engaged for six months. They broke up at the end of last year. November maybe. Obviously not meant to be. He rubs his eyes. Doesn't want to talk about this.

"And . . ." Sophie's voice is soft. "Did she end it?"

"Yep," he says. He explains he was a bit blindsided. It feels wrong to be talking about Caitlin while lying naked next to another woman. He wonders whether Caitlin has spoken about him with Josh after sex. It still makes him feel sick.

"I'm sorry . . ." She tries to make it sound sincere. "Do you think . . . do you think you're over it?"

No. He's not. He's still hanging on to remnants of a friendship because life without her is not livable. They work together. He can tell when she's approaching, just by the way her silver bracelets rattle. It's the idea of her, rather than the real her, that he can't let go of. But the world keeps spinning and people ask whether he's tried Hinge and are sure not to bring up the new guy in Caitlin's Instagram stories, as if any of this is normal.

Not long after the phone call from Caitlin in Perth, he'd received a message from Josh—he had wanted to meet up. Talk. After being back in Sydney for a few days, Patrick had agreed. He didn't know why. Maybe he'd wanted to shout at him. Or had thought that if Josh saw his face, he wouldn't be able to continue things with Caitlin. Or maybe Josh even asking to meet up had been a welcome reminder that someone actually saw him. That he wasn't completely invisible.

They'd met at a café in Erskineville. He'd been in the process of moving. As he'd walked up to Josh, sitting there on a stool outside in the sun, he'd had just one thought. *I like this guy.* Always had. And the fact that Josh was now fucking Caitlin didn't change that. Patrick could convince himself he hated him from the confines of his bedroom, where he could torture himself with scenes he'd invented. But that had changed when he'd looked Josh in the eye. He liked the way Josh spoke. Had forgotten how funny he was. *I understand why she likes him.* Who was he to prevent a relationship between two people who wanted to be together?

So now he is friendly with them both. What keeps him up at night isn't hate or anger but an overwhelming sense that he lost. Josh won. It makes him want to be someone other than himself. It doesn't matter that Sophie appears to like him. It's not her opinion that matters.

"Good question," he says. He can't be bothered to lie. "Probably not. Don't think I'll ever be. Six years is just a long time . . ."

Silence. She moves away from him so their bodies are no longer touching.

"Do you wish you were still with her?" Her voice feigns a light curiosity.

"No . . . it's not like that," he says, trying to convince himself as much as her. Then the words come out just as he's thinking them. What they had they can't get back. Maybe it was never right. The Caitlin of now isn't a person he wants anymore. He wants the Caitlin of five years ago and she doesn't exist.

Some days he believes there were parts of their relationship that never worked. He's found himself saying she was always high-strung and her career was always going to come first. People nod. They'd stopped really seeing each other—had become as used to the other as their own reflection. The thought had crossed his mind when he'd proposed to Caitlin that he had no one to compare her to. Was this it? Would he die only having had one real relationship? But perhaps his brain was playing tricks on him. Finding things in his past to justify the present, as though he had any agency in it whatsoever.

There are things he's discovered about himself. If his life was a house, Caitlin was once every brick. A structure built around him without his noticing until it was finished. Then it collapsed. He's having to build it back—one brick is his running, another his roommates. Sometimes he discovers gaps he wasn't expecting and finds something new to fill them with, like a friend he's neglected or an Xbox game she'd have rolled her eyes at. Whatever is being built will hopefully be more to his taste, without compromise.

"You know what the hardest part of the whole thing actually was?" He turns to her, holding his head up with his hand. "The day I realized I didn't want her anymore. That's when all hope was lost. Because no matter what, if she changes her mind or if circumstances change, none of that matters. Because I don't want it."

It was the hardest part but also the most freeing. He feels like he'd once had plans every night for the rest of his life and suddenly they were all canceled. He's not even sure he wants to be in Australia anymore. Maybe he'll move to the United States and work in software development. Or a different industry entirely.

"Yeah, I think I understand that," she says, reaching out and putting her hand around his wrist.

He kisses her hand and she smiles for a moment, before silently sliding herself out from under the sheets and pulling on her jeans. The room is black and cold. He can barely see her silhouette. A voice then comes from over near the door.

"See ya," she says, tiptoeing into the hallway and gently making her way down the stairs. He doesn't move. He knows he won't see her again.

And as he lies on his back staring up into the darkness, he realizes he feels nothing.

Claire

The next few months go by in a fog.

At one point, she sends a barrage of messages to Maggie late at night, demanding she tell her exactly what happened with Tiff. Trying to convince her that at the very least she deserved closure—even though she knew there would never be any such thing. Maggie had responded, saying she had never cheated. She'd never been in a relationship with Tiff, nothing had ever happened. And then Maggie had blocked her number.

Then there was the night she went to pick up a pad thai from down the road. Her parents had been out. She hadn't eaten all day. It had been days since she'd looked in the mirror, but she knew her eyes were dark and sunken, her hair knotted and greasy. She'd worn what she'd slept in—a jumper and tracksuit pants, a pair of Ugg boots pulled on before she left the house. She couldn't remember if she'd brushed her teeth. Probably not. They'd felt furry. She'd pulled up outside the restaurant and as she'd slammed the driver's-side door, she noticed the seat belt had become stuck. With a grunt, she'd yanked the door open again, tossed the belt in, and then proceeded to shut the door closed on her thumb. This shit was constantly happening to her. The big pain was compounded by a series of small pains, because she was Claire and life was playing an elaborate game called Just When You Thought Things Couldn't Get Any Worse, Guess What?

She'd sworn and her eyes tingled. Suddenly she had lost her appetite and wished she was at home in the dark, but she was already here and she could see an order that was probably hers sitting on the counter, waiting to be picked up. Her head had been down when she'd heard it. The accent. Voice deep for a woman. It was like how you can hear your own name from the other side of an open-plan office. She had just been able to catch the end of her words, which had been spoken to a person right beside her. Instinctively, she'd turned to her right, sure she had imagined it. But walking from the other direction toward the restaurant had been Maggie. And Tiff, walking close enough to her that she could have been Maggie's shadow. Maggie's expression had dropped when she'd seen Claire. There had been no warmth in her eyes. Just fear. Maybe some disdain. And maybe, just maybe, a hint of pity.

Claire had hurried in, grabbed the bag, and nearly forgot to pay. Someone was shouting at her and she couldn't understand. Pay. You need to pay. So she'd paid, muttered, "Sorry, yeah, thanks, sorry," and then slid back out the door, wishing she could choose to disappear. It had *not* been how Maggie was meant to see her. Her hands had been shaking as they'd gripped the steering wheel and she'd only gotten to the end of the street before she'd stopped in silence. She'd rested her forehead against the wheel, closing her eyes as though that would somehow block out the images of Maggie and Tiff driving home with Thai in their laps. Then discussing whether or not they needed bowls. Then cuddling up beside each other on the couch to talk and laugh and touch and fall asleep knowing that someone loved them.

After that, Claire had stopped leaving the house. Toowoomba was too small. Whispers had spread that Maggie was now living with Tiff's family, who were under the impression the two were good friends.

"How can they be that stupid?" she'd said to Lauren one night on the phone.

She'd replied, "Hang on, I'm going to send you a photo." When Claire's phone pinged, she had stared at the photo in disbelief.

It was Maggie. In a dress cut just above the knee. Her chocolate-brown hair was straight and to her shoulders, smokiness framing her small blue eyes. She was standing with a group of women, Tiff included, who looked like they'd spent a Saturday afternoon at Grand Central Shopping Centre buying whatever was in the display windows. Maggie didn't even know how to stand in a dress. Her athletic calves were positioned awkwardly and her narrow hips and broad shoulders were exaggerated by a dress so clearly designed to do the opposite. The whole look was incongruent.

She'd brought the phone back to her ear and told Lauren about a charity event Maggie had been a part of in London. One of her clients had been diagnosed with brain cancer, and in order to raise money for research, Maggie had put up flyers around the gym that said: "If I raise £1000 for brain cancer research, I'll put on a dress." For Maggie, it was far more daring than running a marathon or shaving her head. Committing to wearing a dress—which also included getting her makeup and hair done—was the most outrageous pledge she could make. Claire had been beside her at the function night a few months later, clapping like she was at a circus, when Maggie had emerged onstage in a hired ballgown, with the stiffness and self-consciousness of a pet who has been dressed up against its will.

And yet now Maggie was voluntarily dressing like a woman. Claire had revisited the photo—a screenshot from Maggie's Instagram account—several times over the next few days. She'd stared at Maggie's face. Had she really known her at all? Had parts of Maggie always been figments of her imagination? What did it mean if someone could metamorphose so quickly, forging an entirely new identity, reflecting back whatever their partner desired?

She'd said to her mother one night that it would actually have been easier if Maggie had died. In all honesty, she wished she was dead. At least then it wouldn't be possible to run into her. People might more easily understand her grief. There's a victimhood in losing your wife that appealed to Claire. And that felt true. To be broken up with in life, rather than deserted by death, brought with it a grief indistinguishable from self-loathing. She hated herself so completely that it was all she could think about. Her face. Her hands. Her voice. She had no hobbies or real beliefs. There would be more dignity in her position if she could stand up tall and say, "I deserve better than Maggie." But the problem was, deep down she knew she didn't. Maggie was better than her and that's why she'd left. She'd moved up, and if Claire ever dated again, she'd inevitably move down.

Her mother gently suggested over dinner one night that Maggie might have been a little controlling.

"Did you ever feel that?" she asked, almost in a whisper.

Claire didn't react, but her mind delivered her a flash of an Irregular Choice shopping bag, and how ashamed she'd felt sliding it across the counter at the confused sales assistant. Maybe she had been.

Weeks pass and then months. She starts studying for a diploma of education, mostly so she has an answer when people ask what she's doing. And why she isn't working. She buys self-help books with the money that's left in her bank account. She does what the experts say. Deletes all the messages. Doesn't attempt contact. She throws out all the reminders and bins all photographs of the two of them. She downloads apps that send her positive affirmations. The notes on her phone fill with quotes about self-love and why a breakup is the best thing that will ever happen to you. She follows Facebook and Instagram accounts dedicated to personal growth. She meditates and journals and says to the mirror, "I am okay, I am over it," but the person staring back at her knows that isn't the truth.

Saturday nights become the saddest of all. When you're in a relationship, you don't need plans. The plans are always already there. The things you need in order to be human—from conversation to touch to sex—are features of everyday life. When she finally changes her relationship status on Facebook from married to single and has to click a button to confirm the change, she is aghast. This is more than a box you tick. She is selecting a lower quality of life. One where no one chose to love her. No, she doesn't *want* to save changes. But for six months not one minute of her life had resembled anything she wanted.

She's on the toilet when she downloads Tinder. It feels like opening the fridge when you're not hungry, just to see what's inside. But often once you open it, you find yourself reaching for something anyway, satisfying a desire you can't quite identify. She uses three photos that look least like her, so any compliments she receives will belong to a woman who doesn't exist. When the app prompts her to select whether she is interested in men or women or both, she hovers over the button for some time before clicking on "Both"—not because she is, but because it feels like a way to delay a decision. It almost feels like catfishing, except through angles and filters and lighting.

The pool of lesbians in Toowoomba—let alone lesbians she is even moderately attracted to—is even shallower than she'd anticipated. In the end, she mostly speaks to men. Men seem less scary. Like maybe they won't break her heart. So men it is.

Conversations are opened and questions are asked, but she quickly realizes she doesn't have all that much to say. No rich inner world another person might be mesmerized by. She is a two-dimensional person in a world full of three-dimensional people. Boring. Empty. Flat. When a guy named Amir pushes her to meet up one weekend, she deactivates the app. She knows she won't be able to handle the way his face falls when he lays eyes on her in real life.

Instead, she starts to go out with Lauren and Pia. She drinks until she forgets who she is. She makes eye contact with a man standing beside her at the bar but he quickly averts his gaze. The whole thing is humiliating.

One Saturday night, she's in the corner of the Spotted Cow Hotel with one of Pia's friends, Huw, and he leans in and asks what she's doing tomorrow. Before that moment, she'd never even considered being interested in him. His breath smells sour and his forehead is too big for his face, but he's warm and kind and maybe in order to not be lonely she has to adjust to a future that looks like

Huw. He buys her a drink and she asks about his work. She talks about studying and he doesn't seem bored by it. They laugh a few times. For an hour, she doesn't feel alone. Someone sees her. His hand brushes her knee at one point and she's suddenly reminded that she has a knee. She drinks too much and calls her mum crying in the early hours of the morning, asking if she can pick her up. She does. But they don't speak in the car.

When she wakes around lunchtime the next day, something pierces through her numbness. Huw. She wonders if he's thinking about her. Imagining how she spends her Sundays, placing himself beside her and playing with how that might feel. She wants to ask him if he thinks she's pretty. Or funny. Or clever. Actually, she doesn't want to ask. She just wants him to say all of those things. To be told by someone else who she is, so she can be reminded.

By the evening she's numb again so types out a Facebook message, her fingers seemingly having a mind of their own as they dance across the keyboard. "Hey," she writes. "Just wondering if you wanted to go out to dinner this week or something. X." An hour passes. Then another. He's out. Or his phone is dead. Or he doesn't want to look too interested so will probably just wait until the morning.

By the next day, still nothing. She checks whether it sent. He's been on Facebook. Instagram. She writes in the journal with the polka-dot cover she keeps under her bed: "Did I just get rejected by someone I didn't even want?"

She plays games. Seeing how long she can go without looking at her phone. Leaving it in her bedroom. Then switching it to airplane mode. But after every break, it only becomes more agonizing to press the home button and see an empty beach staring back at her.

The smell of roast potatoes is wafting through the air when her phone vibrates. It's him. "Ah! Sorry, Claire. Must have missed this.

I just see you as a friend. I really like you and wouldn't want to mess the friendship up. Does that make sense?" And so came the feeling of pressing on a bruise.

"I thought I was done with this shit," she writes in her journal. "I spent the last five years letting myself go because I thought the race was over. I want to skip over this stage. The part where you stand in front of a stranger and look at them and say, 'What do you reckon?' gesturing to who you are and they say, 'No, thanks,' and reject all of it. The face you've had your whole life and are stuck with. Your body. Your memories and the way you tell stories and how you spend your time. It's just a no. Not even a maybe. They're sure.

"I'm exhausted. I want to fast-forward and find myself three years into a relationship, where I'm not doing this bullshit dance, holding my breath every time they learn something new about me. I want to skip the part where we both have to pretend we're not human, putting on this mask and waiting to see if it's safe to pull it off. Every day I wake up and think, I cannot believe I am starting again."

After Huw there's Jordan. And Nathan. And with each, she asks for too much. A date. A phone call. Some sort of validation that makes her sound needy, mostly because she is needy. And she learns that nothing turns someone off more than learning that the person you're sleeping with once a week after too many drinks needs something from you.

The sex is mechanical. Sometimes painful. Her body is always cold. She floats above herself and watches from the ceiling, making sure she makes the right sounds and moves her head as she should, never making eye contact for too long. They don't like that. They like it when she turns over and they can pretend she's anyone else. *It's funny*, she thinks, *how something so intimate—your bodies couldn't be closer—can be so unerotic.* She feels nothing when they whisper in her ear or spit on their fingers, moving her around like a pillow that's never in the right position. Afterward, she waits a little while. Each time she thinks they might roll over and say something. Tell her she's sexy. But they never do. So once the room has fallen silent and they drift off to sleep, she gathers her strewn things from the floor and pulls them back on in the dark. She wants to be in her own bed, where she expects nothing of anyone.

Pia's hosting a party at her place and even though it's seven o'clock at night, Claire still has the bleariness of a hangover from the night before. Her voice is croaky and shame has been stirring in her stomach all day, delivering flashes of memory. She'd been at the Spotted Cow again. There's a guy she often sees there and after several drinks, she'd tapped him on the arse on her way to the bathroom. Every time the incident replays, she squints her eyes closed and shakes her head, wishing it away. She hates herself.

The more white wine she drinks, the more she forgets what happened last night. It's freeing. She sits on the sofa in the back room waiting for someone to join her. Eventually, a guy named Joey sits down. He asks how she knows Pia. She explains, looking into his big blue eyes, sprinkled with flecks of yellow. He's an electrician. His forearms are tanned, covered in a layer of blond hair. She spots a number of tiny white scars and asks him one by one where they came from. Every second story he tells her is made up, and she wipes tears from her eyes, laughing so hard she needs to pee. She excuses herself for a moment to go to the bathroom.

Please don't let this go wrong, she pleads silently to God knows who, taking a deep breath. *I can't take one more rejection. My self-esteem can't take it. Let this person like me back. Please. Give me what Maggie has.*

She makes her way back out to the lounge and tops up her glass. They talk about London. The course she just dropped out of. His staffy. She lets herself lean in. Ask questions. Hope. She lets herself hope.

It's only when Pia walks past the doorway with a garbage bag that they realize the party's over. They didn't even notice the chatter die down and the music stop. They mumble thank-yous to her and stumble out the front.

Joey pulls out his phone to call a cab.

"So, Joey." She can taste the dryness of wine on her tongue. "My parents are away. Do you want to come and hang out at mine for a bit? It's ten minutes that way." She points down the street. Realistically, it's more like twenty.

He looks up from his phone and raises his eyebrows. Stares at her for a moment. "Oh shit, Claire. I didn't mean to lead you on if that's what you thought this was." All she wants is for him to stop speaking. "I'm sure ninety-nine percent of guys would take you up on that offer. But I'm not going to. There's a girl . . . things are complicated." He puts his arms around her and says, "I'm sure I'll see you soon. Get home safe."

And with that, she turns around and walks home alone in the dark, the sound of her heavy sobs echoing through the empty streets of Toowoomba.

Epilogue

ஃ

AND THEY MIGHT HAVE CROSSED PATHS.

They might have walked past each other in airport terminals.
A woman in her forties, a woman in her thirties, and a man in his
twenties might have all decided to holiday by the same beach, leaving footsteps in the same stretch of sand. They might have visited
the same crowded café on a Saturday morning, full of people sitting
up straighter than they were, couples and gurgling babies and families, all symbols of love functioning as it should.

And Ana would drag her eyes away from the couple at the next table and focus on her three children. Life is not about what could have been, but rather what is. And Louis would flash her a grin, the right side of his mouth rising higher than the left, just like his father's does. It's a smile she wouldn't trade for anything. She doesn't see the way the man puts his arm around his girlfriend and kisses her on the side of the head, whispering something into her ear.

But Patrick would. He would wonder whether that exists in his future or only in his past. How does someone get that back? Is it a curse to want it too badly? He'll check his phone to see if the girl he's speaking to has replied yet. She will have. Maybe he feels something. His friends start pulling out their chairs, ready to walk down to the beach. And he remembers that fun things exist outside of her. Because while she was the common denominator in all his happiest memories, so was he. He was there too.

Claire wouldn't see any of this, her head behind a laptop screen, the words coming faster than she can catch them. She'd be away with friends but would've taken the morning for herself. She's writing a one-woman play about what happened with Maggie. It makes her feel like she's rediscovered a part of herself she lost for a while. "Art helps when love has failed us," Alain de Botton says. She has found that to be true.

The three would likely not have done more than smile at one another politely. But if they'd spoken—asked questions beyond the rudimentary—they would have learned that the roots of their suffering grow from the same soil. That their loneliness binds them rather than isolates them.

And isn't that the ultimate irony? That nothing makes us more human, more united with every person and every culture in every period of history, than the very emotion that tells us: I am all alone.

On Romantic
Rejection

~

*T*HERE'S A BLACK LEATHER BOOK THAT LIVES UNDER MY bed and I write in it when I hate myself.

Many of the pages are filled with thoughts I had following romantic rejection. I've never let anyone read them before. The words aren't poetic or especially insightful. They don't possess any supreme wisdom.

There's a page that has a lot of capital letters. It shouts, "I AM IN PHYSICAL PAIN AND HAVE BEEN ALL DAY. I CANNOT <u>CONTROL</u> THIS SITUATION. ALL DAY HAS BEEN WAITING. I FUCKING HATE WAITING."

I told you it wasn't very profound.

The following page reads: "Do not do this again. It is not worth it. It never is. Why can't this happen for me? It is all that matters. It took such guts. And I haven't recovered. I never do. It always still hurts. I am always still angry. What is it about me?"

If these sound like the ramblings of a mad person, it is because they absolutely are the ramblings of a mad person. I keep shouting at the page, "PLEASE MAKE SENSE," as though it will speak back, revealing something I'd missed.

The pages get worse. I decide to embark on a list of "Things That Went Wrong" that might explain why this person, let's call him Joshua, decided to leave me. They include:

He wasn't attracted to me
He didn't like my body
His friends didn't like me
I was too clingy
He resented paying for dinner
He saw my anxiety and lack of confidence
Maybe I drank too much

I also have specific details about conversations we'd had that I figured could've turned him off me. Questions I asked that might have been inappropriate. I am approaching him—or us—like a test I failed, and I'm hoping to identify the errors so I know what mistakes not to repeat next time.

But that list, unsurprisingly, does not make me feel better. I decide instead that the error is much simpler. It's me. I am the error.

When you are romantically rejected, the thing that seems to have failed is the very essence of you. You reason that perhaps they saw you as a pool of water they didn't especially want to dive into. The world beneath the surface didn't look inviting. They weren't convinced they'd see themselves when they reached the bottom.

You find yourself obsessing over how your nose casts a shadow over your top lip. Or the ratio of your breasts to your bottom or the way your stomach jiggles when you walk. But it penetrates deeper than that. It feels as though it must be the experiences you've collected and the decisions you've made and the family you come from and the way your mind has you formulate sentences.

The British writer and poet Warsan Shire said, "I won't glorify or romanticize heartbreak, for me it was a kind of death and I was forced to keep living." As dramatic as it might sound, it does feel as though our future has been erased. Every heartbreak we experience represents an unlived life. A road that turned into a cliff and we're shaken and bruised, reeling from the shock of being thrown from a path we trusted.

This seems to me like a reality we're not taking seriously enough.

I can tell you that all of this is an evolutionary response. That romantic rejection is a form of exile—and when humans are banished from the tribe, they die. That love releases chemicals with fancy names and they're addictive and when you're deprived of them, you go into withdrawal. That it's normal to feel like you'd do just about anything to have another hit. I can tell you that your muscles swell and your neck stiffens and—you're not imagining it—it really does feel like your chest is being squeezed by a single unrelenting hand.

But does putting an explanation around a feeling change how much it hurts? Does it feel any less personal?

A year into a project about heartbreak, I can tell you it doesn't.

I'm also going to tell you something that isn't new but has been forgotten in a culture that is both intolerant and impatient when it comes to emotional discomfort.

There are people you know—perhaps you are one of them—harboring romantic wounds, both fresh and old, who are not okay. And not the kind of not okay that can be fixed with an inspirational quote or by downloading a dating app. Studies from all over the world have found that one of the leading risk factors for suicide, particularly in men, is relationship breakdowns. According to the Centers for Disease Control and Prevention (CDC), "intimate partner problems" is the most significant single risk factor for suicide in men under thirty. In 2003, Dr. Augustine Kposowa, a sociologist at the University of California, Riverside, found that divorced men were nine times more likely to die by suicide than divorced women. A study by the University of Ulster in 2013 found that up to seventy-eight percent of the deceased they followed up on had experienced relationship difficulties or a breakup in the period prior to death. That's almost four in five.

In multiple studies it has been determined that the ending of a relationship is the "most common concern" associated with suicidality in adolescents. The problem is that these breakups are often seen to be trivial and meaningless by parents and peers, and therefore critical warning signs are missed.

Our cultural response to heartbreak is vastly insufficient. We say things like "It wasn't meant to be" or "Everything happens for a reason" or "There's plenty of fish in the sea" or "Time heals all wounds," all of which mean nothing, some of which aren't even moderately true, and the last of which sends the message, "I'll let you get on with it then."

Heartbreak does not seem to be a brand of grief we respect.

And so we are left in the middle of the ocean, floating in a dinghy with no anchor, while the world waits for us to be okay again.

Women do what the movies tell us to. We eat ice cream and cry to our friends and wait for our very own montage, where we put the pieces of our shattered selves back together in thirty-five seconds, color our hair, and lose five kilos. It's a flawed script. But at least it's a script.

Men have no blueprint for how they're supposed to behave. No vocabulary for the pain they feel in their bodies. Women at least have been conditioned since childhood to understand that eventually they will have their hearts broken. It comes as more of a surprise to men. A dagger to the heart they don't expect to hurt so much.

And we wonder why a relationship breakdown is a risk factor for suicide in men. Perhaps it's because they endure something exceptionally painful and have no words at their disposal to express it.

This book is an attempt to offer a vocabulary. To put words around the unsaid, so they may be used by people who most need them. To position heartbreak as something that belongs to men too. It belongs to anyone who takes one of the biggest risks we ever take—falling in love.

We trivialize discussions around whether to delete an ex-lover from our social media circles or whether to throw all of their things in a box and leave it on their doorstep. But these are our desperate attempts to design a ritual around a significant life event that lacks any. When someone dies, we gather at a funeral. We wear black and might watch as a casket that looks both too big and too small is lowered into the ground. Rituals are markers of time. They give structure around the structureless. Graduations and weddings and farewells and birthday parties announce to the world: this is a thing that matters. They formalize that one chapter has ended and another is about to begin. There isn't a culture on earth that exists without ritual. It is fundamental to who we are as human beings.

And yet we have no rite of passage when it comes to the ending of a significant relationship. We do not get to write a eulogy or throw a bouquet. We must, to some extent, make up our own.

In West Africa, they do. Specifically, the country of Burkina Faso. The teacher and author Sobonfu Somé writes about a ritual of grief designed to purge oneself of hurt and pain, particularly after the loss of a significant relationship. It's understood that the denial of emotion, the act of declaring "I'm fine" when you're not, can result in a kind of spiritual drought, which gives way to emotional confusion and even certain illnesses. The idea is to keep the grief moving, to do something with it, rather than suppressing it so deeply that it calcifies.

Those involved in the ritual create a grief altar. Drumming and singing begin to fill the air, with everyone repeating the same chant, which roughly translates to "I cannot do it alone." No one is allowed to visit the altar unaccompanied, ask questions, or offer advice. The point is to bear witness. To hold space. People sob and moan and scream and stomp their feet and wrap their arms around each other.

In West Africa, this ritual takes place over seventy-two hours and occurs regularly. You do not have to announce why you are there. It is understood that grief is a way of surviving life and that a straight line can never be drawn beneath it.

So what do some of our rituals look like? Packing away their things. Deciding to cut contact, at least until the sharpness of the pain subsides. Writing a list of all the things you secretly always hated about them. But there's also something to be said for needing to sit in the mess for a while. That's what this book endeavors to do. To be a kind of grief ritual. The time and space we all need to fully feel and explore and not demand happiness of ourselves when we're so desperate to feel a little bit sad.

I suppose part of the ritual is also unpicking ourselves.

In the wake of my specific heartbreak, I wondered if I should quit my job. Do something more interesting. More noble. It's why we all cut our hair too short or decide now is the best time to get a full fringe. We hate our hair because we imagine they probably hated our hair. We buy clothes we wouldn't ordinarily wear and do our makeup slightly differently. They evolved beyond us and we want to evolve with them.

We live in a culture that tells us to self-examine. Obsess ourselves with self-improvement. Do better. Be better. Find fault and eliminate it. Don't start next week when you could start today. And what's the common denominator in all your failings? You are. If this were a science experiment, you'd be the control variable. You are the thing around which your world revolves and therefore everything that happens in your world is a reflection of you. A manifestation of you.

But of course this isn't, logically, the case. I sat in front of a psychologist once and listed off all my romantic failings, explaining to her that I was the constant. What was more likely—that there was something wrong with the last six men I'd dated or that there was something wrong with me?

She paused and two lines appeared between her eyebrows.

"To me," she said, "it just sounds like you've had a string of bad luck."

In all my analysis, I had never considered the role of luck. Sometimes, though, awful things just happen. We can do our best to find meaning in them and decide how we're going to respond. But to believe rejection is entirely about us is to overestimate the role we play in anything. There are dozens of variables that come together in a relationship. Timing. Emotional maturity. Anxieties. Different priorities. A lot of people are unaware that the experience of love is meant to change. We go from a period of infatuation, when we can't keep our hands off each other, to companionate love. No relationship can sustain butterflies for a lifetime. No relationship is meant to. And so, many relationships fall apart during that transition, when sex and passion give way to friendship and commitment. It might take someone several relationships to learn that infatuation always passes. Or they might decide they never want it to pass, and so they jump from one relationship to the next, never letting their feet quite land on the ground. That's not the fault of the person they reject, although I bet for a while it feels like it is.

The author of the 2012 novel *Truly, Madly, Deeply*, Faraaz Kazi, says, "The most difficult aspect of moving on is accepting that the other person already did." As we are thrown against our will into the cataclysmic disaster that is heartbreak, we know just how hard it is to move on from someone. That chaos is perfectly juxtaposed with the other person's order—their lives operating as they always have. We call in sick and they go to work. We retreat to corners of the house where no one will find us. They get on a plane to Ibiza. Crippled by our own passion, we become acutely aware of just how indifferent this person is toward us. We can't understand how they tucked everything they once felt for us away into a back pocket and forgot about it. As though it never existed. We keep fantasizing that they'll find their old pair of jeans and pull them on, only to rediscover that feeling they'd misplaced.

What I've discovered through the process of working on this book is that you cannot write about heartbreak without first writing about love. The former does not exist without the latter.

Joshua and I met through a friend. Our first date was at a saloon-style hipster bar in Newtown he'd suggested and I pretended I'd heard of when I hadn't. I wore red lipstick but wiped it off on the train, deciding it was too much. I was late and he was sitting with his back toward me when I walked in. There were lamps hanging from the walls illuminating every table that softened our faces and made our eyes look colorless. I told him stories about the school I was working at that made me sound as though I was a good teacher. He was a musician, which made me look at him differently. Like he could access a world I couldn't.

Alain de Botton writes in *Essays in Love*, "Perhaps it is true that we do not really exist until there is someone there to see us existing, we cannot properly speak until there is someone to understand what we are saying, in essence, we are not wholly alive until we are loved." I did not know what my life looked like at twenty-four until I had him to perform it to. He forced me to construct a narrative in which my life was wonderful. The kind of life you'd want to get closer to. It was an experience I very much enjoyed, even if it was contrived and entirely for another person's consumption. As we messaged back and forth, I began to wonder: does a student of mine even say something funny if there is no Joshua for me to recount it to?

And so we met again and I behaved like my week had been full of things that weren't him. I became the person he saw me as. It was as though every moment we spent together he was composing a sketch and I was contorting myself to fit inside the lines. Falling in love is an exercise in narcissism as much as it is anything else. I liked him. But it was the person I saw reflected in his eyes I became most addicted to. She began to look more beautiful. She was funny and clever and suddenly her life was this quirky screenplay with interesting characters and subplots. This protagonist, with her eyes and her hair and her laugh, was lovable. She had idiosyncrasies that were accidentally lovely. But the problem with lovers is that we're not seeing a person but an illusion, and then we try to live up to those illusions only to discover we're too human.

Everything I'd done up until that point, I decided, was in preparation to meet him. Every country I'd visited and every subject I'd studied. The time I put my shoes in the microwave as a three-year-old and then called out to my mother because there were sparks flying everywhere only happened so that I as an adult could tell him about it. I told my family about him. My friends.

Paula Boock writes in *Dare Truth or Promise*, "'I'm in love...' she said out loud in amazement, because she knew that this was a life-changing thing and life-changing things should be said aloud." The compulsion to shout my feelings from the rooftops wasn't figurative. I quite literally felt it necessary. Everyone should know because nothing more important had ever happened. I'd found my person. A significant other who made my life meaningful. The process of building a relationship is always inventing certain futures, and what lay ahead of us was too magnificent to put into words. Conversations under blankets in the dark and summer days with no shoes on and stopping on the side of the road to look up at the stars and listen to the silence of a cold Friday night.

"To love someone," David Levithan writes in *The Lover's Dictionary*, "is to live with the fear of who you will become without it." I lived in a state of perpetual terror.

That's why when it happens, it can feel like a nightmare. Because you've dreamed it. You've developed an obsession about it *not* happening. The only way to sleep and move moment to moment is to tell yourself it can't. That tomorrow will be the same as today. If we did not buy into that mythology, at least to an extent, we'd all go mad. The ground is constantly shifting beneath our feet but we like to pretend we're in control of the lever.

It was a Sunday afternoon and the sun was a little darker in the sky. My weekend had consisted of checking my phone and trying not to check my phone. We had been meant to go on a picnic on Saturday and I'd shaved my legs and washed my hair. But then he'd sent me a strange message asking what I was up to, and I had to try to communicate: *I'm currently free by a remarkable coincidence but if you're not then I'm not but if you are then so am I.* He'd said he was going out. I can't remember where. His message left me uneasy. I felt angry but didn't say so. I just didn't reply for a few hours and then asked what plans he had for the rest of the week.

But by Sunday afternoon, it had been twenty-four hours and I hadn't heard back. At one point, I'd considered calling. I just wanted him to *tell* me if this was over, so I could feel pure sadness rather than this sadness laced with hope, which is also known as anxiety. I couldn't sit still. One moment, I would decide things were absolutely fine and I was overreacting and I'd start planning where we'd go for dinner next week. The next moment, a tug in my stomach would tell me that nothing was fine, that he'd changed his mind about me, and that I'd never see him again.

And then came the phone call.

The pitch of his voice gave me the answer. He'd seen his ex-girlfriend. They wanted to try things again. I remember he said their relationship "deserved" that after how many years they'd been together. I listened quietly and tried not to cry. The part of me that still wanted him to like me said, "I understand," and I wished him, in a tone that sounded sincere, the best of luck. After I hung up, I cried myself sick.

"It is forbidden to love where we are not loved," Sharon Olds writes in the poem "Material Ode," published in her 2012 book *Stag's Leap*. In a single moment, the affection you feel for a person goes from being acceptable to pathetic. You're holding this enormous slab of concrete with nowhere to put it down. The other person seems to have broken a pact. The lover's contract. It was implied that neither person was allowed to change their mind.

I told my friends what had happened. I felt humiliated, as though I was confessing to them that I wasn't lovable after all. What I didn't tell them was what happened a few months later.

For days and then weeks, I became convinced the perfect person had slipped through my fingers. I thought about him when a student said something ridiculous at work, and I realized I had no one to tell. I thought about him when I walked my dog up Mons Street, not because he'd ever been with me when I walked my dog, but because I'd gotten into the habit of always thinking about him when I walked my dog up Mons Street.

Then, on a Friday night, he sent me a message.

It was casual. Maybe asking what I was up to. The high came back immediately. I replied and then he replied and said things had ended—for good this time—with his ex-girlfriend.

The universe owed me this. Two months of suffering had been worth it if it meant we'd end up together, this hiccup a funny little aside in our creation story.

But the messages became disjointed again. A plan was made for Saturday, but then on Saturday he behaved as though that conversation had never happened. He was free the following Friday but then over the course of the week became unfree and maybe that was my fault for not making it clear enough that I'd like to see him on Friday.

Then, finally, a Saturday afternoon came. We were meant to do something just us, but then his housemates were throwing a party and I didn't know whether that was an invite or a cancellation. He asked me to come. I wouldn't know anyone but him. But all I wanted was that feeling again. And I knew that if he just saw me, then all those feelings would come back and this would stop being so complicated.

I wore a red shirt, denim shorts, and white Vans. My sister dropped me off at his place in Newtown and when he met me at the door he looked different. Sadder. Distracted.

He brought me out into a courtyard and told half a dozen people my name. And then he left me there. I spoke to the guy sitting next to me, trying to make small talk with a stranger. They told stories about people I didn't know and I laughed when I thought I was meant to. Still, Joshua was gone.

I stood up, pretending I needed the bathroom but really just to see if he was still in the house. He was. Chatting to a friend in the kitchen.

"I wondered where you were," I said, smiling.

"I'm in here," he said. Not smiling.

I discovered that night that even harder than romantic rejection is spending time with a person who is not interested in you anymore. I also learned that heartbreak makes you do awful things to yourself. For three hours, he didn't look me in the eye. Didn't touch me. Didn't ask me a question. I examined myself in the bathroom mirror wondering if there was something awful smudged on my face. What had I done? How had I failed? Again?

With tightness in my throat, I told him I better go. I don't think he gave me a kiss on the cheek. He might've waved at the door. And as I walked down the street on a Saturday night, hot tears fell from my eyes. He had done it again. How could I have been so stupid?

To this day, when I drive past that street I once trudged down alone, I feel a stab in my chest. A jolt. A kind of romantic trauma.

But I also feel a hint of gratitude.

First, because it doesn't feel so bad anymore. I am grateful it is not that Saturday afternoon. That the sun has set and risen a number of times since.

And second, because it reminds me of a language I speak. A language I'm well versed in and never want to forget.

The more we allow ourselves to feel romantic rejection and let the grief pass through us, the better use we are to others. The language of heartbreak becomes a gift we are able to pass on from one person to another.

One thing I recognized in Ana, Patrick, and Claire was the profound sense of aloneness each of them felt in their grief. It felt for each of them like no one understood.

And there's some truth in that.

I found a line in my black leather book that reads: "It's impossible to recall a feeling after you have felt it. You are really only imagining it."

I'm not sure whom I thought I was speaking to. Perhaps my future self, writing this book. My past self was right. I don't feel the sharpness anymore. I can only imagine it. Since I wrote it, I've fallen in love again. The despair feels like a long way away.

But isn't that just the point?

That, as the poet Rainer Maria Rilke put it, "no feeling is final"?

The world is full of broken people who have put themselves back together.

Love is magic and heartbreak is the price we pay. If magic can strike once, it can and will strike again.

And the real magic happens when the person on the other end loves you back.

Acknowledgments

❦

I KEEP PUTTING OFF WRITING MY ACKNOWLEDGMENTS because every time I think about them there's another person I realize I want to thank.

To my publisher, Cate Blake. Thank you for believing in my idea and understanding it before I fully understood it. To Brianne Collins and Emma Rafferty at Pan Macmillan for taking such tremendous care with my manuscript. My primary insecurity came from not knowing how my messy words would turn into anything that resembled the books piled up next to my bed. The secret to how it did is Emma, Brianne, and Cate, who picked my work apart and told me that, sometimes, a stool is just a stool. Thank you for your honesty and for caring about my work as much as I do.

To my US agent, Daniel Lazar, who helped me find the perfect home for this book in the United States. To Serena Jones and the whole team at Henry Holt, who believed in this book and took a chance on a debut author. Thank you so, so much.

To my mum and dad, Anne and Peter, who asked how the book was going even though I'm sure the answer was really, really boring. Thank you to my brother Nick for his interest and my brother Jack for giving me potentially the best advice I got all year. It was to set a timer, and measure your progress based on minutes spent sitting in front of the laptop rather than on words on a page. Not sure I would have completed my book without that approach.

To my pop, Philip Stephens, for our lengthy chats during COVID lockdown. For telling me about that one time he had to write a manual at work and it was the worst six months of his life. Thanks for . . . understanding.

To my sister, Clare, for reading more than anyone else did, out of context and when she was in the middle of something else. Thank you for always being encouraging and giving me the motivational talk I needed when I know you really, really couldn't be fucked.

To my family at Mamamia. Ugh. You know I hate getting sentimental. To Mia Freedman, who gave me a chance when no one else would. To her and the team who invested in training me when they had way more interesting things to do. To Holly Wainwright, who has given me invaluable advice and shown me what's possible. It is because of her I believed I could write a book in a year while working full-time. Not sure whether I should thank you or yell at you for that. Thank you for our discussions on *Mamamia Out Loud* three times a week. And to our community of Out Louders who have cheered me on, sent me messages of encouragement, and some who are even "characters" in the book. Thank you for your enthusiasm and generosity.

Thank you to Jacqueline Lunn, who taught me more about writing than just about anyone else. To Elissa Ratliff, Keryn Donnelly, and Belinda Jepsen for the brainstorms and the creative inspiration. To my friends who have always spoken about heartbreak so openly and made me realize there was a book in this. To Andi, Hugh, Luke, Kim, Tai, Charlie, Ellie, Greta, Charlotte, Rory, Julieann, Kara, Lisa, Dani, Scott, another Lisa, Andrew, and all the other people I definitely forgot to name.

To the brilliant, inspiring Australian authors from whom I have learned everything. I have discovered that there are no people lovelier or more humble than writers, who are genuinely stoked whenever anyone tells them they've read their book. Thank you to all the authors who came on to my *Book Club* podcast, which was basically just a personal project to collect as much advice and wisdom as I possibly could. I was overwhelmed by their encouragement. Thank you to Trent Dalton, Sally Hepworth, Jane Harper, Peter Fitz-Simons, Richard Glover, Rick Morton, and Sophie Hardcastle for their guidance, but mostly for writing bloody incredible books that I picked up whenever I felt stuck.

And to my partner, Luca, who hasn't panicked (yet) that I wrote an entire book about heartbreak. I have discovered so much about what a bad relationship looks like since being in a wonderful one. Thank you for giving me a cuddle while I cried and said, "It turns out I'm really, really bad at writing a book." You talked me through some of the most difficult parts of this project and I absolutely could not have done it without you. Which brings me to living with your family while actually writing the book, during the strangest time in any of our lives. Thank you to Mia, Jason, Coco, Remy, and of course the dogs, Bella and Harry.

You know you've probably gone on a bit when you start thanking dogs.

And finally, thank you to Ana, Patrick, and Claire. This book doesn't exist without you. Thank you for answering my strange questions and for always being open to talk. Thank you for your profound generosity and insights. Thank you for sharing your darkest moments, which so many of us have had but rarely talk about. Your experiences mattered and continue to matter. Every reader is privileged to have been invited into your worlds.

About the Author

Jessie Stephens is a Sydney-based writer and podcaster, with a master's degree in history and gender studies. She's the assistant head of content at Mamamia and cohost of the podcast *Mamamia Out Loud*. She also hosts Mamamia's *True Crime Conversations, CANCELLED*, and *Book Club* podcasts, where she's had the pleasure of interviewing some of her favorite authors. *Heartsick* is her first book.